ABANDONED
MANITOBA

ABANDONED MANITOBA

From Residential Schools to Bank Vaults to Grain Elevators

GORDON GOLDSBOROUGH

GREAT PLAINS
PUBLICATIONS

Great Plains Publications
233 Garfield Street
Winnipeg, MB R3G 2M1
www.greatplains.mb.ca

Great Plains Publications gratefully acknowledges the financial support provided for
its publishing program by the Government of Canada through the Canada Book Fund;
the Canada Council for the Arts; the Province of Manitoba through the Book Publishing
Tax Credit and the Book Publisher Marketing Assistance Program; and the Manitoba
Arts Council.

Design & Typography by Relish New Brand Experience
Printed in Canada by Friesens
Third printing, 2017

LIBRARY AND ARCHIVES CANADA CATALOGUING IN PUBLICATION

Goldsborough, Gordon, 1959-, author
    Abandoned Manitoba : from residential schools to bank
vaults to grain elevators / Gordon Goldsborough.

ISBN 978-1-927855-48-5 (paperback)

    1. Abandoned buildings--Manitoba. 2. Abandoned
buildings--Manitoba--Pictorial works. 3. Manitoba--History.
4. Manitoba--History--Pictorial works. I. Title.

FC3237.G64 2016   971.27   C2016-902045-2

Contents

The grain elevator on the cover of this book was built by United Grain Growers at Brookdale, northeast of Brandon, in 1938. It closed in 1978 when the adjacent rail line was abandoned by the Canadian Pacific Railway. The building was sold to a local farmer who used it into the 1990s. It was demolished in early 2013, six months after I took this photograph. GOLDSBOROUGH

Foreword

Gordon Goldsborough is a walking, talking, insatiably curious story-telling machine and, because he is, "Abandoned Manitoba" has grown into the most popular and most talked-about regular feature on CBC Radio Winnipeg's Weekend Morning Show. I discovered his storytelling gifts when I first met him more than 10 years ago at The Delta Marsh Field Station. I was curious about the place but had never been. A mutual acquaintance arranged for me to drive with Gordon to the Marsh to get an insider's look. Gordon has had a life-long love affair with Delta Marsh. He wrote his doctoral dissertation on it and was the director of the station from 1996 to 2010. Sadly it was deeply damaged in the flood of 2011 and has since closed. (You've probably already read Gordon's magnificent best-seller *Delta: A Prairie Marsh and its People.*)

Heading to the Marsh that day I was expecting to learn a few things about birds and fish and cattails but I didn't know about the encyclopedic mind that Gordon possesses.

I spent a day with him and he talked the entire time, spinning his web of wonder about all things to be found there: abandoned military vehicles buried in the sand dunes, experiments with carp cages to keep these aggressive invaders out of the marsh, the majesty of Mallard Lodge and Donald Bain the man who built it, and the strangeness of the ecosystem of the vast shallow and little-understood Lake Manitoba. Everything he knew was fascinating to me. I was hooked and I wanted more. But how to get it?

My dream came true a number of years later, after I had assumed the role of host/producer of The Weekend Morning Show. Jan Harding-Jeanson and I were puzzling over a way to create a new feature that would allow us to delve deeply into Manitoba's past and tell stories of some of the people who helped to create our unique part of the world. Jan is the exceedingly capable associate producer, technician and director of the show. She agreed to do some research and fish around for ideas. She found herself

exploring the website of the Manitoba Historical Society. It's a treasure trove of just what we were looking for. We called the MHS to see who had gathered that treasure trove. Why it's Gordon Goldsborough they told us.

We asked him if he would agree to come by the show to tell us a couple of his favourite stories. We discovered from his first visit on June 28, 2015 that he doesn't have just a few stories. He has a bottomless pool of stories — stories he has discovered, researched, photographed and written himself. And he was eager to share them with CBC listeners. We tried him out for a few weekends and he just kept coming back with more. Before too long we asked if he'd appear every weekend and he enthusiastically jumped in. That was more than a year ago and he keeps turning up with more and more amazing stories. No-one in Manitoba has driven more backroads, trudged across more fields, poked around more decaying foundations, spotted more overlooked places, asked more questions of total strangers and snooped through more obscure historical documents than Gordon.

We have a unique working relationship. He arrives at the studio and I never know until we sit down at the microphones what story he plans to tell. Usually the week before he has given me a cryptic clue on the radio about what he has planned but he tells me nothing else. Jan sparks up the theme music ("Back in Manitoba" from Winnipeg's Ashley Robertson) and away we go. I ask "Gordon where are we going today?" And off he goes. I prepare no questions and do no research. I just listen, ask a question or two, and the story pours out.

How he does his work for the Manitoba Historical Society is astonishing. He does all of this as a volunteer. His full time work is as a professor of biology at The University of Manitoba. Every weekend you can find him in his Suzuki 4x4, with his note pad on his lap, his GPS sparked up and his camera-equipped drone at the ready chasing stories. He's the sleuth of Abandoned Manitoba.

TERRY MACLEOD, CBC RADIO

The elusive bank vault at the site of "Old Deloraine," now ensconced in a farmyard southeast of town, August 2007. GOLDSBOROUGH

Introduction

The online service called Reddit is essentially a forum where people can share and discuss topics of mutual interest. Almost any subject, no matter how arcane, can be found on Reddit. One of its forums, that I peruse occasionally, is called Abandoned Porn. No, it is not about what you may be thinking. In Abandoned Porn, you will finds thousands of photos, taken all over the world, of places and objects that are abandoned. Houses, ships, aircraft, and factories; they are all there. I am especially intrigued by photos taken inside shopping malls, those denizens of the 1970s that are fast disappearing. It is hard to describe why it is fascinating to see things that were once cherished in an advanced state of decay. But much as I enjoy looking at the photos on Reddit, I also find them frustrating because they almost never provide the backstory that I crave. WHO created these things? WHEN did they thrive? WHY were they abandoned? WHAT does their abandonment tell us?

WHERE are they located? To me, there is a lot to be learned from studying abandoned things. In my opinion, telling the story of these lost and discarded places imbues them with deeper meaning. For me, abandoned places tell us something interesting and informative about the past; what worked and what obviously didn't. Hence this book. Here, we will visit places around Manitoba that, for one reason or another, no longer serve the function for which they once existed. We will hear their stories and, hopefully, delve more deeply into little-known and forgotten aspects of our province's rich history.

For the past several years, I have been mapping historic sites all over Manitoba. The project started innocently enough. My wife, who at the time was working for an environmental consulting firm, was asked to investigate sites for potential wind farm development in the vicinity of Deloraine. I had not visited that part of the province in some time so I tagged along. Given my long-standing

An abandoned stone house in the middle of a farmer's field in rural Manitoba, March 2016. GOLDSBOROUGH

interest in local history, I thought that I could visit some interesting places in and around the town. I did some research in advance and learned that there was an abandoned bank vault near to Deloraine. In 1883, it had been built by brothers A.P. Stuart and F.T. Stuart in the newly established village before the railway arrived in that part of the province. Deloraine, which had been named for the Scottish hometown of its postmaster, consisted of a store, Land Titles office, grist mill, blacksmith shop, two churches, six agents of various kinds, a law office, a school, and several houses. When the Canadian Pacific Railway arrived in 1886, it passed to the north of Deloraine. In late 1886, most buildings were moved to the new town site two miles away. But the vault, being made of stones and therefore very heavy, could not be moved so it was

abandoned, having served its function for a mere three years. Other buildings abandoned were the mill and town hall (used also as a school). In 1895, the site of what has come to be known as "Old Deloraine" was sold as farmland. The vault ended up in the middle of a livestock paddock. The farmer, recognizing its historical interest in showing what befell many prairie towns founded before the arrival of the railway, built a fence around it to protect the structure from damage from his cattle. And there it sat for decades. In 1974, he carried out some restoration work to repair the mortar holding together its stones.

Wanting to see the bank vault at Old Deloraine, I asked about it at the front desk of our hotel. They had never heard of such a thing, and advised me to check at the town office. In turn, the town's office staff had vague recollections of the vault and sent me off in the general direction. After an hour or two of fruitless driving around the countryside, asking in vain for directions several times, I was ready to admit defeat. Making one last effort, I drove into the driveway of a nearby farm and knocked at the door of the farmhouse. Do you know where I can find an old bank vault, I asked the surprised farmer who answered, who no doubt wondered why someone was knocking in the middle of the afternoon? To my relief, he gestured toward the nearby barn and invited me to walk around behind it. And there it was! The structure measured about eight feet tall, perhaps eight feet deep and 12 feet wide, made of field stones held together by mortar.

There must be an easier way to do this, I thought, as I drove back to Deloraine. In this day and age, with the Global Positioning System (GPS) becoming ubiquitous in so many aspects of our lives, with GPS mapping capability becoming commonplace in our cars and smartphones, it should be easy to find historic places in obscure locations. I was familiar with GPS equipment, having used it for years in my scientific work. At that time, Google Maps was newly available, making it easy for people to create and display all sorts of information on maps that were available widely and freely. All that I needed to get going on this project was one final enticement.

My start came in the form of a challenge. The Manitoba Historical Society, for which I volunteer, had been given a grant to promote awareness of small, rural museums. Soon after the grant was received, the person who had spearheaded the application got a job outside the province, and left the Society holding the bag. Do the project, or give back the grant, we were warned. How do we go about fulfilling the terms of the grant, we wondered? I was reminded of my thoughts on mapping historic sites and proposed that a customized Google Map showing the locations of the museums could be useful, especially if it also showed noteworthy places along the route to those museums. In that way, someone with a passion for local history could indulge in their interests as they travelled, stopping at noteworthy monuments, buildings, cemeteries, and other places on the way to the destination. Initially, I thought that perhaps there would be a few hundred of such sites on the map. But that's when the obsessive aspect of my personality kicked in. Who was I to presume what someone might find interesting? Why not include a wide range of sites, and give people the ability to selectively show only those matching their personal preferences? In that way, a museum trip could become a truly customized experience. That was my objective and the beginning of a project that continues today.

So far, my friends and I have mapped some 6,200 sites around the province, with no end in sight. Thinking back to the bank vault that got me started, I can now report having found four other abandoned vaults, at Arden, Pilot Mound, Holmfield, and Red Deer Lake. Many of the sites we have mapped are still in active use, although their historical nature may not be clear. For instance, innocuous buildings in many of our communities often conceal a fascinating past. Making more people aware of this past, so they can have a deeper appreciation of where we have been as a guide to where we are going, is my motivation. Sometimes, nothing conveys a story better than a site that is abandoned because it emphasizes in a very visceral way that change has occurred: at one time, the abandoned site was valued. Now it is not. That change in attitude is the basis for a story that I want to tell here.

In this book, I present a small selection of the abandoned places that I have visited over the past several years. But first, I should explain how I define the sorts of places we will be visiting. "Abandoned" is not quite the right word but I am hard pressed to come up with a better one. Essentially, my conception of "abandoned" is that it is a place that no longer serves the function for which it was originally designed and which is underused. I do not mean to imply these places were abandoned through willful malice. And not all of the places we will be visiting are

The author in the now-closed Rapid City Museum, May 2013. ED LEDOHOWSKI

The author peering in the window of the former Hayland School, June 2015. ALAN MASON

completely unoccupied and decaying. A euphemism that I often hear about old buildings is that they are being used for "storage" but, in truth, most of them are filled with stuff that will never be removed. (In that sense, some might say that my messy office is abandoned.) So I will embrace three criteria for sites to be profiled here:

1. The site should have some vestige of its former use. Quite often, when I visit the site of some former building, I find absolutely nothing left: no concrete rubble, no remnants of an access road, no commemorative monument. I will mostly exclude such places here. I think it means something to be able to see authentic history, to walk in the hallway of an abandoned building, or to KNOW with certainty that you are standing where someone else stood years ago.

2. The site must be special, either one-of-a-kind or a particularly good representative of a class of sites. For example, there were over 2,000 one-room schoolhouses that operated in Manitoba during the 20th century and several hundred still stand today, in varying stages of disrepair. I will not be showing you all of them. Instead, I will pick one, or maybe two, really interesting ones and, if your curiosity is piqued, maybe you will be enticed to go out in search of others. I can help with directions.

3. The site must demonstrate something interesting or important about Manitoba history. For example, there are LOTS of vacant houses in rural Manitoba and I am sure there is a sad story for each and every one. But unless someone noteworthy lived there, or there is something important that the house shows us, or the building is in some way architecturally unique, I will not bore you with all those stories.

I am challenged occasionally about the wisdom of promoting awareness of abandoned sites, on the grounds it may attract those with malicious intent or who may be injured while trespassing at a site with dubious structural integrity. I respond in two ways. First, everyone should act responsibly. For their part, owners of abandoned sites should be aware they are responsible under the law for ensuring there are no obvious hazards on their property that could harm trespassers. Putting up a "no trespassing" sign is a good start. But this does not put the onus solely on them. Those keen to see things on private property should obtain permission before making any attempt to enter. Trespassing is bad for everyone, especially those who may follow you. Otherwise, be content to view a site from afar, on public property such as roads and rights of way. My second response to the naysayers is that "security through obscurity" is never a good strategy. People are deluding themselves if they think that not talking about a site makes it secure in this age of instantaneous, global communication. Sooner or later, if there is something interesting about a place, someone will find out and spread the word via places like Reddit. Likewise, I think it is highly unlikely that vandals will use this book as a basis for finding targets. If nothing else, vandals are lazy and will not drive for hours merely to cause willful damage when there are easier, closer places to go. (In my experience, most vandalism is caused by locals, not visitors.) And to the potential treasure-hunters, I say this: do not visit the places profiled in this book with expectations of booty. The "treasure" in these places is not that they are monetarily valuable—most are not—but that they tell us something important about Manitoba. In this spirit, I encourage you to go out and explore our beautiful province. Along the way, learn, share, respect, and, above all, enjoy the experience!

SS *Alpha* Shipwreck

People have romantic notions about the period in the 19th century when steamboats plied the waterways of the North American interior. Most of those notions are founded in the American experience, on mighty rivers like the Mississippi and Missouri, as popularized by Mark Twain and other writers. Steamboats frequently sank and, in rare cases, well-preserved boats with their cargo intact have been discovered and put on display. In Manitoba, the reality was much less romantic. The steamboat *Alpha*, which sank in the Assiniboine River in 1885, in what would later be Spruce Woods Provincial Park, is a case in point.

Steamboats provide us with a rare glimpse into life in Manitoba at the cusp of the modern age, as the fur trade that had held sway for centuries was giving way to today's agro-industrial society. Manitoba's steamboat era began in 1859 with the *Anson Northup*. Built in unorganized territory that would later become the state of North Dakota, it reached Upper Fort Garry on 10 June 1859, winning a prize for the first steamboat to travel on the Red River to the colony. It operated until 1862 when it sank in Cook's Creek. Other steamboats that operated in Manitoba through the 1860s and 1870s were, in alphabetical order, the *Cheyenne*, *Chief Commissioner*, *Colvile*, *Dakota*, *International*, *J.L. Grandin*, *Keewatin*, *Lady Blanche*, *Lady Ellen*, *Lily*, *Maggie*, *Manitoba*, *Marquette*, *Minnesota*, *Northcote*, *Prince Rupert*, *Selkirk*, *Swallow*, and *Victoria*. It was a tough life and Manitoba steamboats did not last long, succumbing to the effects of fire, ice, or river hazards. Their average lifespan was 12 years but some lasted as few as two. By the early 1880s, steamboats had been mostly displaced by railways as the transportation method of choice.

Despite their short history in Manitoba, the allure of steamboats has ensured they have not suffered for lack of attention from historians. In 1959, the Historic Sites Advisory Board of Manitoba (precursor to today's Manitoba Heritage Council) installed a commemorative plaque for the *Anson Northup* in Winnipeg's Kildonan Park. The acknowledged expert on all facets of steamboat history was freelance writer and historian Molly Basken, who wrote magazine articles about them during the 1950s and early 1960s. And for steamboats operating on the Assiniboine River, Roy Brown was your man. He made a name for himself as a member of a popular dance band in the 1930s and 1940s, then turned to television as the host of a variety show on Brandon's CKX. During the 1970s, as executive director of the Westman Branch of the Tourist and Convention Association of Manitoba, he looked for interesting stories drawn from the history of western Manitoba. He wrote three slim booklets in the 1970s and

The only-known photograph of the SS *Alpha*, on the upper Red River, circa 1878. ARCHIVES OF MANITOBA

The three-year-old steamboat *Assiniboine* was able to travel on the streets of Emerson during a catastrophic flood in 1897. It was dismantled in 1900 and its parts were used to build another steamboat, which was destroyed by fire four years later. GOLDSBOROUGH

early 1980s, before his death in 1985, on the history of the Fort Brandon fur trade post, about his experiences playing in the dance pavilion at Clear Lake, and on his effort to document the history of the *Alpha*.

An advantage that Roy Brown had in the 1970s, as he was researching the *Alpha*, was that there were still people alive who remembered it, or thought they did. Human memory is a fickle thing, and some of Brown's "facts" based on foggy recollections are dubious. Our advantage today is that first-hand details on the day-to-day activities of the *Alpha* are far more accessible than in Brown's day. Daily newspapers that faithfully reported the goings-on of the steamboats, their arrivals and departures, and the cargo manifests, are available at the Manitoba Legislative Library. Although the newspapers contain a wealth of information, until recently, one faced the daunting task of reading

thousands of small-print pages to find it. Fortunately, access is now much easier, as commercial and non-profit projects have scanned or photographed these newspapers then turned the resulting images into machine-searchable text. Now, within seconds, we can find numerous daily references to the *Alpha*, allowing a richer story to be told about its 12-year life on the rivers of Manitoba.

The *Alpha* was constructed at Breckenridge, Minnesota and launched into the Red River on 4 July 1873. Its owner was J.W. "Flatboat" McLane of Winnipeg. The hull, made of Wisconsin oak, measured 105 feet long (lengthened to over 120 feet during the winter of 1881-1882, at Brandon), 24½ feet wide, with a draught of 12 inches. A stern-wheeler, the boat was propelled by twin, 12-horsepower engines driven by steam produced in a single, large boiler below deck, fueled by wood. Because it had to carry firewood on the main deck, space for freight was limited, so it frequently towed one or more barges upon which hundreds of tons of cargo—bags of grain, barrels of pork, bundles of furs, and myriad other items—were piled. Staterooms could accommodate 12 to 30 passengers although the numbers varied between trips and often the *Alpha* would arrive at Winnipeg with nothing but cargo. The boat was well-designed for operation in shallow water, such as was common on the Red and Assiniboine Rivers. But it was still prone to beach on shallows whose positions changed year-on-year with erosion and deposition of sediment. And its hull could be punctured by submerged hazards such as rocks and snags (waterlogged tree trunks).

The *Alpha* was operated by a crew of at least eight men. The Captain (or Master) was a jack-of-all-trades who had overall responsibility for ship operation and management of the crew, including hiring and firing. The Mate spelled off the Captain, supervised loading and unloading to ensure proper weight distribution, and performed odd jobs as needed, such as helping with repairs following an accident. Two pilots who were supposedly familiar with the river navigated the boat to its destination, while two engineers ensured the thrust from the engines to do so. The Clerk was the business manager and bookkeeper aboard the vessel, responsible for selling tickets to passengers, maintaining records on cargo, and ensuring overall smooth financial operation on behalf of the owners. The Steward ensured that passengers were fed and otherwise kept happy, aided by a Cook as necessary. There were a varying number of deckhands to load cargo and fuel (and probably help to cut trees along the riverbanks when the firewood supply ran low), and manhandle the boat around river hazards. Many, and perhaps most, Manitoba steamboat captains were American, for the simple reason that they had more experience founded on the longer and more intensive use of steamboats south of the border. At least two *Alpha* captains during the 1870s were American—Thomas Townsend from St. Louis, Missouri and Alexander Griggs from St. Paul, Minnesota.

The *Alpha* encountered its first impediment to travel on the Red River during its maiden voyage.

American export rules prevented Flatboat McLane, as a British subject, from operating in American waters (although no reciprocal restriction applied to American captains operating in Canadian waters). With no recourse, McLane was forced to sell the *Alpha* to Norman Kittson of St. Paul, Minnesota (ironically, of Canadian birth) who put it into service with his Red River Transportation Company. In its early life, the *Alpha* plied the waters of the Red River between Moorhead, Minnesota and Winnipeg, a trip that

Built at Moorhead, Minnesota in the spring of 1875, the SS *Manitoba* was, like the *Alpha*, based at Winnipeg and operated for a time by the Winnipeg & Western Transportation Company. It was crushed by ice on the Shell River, in the North West Territories, in 1885. GOLDSBOROUGH

would typically take over a week. In May 1876, for instance, it arrived in Winnipeg nine and a half days after leaving Moorhead, carrying a record-setting 675 tons of freight, including flour, unprocessed oats, merchandise for sale by Winnipeg merchants, and a 1,200-pound

Winnipeg & Western Transportation Co., Limited.

—

For Fort Ellice, Rapids, Portage la Prairie, and all intermediate points.

STEAMER ALPHA,

ALEX. GRIGGS, MASTER,

Will depart for the above on

Thursday Evening, June 12th.

june9-14

An advertisement in the *Manitoba Free Press* on 12 June 1879 advertised the departure of the *SS Alpha* from Winnipeg, heading to Portage la Prairie, Assiniboine River Rapids southeast of today's Brandon, and Fort Ellice.

stove—reportedly the largest in western Canada—for the kitchen of the local Grand Central Hotel. In 1878, a consortium of Winnipeg and Montreal merchants, along with experienced (and American) steamboat captain Edwin Holcombe, formed the Winnipeg and Western Transportation Company. It had grand visions of operating on rivers and lakes throughout Manitoba but, in fact, mostly focused on the Red and Assiniboine. It paid the Red River Transportation Company $44,000 for four of its steamboats—the smaller *Alpha* and *Cheyenne*, and the larger *Manitoba* and *Minnesota*. The *Manitoba* and *Minnesota* were put on thrice-weekly runs between Winnipeg and St. Vincent, Minnesota, just inside the US border, while the *Alpha* and *Cheyenne* were primarily tasked to the Assiniboine River, travelling between Winnipeg and Portage la Prairie. In wet years, with river levels high, the *Alpha* went as far upriver as Fort Ellice (near today's St. Lazare, Manitoba) and Fort

Pelly (in present-day Saskatchewan). Occasionally, it went down the Red River as far as Lower Fort Garry.

Travel on the shallow, obstacle-strewn Assiniboine River was fraught with challenge so travel by steamboat was definitely not for those in a hurry to reach their destination. A trip between Winnipeg and Fort Ellice, travelling against the current, about 190 miles straight distance, could take 20 days. A half day's steaming might cover just 50 feet of river. The big advantage of steamboats is that they could carry immense amounts of cargo at relatively low cost compared to the alternative, Red River carts drawn by oxen. In June 1878, a round-trip to Portage la Prairie was completed in a record-setting four days and six hours, and returned with 206 sacks of potatoes, 510 sacks of oats, 232 sacks of flour, 274 sacks of wheat, and 15 sacks of barley. The following year, a passenger aboard the *Alpha*, heading to Portage, described the trip in a prescient letter to a Winnipeg newspaper:

"The steamer Alpha started up the river to the Portage on Wednesday last, groaning under the load of freight, animate and inanimate, bearing away to the far west implements of industry, horses, cattle, carriages, furniture, men, women and children. The Great Lone Land will soon be lone no longer, but will be peopled by a hardy, enterprising race, that will make a great country of the beautiful Province. The steamers on the river facilitate the immigration to a great degree. From point to point, cattle and horses with their loads, wagons, carts and all, were shipped on the Alpha, the terrors of Baie St. Paul having proved too much for their owners. From the thousands who are flocking into the

A man surveys the wreckage of the SS *Alpha* in the Assiniboine River, November 1958 by Chris Vickers.
ARCHIVES OF MANITOBA

country it is not difficult to fancy the time when the railroad will connect the Atlantic and Pacific and the Hudson [B]ay, being the great granary of the country, shipping our produce to the millions of Europeans at a much cheaper rate than by rail. We had good weather on our trip, and it was altogether a pleasant one, rendered so by the very accommodating manner of Captain Sheets, who certainly showed every attention to his passengers. I had no idea there was so much traffic on the Assiniboine. There are several store houses at

Wreckage of the SS *Alpha*, 2003 KEN STORIE

the Portage, and Mr. Drummond has a large one at High Bluff capable of containing many thousands of bushels."

The beginning of the end for steamboats in Manitoba can be dated exactly: 9 October 1877. That was the day a steam locomotive, later named the *Countess of Dufferin*, arrived in Winnipeg aboard a barge towed up from Minnesota by the steamboat *Selkirk*. The locomotive was to be used by the Canadian Pacific Railway to help in constructing its branch line to Dakota Territory and thence on to the rest of the United States and Canada. Completed in December 1878, the Pembina Branch became the major

conduit by which goods and people arrived into Manitoba. The next nail in the coffin of steamboats occurred in the spring of 1881 when hordes of men employed by the CPR descended on Winnipeg. On the 26th of July, the Louise Bridge that enabled trains to cross the Red River was completed. Manitoba was now connected directly to the rest of the country.

In 1883, the *Alpha* was sold for $4,365—depreciated from the $12,500 for which it had been purchased just five years earlier—to William Robinson of the Northwest Navigation Company. Through 1883 and 1884, it was mostly used on the Assiniboine, running between Brandon and Fort Pelly. On 27 April 1885, it departed Brandon bound for Winnipeg, where it was to undergo repairs before being put on the St. Vincent run. About 25 miles downstream of Carberry, in a shallow reach of the river, its rudder was broken off and the hull was damaged so badly that the captain ran the ship aground to keep it from sinking. The crew continued on to Winnipeg by foot to

report the accident to the company. When corporate secretary Frank Drummond and Captain Duncan paddled back to the *Alpha* in mid-May, they found that it had been "perfectly stripped." The identity of the scavengers was unknown. Although newspaper accounts at the time ascribed the thefts to "Indians," later reminiscences would claim that entire barns in the region were built using timbers taken from the *Alpha* wreck. With the prospect of costly repairs, and dubious economic viability for steamboats generally, it must not have been a difficult decision to make. The vessel was abandoned where it lay.

By the time of the *Alpha* loss, the glory days of the steamboat were over. Railways could operate year-round, versus only during ice-free periods by steamboats—and then only when the water was deep enough. Railways went by the most direct route while steamboats had to follow the meanders of prairie rivers. The *Alpha* shipwreck site is, for example, 41 miles as the crow files from Brandon's First

Street Bridge, but 96 miles by water. The *Alpha* sat patiently, wedged in the bank of the Assiniboine River, for some 126 years, partially covered by deposits of silt. In late 1958, noted Manitoba archaeologist Chris Vickers visited the wreck and took a few photos of relic timbers. In 1969, Roy Brown visited the *Alpha* and found its starboard side was under two feet of water, while the port side was buried in the riverbank. He salvaged pieces of the hull. The rudder was displayed at a museum, now closed, in Cypress River and later at the Marine Museum in Selkirk. Brown presented another piece to the Chamber of Commerce at Breckenridge, the *Alpha*'s birthplace. A ship model, made by a high school student from a piece of recovered timber, was displayed at the Manitoba Agricultural Museum at Austin and later at the Treherne Museum. In the fall of 2003, while the Assiniboine was unusually low, Brandon historian Ken Storie found pieces of planking sticking out of the water and fire bricks from the *Alpha*'s boiler. He may be the last person to see the ship because, in the spring of 2011, a disastrous flood in the Assiniboine valley destroyed bridges and scoured the riverbanks. The last vestige of Manitoba's steamboat era has probably been washed away forever.

SOURCES

"The river," *The Manitoban and Northwest Herald*, 26 July 1873, page 3.

"The new steamer Alpha," *The Manitoban and Northwest Herald*, 20 Sept 1873, page 2.

"Steamboat news," *Manitoba Free Press*, 1 April 1875, page 7.

"City and provincial news," *Manitoba Free Press*, 16 May 1876, page 3; 18 May 1876, page 3; 5 June 1878, page 1.

"The Alpha on the Assiniboine," *Manitoba Free Press*, 4 May 1878, page 1.

Ten Years in Winnipeg: A Narration of the Principal Events in the History of the City of Winnipeg by Alexander Begg and Walter R. Nursey, Winnipeg, 1879.

"Steamboat mishap," *Winnipeg Daily Times*, 30 April 1885.

"Stripped by Indians," *Brandon Sun*, 20 May 1885, page 5.

"City and province," *Manitoba Free Press*, 20 May 1885, page 4.

"Steamboating on the Red" by Molly McFadden, MHS *Transactions*, Series 3, 1950-1951 Season. [http://www.mhs.mb.ca/docs/transactions/3/steamboating.shtml]

Fire Canoe: Prairie Steamboat Days Revisited by Ted Barris, McClelland and Stewart, 1969.

"Steamboats on the Assiniboine" by Roy Brown, *Brandon Sun*, 12 May 1979, page 9.

Steamboats on the Assiniboine by Roy Brown, 1981 [reprinted 2007 by Daly House Museum, Brandon]

Steamboats on the Rivers and Lakes of Manitoba, 1859-96 by Martha McCarthy, Manitoba Historic Resources Branch, Research Report, 1987.

The Alpha Revisited, False Starts: Settlement Stories From Western Manitoba by Ken Storie [www.virtualmanitoba.com/FalseStarts/Alpha]

ACKNOWLEDGEMENTS

I thank historian Ken Storie of Brandon for his excellent work in documenting the life and death of the steamboat *Alpha*, building on the past research of the late Chris Vickers and Roy Brown. Georgette Hutlet (Manitoba Agricultural Museum) put me on the trail of the *Alpha* model at the Treherne Museum. And I am especially grateful to the people who created NewspaperArchive.com and Newspapers.com, as their digitized collections of Manitoba newspapers from the 1870s and 1880s were invaluable. For readers wanting a fact-filled book about steamboating, albeit from an American perspective, I recommend *The Steamboat Era: A History of Fulton's Folly on American Rivers, 1807-1860* by S.L. Kotar and J.E. Gessler (2009).

Atkinson House

Many of Manitoba's early European immigrants occupied makeshift structures until they could build something more substantial. A story in my family, for example, is that my great-grandfather spent his first few nights in a beaver lodge. Settlers on the open prairie, where wood was scarce, built temporary structures called soddies or semlins by covering stacked sod-block walls with a sod roof.

The first Slavic settlers in western Manitoba constructed tent-shaped "buddas" using thatched straw. Eventually, these first-generation homes were replaced by more robust, permanent ones made of stones, bricks, logs, or sawed lumber. In time, some settlers expanded or replaced their second-generation house with a larger one as a conspicuous demonstration of their material success. This seems to have been the motive of English settler Arthur Atkinson when he built an impressive mansion near Hamiota. Unlike other such homes which remain in use today, his house has been vacant for over 50 years. The reason for its abandonment is, I suspect, a common one for many of the houses built during those early days of settlement.

Under the system used by the federal government to settle the arable lands of western Canada, new farmers were eligible for a grant of 160 acres. This meant that, in theory, four families could occupy each square mile. In time, as farms grew larger in size, the number of people living on the landscape dwindled. Today, we see scores of abandoned farmsteads in some parts of the province and each one conveys a story of initial hope and ultimate failure. In choosing a farmhouse to profile here, I was looking for a good example of a third-generation building. I found what I was looking for, oddly enough, at a banquet in Winnipeg. I told a fellow sitting beside me about my fetish for abandoned buildings, and he told me about an

OPPOSITE View of the Atkinson house exterior, August 2014.
GOLDSBOROUGH

View of the Atkinson house, probably in the late-1920s.
TED DELLER AND RHONDA MCDOUGAL, FROM THE COLLECTION OF NORMAN AND GRACE TURNBULL

interesting one beside his livestock feedlot near Hamiota. I made a mental note to look at it the next time I was in western Manitoba and I did some research in preparation for that visit. An historian at Hamiota advised that the building had been built by Atkinson and that information about it could be found in the local history book. By the time of my visit in August 2014, I had learned about its builder and his tragic past. It was no mere soddie or budda and was, in fact, far grander than most other abandoned farmhouses I had seen. Clearly, its owner had been someone of means.

Born at Whittlesea, England in February 1870, Arthur Atkinson immigrated to Canada in 1892 and worked in Ontario, later moving to the Hamiota area where he worked for a local farmer. When he had saved enough money, he bought his own farm about two miles southeast of town on a site known as "Old Hamiota"

An example of a "budda" temporary shelter made by some of Manitoba's early settlers, recreated in 1978 near Oakburn by the Parkland Ukrainian Pioneer Association. GOLDSBOROUGH

Like numerous old buildings around Manitoba, the former Ascension of Our Lord Ukrainian Catholic Church at Pulp River in the Rural Municipality of Mountain, photographed in June 2015, is covered with insul-brick siding. GOLDSBOROUGH

because it was near where, from 1884 to 1890, the first post office had operated. He later enlarged the initial 160-acre farm by purchasing another 160 acres nearby, and hired a man to help with its operation. Atkinson was a member of the Hamiota School Board, as well as the Methodist Church, Canadian Order of Foresters, and Loyal Orange Lodge. In August 1898, he married 22-year-old Ida Levins, whose family had moved to the Hamiota area from Pennsylvania a few years earlier. The Atkinsons had six children, four of whom lived past infancy: Ethel Hope (born in 1900), Ernest (1902), Orison (1904), and Ellen Grace (1905).

In 1913, Atkinson replaced the modest house that he had built where he first started farming. His grand new house sat atop a small hill that gave it a commanding view of the surrounding countryside. It was a large, two-storey building with a full basement and a full-height attic. (Some people today consider it is a three-storey house, perhaps because of the spacious attic.) On the outside,

massive verandahs wrapped around the building's south and west sides. Inside, it featured all the latest conveniences. Heat was provided by dual, coal-fired furnaces in the basement and running water was piped throughout the house, including to indoor toilets and bathtubs, from a large cistern buried in the basement floor. A dumbwaiter carried laundry and supplies between the basement and the two upper floors. It was one of the few farms in the area to have a telephone. It would have seemed right at home among the mansions in the tony areas of Brandon and Winnipeg. By all accounts, Arthur Atkinson was a shining example of a settler who had come to Canada with nothing and, by dint of hard work, had become a successful farmer.

On 17 July 1924, Arthur Atkinson died suddenly, at the age of 54. Newspaper accounts the next day were frank in describing the circumstances. He had suffered a severe illness that had kept him from farming for a prolonged period. The resulting financial shortfall led to bouts of

A wedding party for Norman Turnbull and Ellen Grace Atkinson on the verandah of the Atkinson House, June 1926. TED DELLER AND RHONDA MCDOUGAL, FROM THE COLLECTION OF NORMAN AND GRACE TURNBULL

depression and despondency. On the morning of his death, Atkinson told his hired man that he did not intend to work that day. Soon after breakfast, family members were alarmed to see him walking toward a buggy shed near the house, carrying a gun. They hurried toward the shed but were too late. Atkinson died instantly from a single gunshot wound to the head. After a well-attended funeral in the Methodist Church, he was buried in the Hamiota Cemetery.

The Atkinson family carried on as best they could. In 1926, Grace Atkinson married an ambitious young farmer, Norman Turnbull, at the family home and the newlyweds operated the Atkinson farm until the spring of 1934 when they moved to their own farm near Binscarth. (Two years after the move, Turnbull was elected to the Manitoba Legislature, serving until 1949, including terms as a cabinet minister in the governments of John Bracken and Stuart Garson.) As the Turnbulls moved out, the executor of Atkinson's estate sold the house and property to Thomas Strachan who farmed there until the mid-1940s

The Atkinson family, August 1912, the year before moving into their grand new home. From left to right: Ellen Grace Atkinson (later, wife of Norman Turnbull), Arthur Atkinson, Ida Levins Atkinson, Orison Atkinson (front), Ernest Atkinson (rear), Ethel Hope Atkinson. TED DELLER, FROM THE COLLECTION OF NORMAN AND GRACE TURNBULL

The kitchen of the former Atkinson House with a hole burned through to the basement, August 2015.
GOLDSBOROUGH

The Atkinson House featured two furnaces, seen here in August 2015. GOLDSBOROUGH

when he moved to Hamiota. Then, the building was occupied by a succession of families: the Johnsons in the mid-1940s, the Hodgsons from around 1948 to 1957, and the Grays from 1957 to November 1960. I suspect the Grays moved out in late Fall because they could not face the prospect of another winter in a very cold house. The Atkinson House had little or no insulation in its wood and brick walls other than what was provided by the materials themselves. With its large interior spaces, the building was difficult and expensive to heat. Though it had been a showpiece and technological marvel for its time, it was poorly suited to Manitoba's climate.

The lack of insulation in the Atkinson House was not unusual for its time. Few, if any, buildings constructed before the mid-20th century were insulated, their owners going on the assumption that the heating system would be sufficient to keep them warm in winter. In 1919, University of Manitoba professor Reginald Buller wrote to a colleague in Ottawa with a suggestion for a post-First World War project for government scientists:

"In a city like Winnipeg there are many so-called cold houses where a large amount of coal is burned up but no satisfactory heating secured. There seems to be but little doubt that such cold houses are due to faulty construction, and the faulty construction may simply be due to ignorance. It seems to me that the investigation of the loss of heat from houses is a first-class peace problem ..."

Through much of the twentieth century, impromptu solutions to improve the warmth of existing Manitoba houses included covering their walls in corrugated cardboard, layers of old newspapers, and fiberboard, or filling interior spaces with wood shavings, sawdust, or flax straw. Through the 1930s, inventor Soffanius Thorkelsson used wood waste from his Winnipeg box factory to make a wool-like product for insulating the walls of hundreds of local homes. From the late 1930s to the early 1960s, a Winnipeg firm manufactured rolls of asphalt-based

The living room of the former Atkinson House with a fireplace and stairs leading to the second floor and attic, August 2015. GOLDSBOROUGH

widely during the same period, such as vermiculite (sold in Canada since the 1930s as zonolite) and urea-formaldehyde foam (primarily in the 1970s), have been taken off the market due to concerns they may adversely affect human health.

As time rolled on and the uninsulated Atkinson House sat empty, it fell into ruin. When I visited it in 2014, it had been unoccupied over 50 years. Walking toward the house through the tall grass, I saw that once-conspicuous verandahs had fallen away or been removed. All the window glass was long gone, along with most of the shingles from the roof. Numerous gaping holes revealed that the exterior walls were made of timber beams and stacked fired-clay blocks, neither of which provided much insulation, while the interior walls were wooden studs covered with lath slathered with plaster. The building has been used for impromptu parties and, at some point, a bonfire had been set on the wood floor of the kitchen. The fire had burned through to the basement but, amazingly, had not destroyed the rest of the building. As I walked up the staircase to the attic, I remembered being told that old buildings like this one were havens for turkey vultures, scavengers that feasted on the dead and decaying carcasses of other animals. The amount of road-kill along highways today, combined with an abundance of abandoned buildings with attics accessible to the sky, was

siding called "insul-brick" that made a building's exterior look somewhat like real brick while providing a bit of insulation value. Available in a range of colours, insul-brick required no painting or maintenance, and is very durable, still intact on some Manitoba buildings over 60 years after it was installed. Ultimately, the best solution is to install insulation in homes during construction. The use of fiberglass batts for insulation began in the late 1940s and, today, it is ubiquitous. Fiberglass has distinct advantages over wood-based products, most notably that it is fireproof, is inedible to pests, and will not rot, mildew, or absorb moisture. Other insulation products used

providing excellent nesting habitat for the vultures and their populations were growing. Although turkey vultures will not normally confront a human, I was not excited about finding one here, especially if there were chicks in its nest. Reaching the attic, where I saw no evidence that insulation had ever been added to the floor or roof, thankfully I also saw no vultures. But there were definite indications that some large animal had taken up residence because the place had the funky aroma of animal feces. The floor looked none too stable either. Certainly, it was no longer capable of supporting the weight of a large billiards table that I was told once stood up here. Who told me so? That's where the story becomes personal to me.

As I had learned the story of the Atkinson House, elements had sounded vaguely familiar. Eventually, it came back to me: one of my good friends, in fact one of my former graduate students with whom I have worked closely, was Arthur Atkinson's great-granddaughter. Years earlier, she had told me about the house and its tragic past. That is why, when I visited the house in 2014, it was with the two-fold purpose of seeing the remains of a once-grand house that had been the pride and joy of a successful farmer, and to be able to tell my friend about the heart-breaking condition of the place where her grandparents had been married. The Atkinson House is an especially extravagant example of the inability of early settlers to acknowledge and accommodate Manitoba's harsh climate, basing their construction on conditions they had known in their home countries. Chilly old houses around the province can sometimes be retrofitted with insulation but it is a difficult, costly, and never fully satisfactory proposition. Those who choose to do it are motivated by a love of history and appreciation for the beauty and solid construction of these old structures, and not by their questionable energy efficiency.

SOURCES

1901 Canada census [Arthur Atkinson], www.automatedgenealogy.com

A.H.R. Buller Fonds [correspondence between AHRB and A.B. Macallum], University of Manitoba Archives & Special Collections.

Death registration [Arthur Atkinson], Manitoba Vital Statistics.

"Suicide at Hamiota," *Brandon Sun*, 18 July 1924, page 10.

"Farmer residing near Hamiota slays himself," *Manitoba Free Press*, 18 July 1924, page 1.

"Late Arthur Atkinson," *Hamiota Echo*, 24 July 1924, page 8.

"Winnipeg manufacturer inventor of wood wool insulation for houses," *Winnipeg Free Press*, 4 August 1934, page 64.

[Advertisement – fiberglass insulation], *Winnipeg Free Press*, 8 August 1949, page 2.

Hamiota, Grains of the Century: 1884-1984 by Hamiota Centennial History Committee, 1984, pages 336-338.

ACKNOWLEDGEMENTS

I first learned about the Atkinson House from Jay Jackson, who raises livestock on the property adjacent to it. Atkinson descendants Rhonda McDougal and Ted Deller provided information about the house, including some great photos during its heyday, from the collection of Norman and Grace Turnbull. I am also grateful to historian Ken Smith at Hamiota who referred me to information in a local history book.

Bender Hamlet

When we consider the history of Manitoba's Jewish community, we tend to think of Winnipeg's North End, with life on Selkirk Avenue and its surrounding neighbourhood. Yet, as early as 1884, Jewish farm colonies were established at several places in rural western Canada. Some colonies in Saskatchewan and Alberta thrived. But four colonies established in Manitoba, two with financial aid from a foundation established by Jewish philanthropist Maurice von Hirsch (1831-1896), did not. The first of those colonies—established in 1903 and abandoned after a 24-year period of occupation—was Bender Hamlet.

The Bender Hamlet public school in 1926 where, in addition to lessons prescribed by provincial education officials, children were given lessons in Hebrew and religious subjects. ARCHIVES OF MANITOBA

Bender Hamlet was about 21 miles northwest of Gimli, roughly half-way between Lake Winnipeg and Lake Manitoba, in the Rural Municipality of Armstrong. Sometimes called Narcisse in commemoration of Narcisse Leven—a French lawyer and President of the Jewish Colonization Association under whose auspices the community was founded—to avoid confusion with the railway siding of Narcisse about two miles west, the more common name recognized its founder, Jacob Bender (1854-1941). Bender had immigrated from Nikolaiev in the Ukraine in 1892 and, by the turn of the 20th century, was working in Winnipeg as a land agent, speculator, and entrepreneur who, despite having no agrarian roots of his own, had grand ambitions of establishing a Jewish farm colony. While on a trip to England in 1902, Bender recruited settlers for his colony. Later, he added a few more from Winnipeg and one from the United States, although all had been born in the Ukraine. Like Bender himself, few had any meaningful farming experience. Among them were merchants, tailors, woodworkers, pedlars, carpenters, and a pair of gardeners. Few Jews from eastern Europe had substantial farming experience because they had been prohibited from owning land.

Like most settlers arriving in Manitoba, Bender secured a quarter-section of land on which to establish a farm, with intentions of acquiring more land as the number of settlers warranted. However, Bender wanted his settlers to live together in the fashion of European villages rather than to be dispersed on isolated homesteads miles apart. So, unlike most settlers, he got permission to divide the quarter section into 19 equal strips, 60 feet wide, one for each family of settlers and the 19th for a synagogue. Living together in this way, 18 families had "critical mass" to hire a Jewish teacher for their school (so Hebrew lessons could be offered in addition to subjects prescribed by the public curriculum) and provide a quorum or "minyan" of ten males required during Jewish rites in the synagogue.

In 1903, the settlers built houses in the European style. All faced north, side-by-side, in a neat row. They

The Bender Hamlet commemorative monument, made from stones delimiting individual family plots, and a plaque from the Manitoba Heritage Council, July 2010. GOLDSBOROUGH

The Bender Hamlet cemetery, September 2015. ED LEDOHOWSKI

also began clearing trees and tilling the soil, which was not ideal cropland, being stony and infertile. Bender's enthusiasm for the colony seems to have waned quickly. Within four years of establishing the colony, he was not actively involved in it, and was gone by 1917. (Bender lived in southwestern Saskatchewan for a time before returning to Winnipeg, where he died in February 1941 and was buried in Brookside Cemetery.) The community's population peaked in 1915, at 182 people, including 39 farmers. They owned an impressive 6,197 acres of land, but only about one-tenth of it, 676 acres, was cultivated. A modest visual record of life at Bender Hamlet comes to us from William Sisler, a Winnipeg school teacher for whom a high school is now named. Sisler took a special interest in the life of Canada's new immigrants, and he spent much of his summers travelling the province to visit their communities. Sisler came to Bender Hamlet in 1916 and snapped a photograph showing the row of houses and a single cow resting tranquilly on a path.

The Bender Hamlet experiment failed for several reasons. The village configuration, while well-suited to social interaction between the settlers, meant that some farmers had to travel up to four miles to reach their land. Isolation caused by bad roads that were only passable when frozen in winter, combined with the absence of a railway (the CNR did not reach the area until 1914), made it difficult to market crops. Agricultural output from the colony was low as a result of inexperience and poor land. Gradually, families moved away and, with each successive departure, conditions became less favourable for those who remained. As an ethnically and culturally distinct group who chose not to intermingle with other settlers in the region, fewer colony members meant fewer potential mates for marriage and greater difficulty in achieving minyan. By 1927, after three consecutive crop losses due to rain, the colony was all but abandoned. Most of its residents moved to Winnipeg or other cities. By 1931, there were just 456 Jews in rural Manitoba, most operating general stores in over 100 small towns across the southern agricultural belt.

I visited the site of Bender Hamlet in mid-2010. I found only a small cemetery (surrounded by a low, concrete fence erected after the overgrown area was rediscovered in the 1960s) and a few building foundations. More conspicuous was a monument made from stones used to mark the lot lines that was erected in October 1986 and dedicated in June 1987. It listed the pioneer families. For just over 20 years, they braved harsh, isolated conditions—physically, climatically, and socially—in search of a better life, and contributed to the rich cultural mosaic that is Manitoba.

SOURCES

1901 Canada census [Jacob Bender], Automated Genealogy.
1921 Canada census [Jacob Bender], Ancestry.
"Mrs. Jacob Bender, resident of west for 42 years, dies," *Winnipeg Free Press*, 13 August 1934, page 5.
Death registration [Jacob Bender], Manitoba Vital Statistics.
Obituary [Jacob Bender], *Winnipeg Tribune*, 15 February 1941, page 27.
"Wapella Farm Settlement: The First Successful Jewish Farm Settlement in Canada" by Cyril E. Leonoff, MHS *Transactions*, Series 3, Number 27, 1970-1971 Season.
"New Jerusalem just a memory" by Ted Allan, *Winnipeg Free Press*, 10 December 1980, page 73.
The Geography of Manitoba: Its Land and Its People by John C. Everitt, John Welsted, and Christoph Stadel, 1996, page 98.
Coming of Age: A History of the Jewish People of Manitoba by Allan Levine, Heartland Associates, 2009.

ACKNOWLEDGEMENTS

I am grateful to Ed Ledohowski and Jean McManus for sharing their photos taken during a visit to Bender Hamlet in the fall of 2015, bolstering my own meagre supply taken before I fully appreciated the importance of the site to the Jewish history of Manitoba.

Grave marker in the Bender Hamlet cemetery, September 2015. JEAN MCMANUS

Birtle Indian Residential School

I was sitting in the Birdtail Country Museum, in the village of Birtle in western Manitoba, perusing a thick scrapbook. It had been compiled by a woman named May Kenny and donated to the museum by her friend, Edith Rusaw, probably after her death. Miss Kenny had been born at East Selkirk and, in 1946, after teaching at public schools around Manitoba for 15 years, she came to Birtle to teach at the Indian Residential School on a hill overlooking the town.

Young indigenous girls on the front steps of the Birtle Indian Residential School, no date. BIRDTAIL COUNTRY MUSEUM

Over the course of the next 25 years, she taught, supervised, helped in the school's garden, and cooked meals, right up to the day before her death in 1968. The scrapbook contains photos of children—some smiling, some not—and a group of staff members. There was Miss Kenny standing on the left, behind Edith Rusaw, who was the Matron. On the opposite side sat Martin Rusaw, Edith's husband, the school's Principal. In the middle was teacher Harry Shafransky, who would later serve for eight years as an MLA. Are these the faces of evil people, I wondered, who could do unspeakable things to innocent children? I reminded myself that it is possible for good people to do bad things through ignorance. Perhaps that is what explains complaints from those who attended the school. Yet, it was a different time, when justice was often brutally and indiscriminately dispensed, and attitudes were routinely coloured by racism, ageism, and sexism. Conflicting emotions fill me as I close the scrapbook and head off to look at the old Birtle Residential School for myself.

The Indian residential school system in Canada operated for roughly one hundred years as an initiative of the federal government. Children were taken from their home communities, away from family and cultural influences, and prohibited from speaking their native languages. The expectation was that the education they received would integrate them as contributing members into broader Canadian society. It is estimated that some 150,000 children passed through the system. Persistent allegations of psychological, nutritional, and sexual abuses were finally addressed by a Truth and Reconciliation Commission appointed in 2008 by the federal government. Manitoba has played a

Teaching staff of the Birtle Indian Residential School, May 1953. FRONT ROW (L-R): Mrs. Rusaw, E. Heinricks, Mrs. Reynolds, E. Bayne, Mrs. Finlay, Mr. Rusaw. BACK ROW (L-R): May Kenny, Mr. De La Mare, Nettie Heppner, Harry Shafransky, Mrs. McGinnis, Hazel Torrie, Mabel Cooper, Fred Finlay. BIRDTAIL COUNTRY MUSEUM

major role in that process; the Commission was chaired by local Indigenous lawyer and judge Murray Sinclair, and the information amassed by the Commission during its five-year mandate led to the establishment of an ongoing National Centre of Truth and Reconciliation at the University of Manitoba.

At one time or another, residential schools operated at several places around Manitoba, in addition to

The homeward trek from school in Birtle, winter of 1964. BIRDTAIL COUNTRY MUSEUM

the one at Birtle: Brandon (1895-1972), Camperville (1890-1969), Dauphin (1955-1988), Elkhorn (1889-1949), Fisher River (1874-1963), Fort Alexander (1905-1970), Norway House (1899-1967), Portage la Prairie (1891-1975), Sandy Bay (1905-1970), The Pas (1914-1933), Waterhen (1890-1900), and Winnipeg (1958-1973). Most were operated by churches, including the Roman Catholics, Presbyterians, Methodists (United), and Anglicans, usually with financial contributions from the government.

The first facility at Birtle for the education of Indigenous children was known as the "Stone School." Built between 1882 and 1883, the two-storey stone structure was used for three years as a public school for the non-indigenous children of Birtle. Then, the government leased it as a boarding school for children from the Birdtail, Keeseekoowenin, Rolling River, and Waywayseecappo reserves. They used it for a year or two then, in 1894, moved into a newly-built, two-storey stone building on the north hill overlooking Birtle. Operated later by the Women's Missionary Society of the Presbyterian Church in Canada, the school's mandate was to provide a general education as well as vocational training at a model farm next to the school. The farm raised dairy cattle, pigs, laying chickens, sheep, and turkeys; grew a variety of root vegetables in gardens around the campus; and cultivated cereal crops and livestock hay on some 600 acres of land, all to offset food costs for the staff and students. In 1935, the federal government provided a grant of $144.50 for each student attending the school. The remaining funds were raised by the Women's Missionary Society.

In June 1930, construction of a brick replacement for the 1894 stone structure was undertaken by the Claydon Brothers Construction Company of Winnipeg. It had a steel skeleton, reinforced concrete floors, and walls made of red bricks and concrete blocks. A full basement contained washrooms, dining hall, kitchen, and laundry. There were offices, classrooms, and dormitories on the upper floors, and a one-storey gymnasium/assembly hall on the back. The floor layout of the dormitory space

Laundry room in the Birtle Indian Residential School, no date.
BIRDTAIL COUNTRY MUSEUM

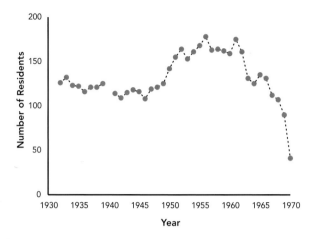

Graph of the number of residents at the Birtle Indian Residential School, 1932 to 1970.
NATIONAL CENTRE FOR TRUTH AND RECONCILIATION

allowed for strict segregation of the sexes. A two-storey residence for the Principal and his family was attached on the west end. After the building was completed by March 1931, the former school building was demolished, although a pile of gray stones from its foundation are still visible. At some point, a one-room schoolhouse was constructed or brought to the site, adjacent to the main building, and used for lower-grade classes.

Several of the Principals (who were invariably male) were Presbyterian clerics and their wives would serve as Matron. They were responsible for the overall operation of the facility, including hiring and managing staff, supervising and disciplining the student body, overseeing maintenance, and managing the daily finances. Teachers were recruited from the ranks of public schools around the province. Most appear to have had no special training to work with Indigenous children. The number of students who resided at the school was variable. From the time the new school opened in 1932, to 1950, the total hovered around 120 per year, with instruction in grades 1 to 8. In the 1940s, one teacher had classes in grades 1 and 2, another had grades 3 and 4, and a third handled grades 5 to 8. There was a dedicated music teacher, sewing instructor, teacher-counsellor, and nurse. Until 1943, students spent a half day in the classroom and the rest in vocational training. Boys worked on the farm—milking cows, cleaning barns, and harvesting crops—while girls learned sewing and cooking, and helped with the laundry. Around

1950, the number of students jumped to around 160 and peaked at 178 in 1956 when the school expanded to include grades 9 to 12. In addition to the three to four teachers, the school had several non-teaching staff members who, along with the Matron, supervised the girls and boys outside the classroom. Other staff made the meals and supervised the kitchen, maintained the physical plant and grounds, did the housekeeping and laundry, and supervised farm operations.

In testimony to the Truth and Reconciliation Commission, some former residents of the school described abusive experiences there. Girls reported being observed by the Principal while they showered. Boys working in the farm complained about being overworked. In 1942, a provincial official was incredulous when he learned that a school truck involved in an accident had been carrying 70 boys. (Luckily, only two were injured.) Discipline in the classroom was tough, with wrong answers eliciting pulled ears and

Teachers and children at the Birtle Indian Residential School, 1946-1947.
BIRDTAIL COUNTRY MUSEUM

shaken heads. Girls and boys, especially the older ones, even siblings, were strictly segregated from each other. Sometimes, students would be transferred to other facilities without asking or informing their parents. It is impossible to know the exact circumstances of each case but it is likely that cultural insensitivity of non-Indigenous teachers affected the way they treated the children under their care. Verna Kirkness, an Indigenous woman who taught at Birtle in the 1960s, recalls:

> "The high-school students often dropped in for a chat. This kind of closeness was frowned upon by the school administration. Instead of being happy to have an Indian teacher in their midst with whom the children could identify, the administrators tried to discourage them from spending time with me. I did not feel welcome at the school."

Locals say they never witnessed abusive behaviour. Then again, abusers would likely be on their best behaviour if they were under scrutiny. After Ms. Kirkness witnessed a student being humiliated by the Principal for

Collapsing wall blocks and debris fill the hallways of the former Birtle Residential School, March 2016. GOLDSBOROUGH

Occasionally, some students ran away from the school or left it in other ways. In 1959, a runaway complained to an Indian Affairs official that he was essentially an unpaid worker who put in four hours a day in the barn, and stoked the furnace with coal before going to bed, in addition to attending classes. As many as four percent of the children who attended residential schools across Canada died at them. In Manitoba, there were cemeteries at the Brandon and Elkhorn schools, and possibly elsewhere. None of the graves were marked. In 1990, a reunion of former staff and residents at Elkhorn erected a monument in memory of those interred there. At Brandon, a monument has the names of eleven people buried in an overgrown cemetery although a recent study suggests there may be many more unmarked graves. A second, older cemetery nearer the Assiniboine River is completely unmarked, as a commemorative monument erected in 1972 by local Girl Guides has disappeared. I have found no evidence of burials at the Birtle site, which of course does not mean that no deaths occurred there.

There were positives along with the negatives. Ms. Kirkness recalls that the school's reputation for being superior to the Brandon Residential School was well founded. At Birtle, children were very well fed with the same food as the staff, much of it produced by the school's farm. But we have little quantitative data on which to base an assessment of conditions at the school. Basic statistics do not reveal anything out of the ordinary. For instance, from the mid-1940s to the early 1960s, each teacher had

taking food from the kitchen, she contacted the Women's Missionary Society who dispatched an inspector. During the week of that visit:

> "…[T]he staff, in general, were perfectly behaved and the principal, in particular, was the most charming person one could wish to have working with the Indian children. I saw him one day skipping down the hall with a couple of the little grade one girls on each hand."

between 30 and 40 students in their classes. This would be considered much too high by modern standards—the average province-wide value in 2013 was 17 students per teacher—but such numbers were typical for public schools in that period.

The number of residents at Birtle dropped as changes to the Indian Act in 1951 enabled construction of on-reserve schools. By 1954, residents in grades 11 and 12 were walking into Birtle to attend the public school there. By the early 1960s, those in grades 6 to 10 also attended public school and, as of the 1962 school year, students in grades 1 to 3 were sent to Brandon. Responsibility for the Birtle Residential School transferred to the federal government in March 1969. The farm operation ceased and its equipment and livestock were sold. By the time the facility closed in June 1970, there were just 41 residents. The main building was sold in the late 1990s to a young couple from British Columbia who held a "cleanup auction" and converted the Principal's residence into their home, with plans to renovate the rest of the building. They lived there for eight years before returning to BC, their plans unfulfilled. In the mid-2000s, a proposal to develop a cultural centre never got off the ground. Consequently, the building has been sitting vacant for more than ten years. In 2015, the owners attempted to sell the 26-acre property, mostly for its land and salvage value. Finding no local realtors willing to take on the sale, they listed it on the internet. News that a former residential school was for sale, coming just before the public release of the Truth and Reconciliation Commission's final report, made national headlines. Two prospective buyers, both offering less than the $79,000 asking price, were dissuaded when they saw the state of the site.

Approaching the building in the spring of 2016, what I saw did not look like the product of gradual decay. Frankly, it looked like it had been the site of a battle. The once-carefully manicured lawns and flower-beds were overgrown, and the building was obscured by unpruned hedges and trees. Derelict vehicles and hardware were strewn about the grounds, along with bricks from walls that had fallen. The one-room schoolhouse by the entrance road was filled with piles of jumbled garbage. There was not an intact window in the place. Inside the main building, large, gaping holes in the walls showed where concrete blocks had been forcibly removed.

The former Birtle Residential School, March 2016.
GOLDSBOROUGH

Basement dining hall of the former Birtle Residential School, March 2016. GOLDSBOROUGH

Ceilings had been charred by fires lit on the floor below. If I was unfamiliar with the male anatomy, the abundant graffiti throughout the building would certainly remind me. Some hallways had at least a foot of miscellaneous rubble on the floor. Either vandals had had a lot of fun wreaking havoc, or they had exorcised personal demons through willful and wanton destruction. I vacillated on whether or not it would be possible to repair the damage, if anyone ever wanted to. Certainly, the structure of the building was intact and a lot of the damage

seemed superficial. But it would be a major (and costly) undertaking.

Some have suggested that the Birtle Residential School should be demolished so those with painful memories of time spent there may get some measure of relief knowing it no longer exists. That is what happened to the Brandon Residential School which, for over 70 years, overlooked the Assiniboine River before the building was finally demolished in 2000. Other residential schools, such as the one on the west end of Portage la Prairie and the one on Academy Road in Winnipeg, have been turned to other uses; in the former case, as a facility of the Long Plain First Nation, and in the latter by a national child welfare agency. I can understand how removing the evidence would be appealing. On the other hand, conspicuous reminders can be a powerful way to prevent recurrence. For example, the Nazi atrocities toward Jews during the Second World War will never be forgotten as long as places like the Auschwitz Concentration Camp remain standing. My own view is that the old residential school at Birtle should survive, whether in its present dilapidated condition or with some restoration, as an ongoing reminder that Canada has not always been as accommodating and congenial a place as we would like to believe.

SOURCES

Birtle Indian Residential School Album, Birdtail Country Museum.

Birth registration [Pearl May Kenny], Manitoba Vital Statistics.

"Women are praised for mission work," *Winnipeg Tribune*, 28 March 1935, page 2.

"Memories of the Birtle Indian Residential School" by Jack Dodds, *Shoal Lake Crossroads*, 27 September 2013, page 3.

Brief Administrative History of the Residential Schools & the Presbyterian Church in Canada's Healing and Reconciliation Efforts, The Presbyterian Church in Canada Archives, September 2010. [http://presbyterian.ca/?wpdmdl=94]

"Residential school survivors share their stories," *Prince Albert Daily Herald*, 31 January 2012 [http://www.paherald.sk.ca/Local/News/2012-01-31/article-2882517/Residential-school-survivors-share-their-stories/1]

Creating Space: My Life and Work in Indigenous Education by Verna J. Kirkness, University of Manitoba Press, 2013, pages 29-33.

"Inside Birtle Indian Residential School 2014" by Reid Dickie. [https://readreidread.wordpress.com/2014/11/19/inside-birtle-indian-residential-school-2014]

"Crumbling former Manitoba residential school property available for $79,000," *Winnipeg Free Press*, 27 June 2015. [http://www.winnipegfreepress.com/local/for-sale-dark-chapter-in-canadian-history-310249561.html]

"Birtle Residential School for sale online," *Crossroads This Week*, 3 July 2015, page 5.

The Survivors Speak: A Report of the Truth and Reconciliation Commission of Canada, Winnipeg: Truth and Reconciliation Commission of Canada, 2015. [http://www.trc.ca/websites/trcinstitution/File/2015/Findings/Survivors_Speak_2015_05_30_web_0.pdf]

Honouring the Truth, Reconciling the Future: Summary of the Final Report of the Truth and Reconciliation Commission of Canada, Winnipeg: Truth and Reconciliation Commission of Canada, 2015. [http://www.trc.ca/websites/trcinstitution/File/2015/Honouring_the_Truth_Reconciling_for_the_Future_July_23_2015.pdf]

ACKNOWLEDGEMENTS

I thank Brenda Samchuk (Birdtail Country Museum) for giving generously of her time during my visit to Birtle in early 2016. Nicole Courrier (National Centre for Truth and Reconciliation) pointed me toward data in their archives on the Birtle Residential School. Ed Ledohowski provided his research notes and photos on the former school and James Kostuchuk (Portage Collegiate) helped with historical enrollment statistics in the public school system. Katherine Nichols shared her research on the abandoned cemetery at the Brandon Residential School.

Bradley
Grave

History is a collection of stories about the past. Some of these stories are strict recitations of easily proved facts. Others are, in whole or part, accidentally or intentionally fictional. Humans are good (or bad, depending on your perspective) at embellishing a story, especially when there are gaps in what is known. So how can we know that the stories contained in books like this one are reliable? The short answer is that we cannot know with certainty, so we decide based on our perception of the author's integrity.

Whenever possible, I have tried to verify the stories presented in this book by using primary sources—ones created at the time of the event being described, by people most likely to know—but I readily acknowledge that this was not always possible, in which case I have used second-hand or, in a few cases, third-hand sources. I have done so reluctantly because, when we are dealing with events that happened long ago, when primary sources are scant or nonexistent, distortions and mistruths creep insidiously into stories, becoming "facts" by the mere act of repetition. This is what I want you to consider as you read the story of F.T. Bradley, a disgraced civil servant who died under mysterious circumstances and is buried in an unusual place near Emerson. First, I will tell the story as it was told to me by a friend at Emerson, then I will reexamine the story with a more critical eye. Lest you think that I am casting aspersions on my

friend, he did not have access to primary sources that place aspects of his story into doubt. The story as he relayed it to me seemed, under the circumstances, quite reasonable. But reasonableness is why such stories get repeated and remembered, even if they turn out to be wrong.

Born at Ottawa in 1845, Frederick Thomas Bradley arrived in Manitoba in 1871, a year after it became a province. Unlike a lot of Ontarians, who came to western Canada looking for opportunities, Bradley already had a job as the federal government's first customs collector on the west bank of the Red River at the Canada-US border. The railway had not yet reached Manitoba. The primary means of travelling here, other than the arduous 530-mile trail hacked through the rocky, heavily wooded, and wet country separating Manitoba and Ontario by surveyor Simon Dawson between 1868 and 1871, was by steamboat from

Frederick Thomas Bradley (1845-1884), the disgraced federal customs officer at Emerson who died under mysterious circumstances and was buried near Emerson. EMERSON MASONIC LODGE, COURTESY OF WAYNE ARSENY

the United States. The Canadian government needed to regulate river trade into its new territory. Bradley occupied a small log building—still standing on the western outskirts of Emerson—that served as the customs office, eventually being forced to move it northward when it was discovered to be in American territory. The office, along with a trading post of the Hudson's Bay Company, formed the basis of the Town of West Lynne, incorporated in 1882. On the east bank of the river, the Town of Emerson was established when, in 1873, Americans Thomas Carney and William Fairbanks obtained land from the Canadian government and named their new community after the American essayist and philosopher, Ralph Waldo Emerson. Emerson and West Lynne vied for dominance until 1889 when they merged into a single urban municipality, the Town of Emerson.

As one of the area's first residents, and a representative of the federal government, Bradley was a respected member of the community. In addition to his government duties, he speculated in land and, by the early 1880s, owned several valuable lots in and around Emerson. He served as the local Justice of the Peace and was responsible for issuing marriage licenses. He was a founding member of St. Luke's Anglican Church and helped to establish its first cemetery. Active in the Masons, Bradley was the first member of Masonic Lodge No. 6, established in 1876, and served as its Worshipful Master several times. In September 1871, he married Caroline Jenkins, the daughter of a senior civil servant at Ottawa, and he brought her

to Emerson. Over the next eight years, they had seven children together, although only two would live to adulthood. The last two children, twin sons, died a few days after their mother, in 1879. Caroline Bradley and four of the Bradley children were buried in Emerson's Anglican cemetery. Bradley remarried to a widow from Quebec but had no more children.

In February 1884, the Canadian Pacific Railway imported a shipment of coal and paid duty amounting to about $4,000. In due course, it was discovered that the money had disappeared. Suspicion immediately fell on Bradley, although he claimed the theft was committed by two clerks under his supervision who, he said, skipped across the American border. Charles Constantine, chief of the Manitoba Provincial Police, came to Emerson and arrested Bradley, bringing him to Winnipeg to appear before a police magistrate. Granted bail, Bradley had no sooner left jail than he became violently ill, went into convulsions, and fell into unconsciousness. His brother-in-law, Winnipeg physician Alfred Codd, was called. Codd pronounced the case a "dangerous one" and had Bradley taken to his home. Bradley was too ill to appear in court but he was represented by a former Attorney-General and Premier Henry Clarke, while the prosecution was handled by eminent lawyer and future Lieutenant Governor J.A.M. Aikins. Bradley's trial was postponed a week, then another three days, to enable him to attend court. On 27 February 1884, Bradley died at Codd's home, at the age of 39 years, never having regained consciousness. Bradley, in disgrace over his impending trial for embezzlement, had taken his own life—perhaps by taking poison that led to the observed symptoms. His body was returned to Emerson. Because suicide was a grievous sin, he was denied burial in the Anglican cemetery that he had helped to found. Instead, Bradley was buried quietly in a piece of farmland on the outskirts of Emerson. No grave marker was placed at the site. Sixteen years later, when the low-lying Anglican cemetery was relocated to higher ground, the Bradleys were disinterred and reburied in the farm field alongside F. T. Bradley and a crème-white gravestone from the cemetery was moved there too. The Emerson Masonic Lodge acquired the title to the Bradley grave site, eventually adding a small marker with Bradley's name, but not his dates of birth or death. When that lodge was dissolved in 1996, control of the site passed to Historic Emerson, an incorporated group of heritage advocates which is now mostly inactive. One of its last members, my

friend, still maintains the Bradley grave along with the Emerson Masonic Lodge building.

There are at least two ways to view the Bradley case. One version is that F. T. Bradley was a dishonest man who, when caught, killed himself to escape justice. A second version is that Bradley was an honest man who was taken advantage of by subordinates and died tragically before he could clear his name. Both versions end with Bradley's suicide and burial in an unmarked grave in a farm field. Unfortunately, we will probably never know for sure which version, or perhaps another variant, is correct. However, using primary evidence in newspaper accounts of the day that are now readily available online or at the Manitoba Legislative Library, we can corroborate or refute aspects of the narrative as it was told to me so, at least, we can set the record straight as much possible. By pouring through pages of the *Emerson International*, *Manitoba Free Press*, *Manitoba Mountaineer*, and *Winnipeg Daily Times* from 1884, I

can offer some corrections to the narrative, as answers to a few questions about the case.

What happened when the embezzlement was discovered?
Bradley was arrested on Saturday, 23 February and arrived in Winnipeg the following day. He immediately appeared before a Provincial Police Magistrate and was released on $10,000 in bail, with the trial set to begin on Monday. The court seized Bradley's assets. He was nevertheless able to provide half of the bail money, and two of his brothers-in-law, Alfred Codd and Donald Codd, each contributed $2,500. Bradley checked into the Queen's Hotel, on Portage Avenue, on Sunday evening and soon began having convulsions in his room. Alfred Codd had Bradley moved to his home, presumably so he was better able to watch over him. Four days elapsed between Bradley's arrest and his death. Meanwhile, the federal government dispatched a customs inspector from Winnipeg to make an initial investigation at Emerson, and

replaced Bradley with a Mr. Clark from the Winnipeg customs office, and eventually a collector from Quebec.

Was Bradley guilty of embezzlement?

Technically, yes. It is unknown how the missing funds in the Emerson customs office came to light but no one—neither Bradley nor the two customs clerks who he implicated—disputed that money was gone or that documents that would have revealed the thefts had disappeared. Early estimates of the amount of money taken ran as high as $9,000 but most eventually settled on $4,700, worth over $200,000 in today's money. Bradley claimed that "I left all the deposits and receipts in the hands of my two confidential clerks." According to the practice of the day, however, Bradley, as head of the office, was ultimately responsible for all money so, whether or not he benefited personally, he was legally responsible. He was quoted several times in newspapers as freely acknowledging this fact. He gave all his assets to the government, or had them taken, and put up $5,000 for his own bail, roughly equal the amount he was purported to have stolen. When Charles Constantine went to arrest Bradley, "The chief, very naturally had expected to find Mr. Bradley missing, and was not a little surprised to find him ready to give himself up to the authorities." All of this seems to imply that Bradley was acting honourably in the face of an undoubtedly stressful situation. A married man, with two young sons, with deep roots and investments in the Emerson community, he hardly strikes one as the sort of man who would resort to criminal activity. On the other hand, at that time the Town of Emerson was on the verge of bankruptcy. In June 1884, it had to lay off all salaried staff and close its public school. (In response, the provincial government appointed E.P. Leacock, described in another chapter of this book, to a Royal Commission to investigate the situation.) Perhaps, like the town, Bradley found himself over-extended financially and dipped into the cash drawer with plans to repay it when his fortunes improved.

What do we know about the other two men implicated in the Emerson embezzlement?

A curious aspect of the story is that few details about customs clerks Thomas Hickey and Frank McGinley were ever published and the focus of attention in the case was primarily on Bradley. There were allegations that Hickey got his job at Emerson through nepotism on the part of Mackenzie Bowell, the federal customs minister (and later the fifth Prime Minister of Canada, from 1894 to 1896), to whom Hickey was a nephew or a cousin, depending on the source. The man who brought the founding charter for the Orange Lodge to Manitoba, as a member of the Wolseley Expedition of 1870, was named Thomas Hickey but we have no way of knowing if this was the same man. We only know that, prior to working in the Emerson customs office in 1884, Hickey was a clerk for the Canadian Pacific Railway at St. Vincent, Minnesota (across the border from Emerson) for "a year or so." About McGinley, we know nothing.

Aerial view of the Bradley family cemetery in a farm field northeast of Emerson, July 2016. GOLDSBOROUGH

The customs office where the Bradley embezzlement was said to have occurred, now a public display at Emerson, April 2016. GOLDSBOROUGH

In January 1884, mere weeks before the embezzlement was revealed, staff in the Emerson customs office—including McGinley but not Hickey—presented Bradley and his wife with gifts and lauded his service:

"We, the officers of your staff working under your supervision as Collector of Customs for Her Majesty the Queen in this ancient and historic Port of Emerson, recognise in you a worthy chief who has on more than one occasion vindicated the honour of the Queen on the frontier in times when Law was not established; and also found you a firm and determined officer when British rights were called into question."

Yet, when the scandal at Emerson was revealed, blame was thrown far and wide. McGinley rushed to

Ottawa to plead his innocence. Bradley claimed in a letter to the *Winnipeg Daily Times* that "Mr. Thomas Hickey has, as I am credibly informed, been living at the rate of $4,000 per annum, while receiving a salary of only $1,000." He also alleged that McGinley and Hickey had absconded to Chicago, whereas a newspaper story in late February 1884 placed Hickey at Portland, Oregon. In mid-March, McGinley was at St. Paul, Minnesota where he reported to police that he had been robbed while playing dice in a bar. His whereabouts after this time are unknown. In 1895, Hickey was said to be living in the United States. Ultimately, Bradley was the only person held accountable for the Emerson embezzlement.

Did Bradley commit suicide?
Unknown, but I think the evidence, admittedly circumstantial, argues against it. When Bradley arrived in Winnipeg under arrest, he told newspaper reporters that he intended to mount a vigorous defense. Why,

then, would he commit suicide before having his day in court? I could find no evidence that an autopsy was conducted on Bradley's body. Even if one was done, it is doubtful that death by poisoning would have been diagnosed given the primitive states of toxicological science and forensic medicine in the 19th century. Bradley's death certificate filed with the provincial government lists his cause of death as "epileptic convulsions." Alfred Codd, Bradley's brother-in-law and a noted Winnipeg physician, told local newspapers that "[t]he main cause of Mr. Bradley's death was apoplectic convulsions and the trouble he had been put to over this shortage in the customs office. He was greatly distressed in mind at the position in which he had been placed, and this no doubt did much to terminate his life." This conclusion seems to have been accepted widely. Newspaper accounts say that Bradley had suffered ill health for some time before his death. They made no mention of suicide which, in itself, is odd because newspapers of Bradley's day

routinely reported suicides, murders, and other grisly demises. Today, if suicide seems a plausible explanation for Bradley's behaviour after his arrival in Winnipeg, would it not have been even more obvious in 1884? In fact, newspaper stories after Bradley's death focused on the high regard in which he was widely held, not on any element of disgrace. Obituaries say that his funeral in St. Luke's Anglican Church was Emerson's largest ever and was attended by "very large attendance of citizens of Emerson, St. Vincent and Pembina, and of settlers from the surrounding country." Emerson historians who have combed through church records find no mention of Bradley being denied burial in the cemetery. Surely a matter of such gravity would have warranted at least a discreet mention?

Who is buried in the Bradley grave site and why it is located in a farm field?
Several members of the Bradley family are buried there. My search of Emerson tax rolls revealed that

Bradley's home was situated on 194 acres of farm land on the outskirts of Emerson where, the local newspaper tells us, he planted 75 acres of wheat. When Caroline Bradley died in 1879, she was not buried in the Anglican cemetery as the popular story would have us believe. Her obituary in the Emerson newspaper stated that she was buried "on Mr. Bradley's place, not far from the residence, and near the graves of two children who had gone before." The grave marker in the field refers to Caroline Bradley and "our loved ones," and lists the four of their children, including the twin sons, who had died by 1879. It is exactly the sort of monument that a grieving husband and father would erect. The grave site is surrounded by a low concrete wall, measuring 16 by 22 feet, with the name "Bradley" embedded on one side. I interpret all of this to mean that Bradley once owned the land where the graves are situated and his wife and children were buried in a family cemetery. When it came time for Bradley to be buried, he joined them but no one saw fit, for reasons unknown, to erect a monument for him. His obituary in the Emerson newspaper noted that, following a brief delay caused by inclement weather, "[t]he body was taken from the church to Oak Lodge Farm, situated in the north part of town and the property of deceased, and buried beside the graves of his first wife and two little children."

What happened after Bradley died and was buried?
Alfred Codd was appointed executor of Bradley's estate. In a copy of Bradley's will deposited with the Manitoba Surrogate Court in April 1884, Codd swore that the value of the estate was about $900. This means either Bradley's land holdings had not yet been liquidated—they had been assessed in 1883 as being worth $21,975—or they had been seized by the Crown in repayment for the lost customs money. An auction of Bradley's personal effects realized over $1,000 for his widow. The Bradley home was occupied by the family of his successor as customs collector, A.M. Phillips, from St. John, Quebec. The later whereabouts of Bradley's widow are unknown, but his two sons by his first wife, aged 10 and 9 when Bradley died, remained in western Canada, dying in 1944 and 1945, respectively.

What other evidence would be helpful?
There are other sources it would be useful to check in hopes of learning more facts about the Bradley embezzlement case, so we could draw more definite conclusions. The local newspapers, which were my main source of primary information, seemed to have lost all interest after Bradley died, so I was unable to find any formal conclusion to the case. Would federal government customs files, perhaps preserved at Library and Archives Canada in Ottawa, describe the outcome of the investigation at Emerson? Would Manitoba Land Titles records show how the Bradley graves came to be owned by the Emerson

Masons? Unfortunately, finding answers to these questions would require more time and resources than I was able to commit. Maybe someone reading this text will be inspired to pick up the investigation. For now, I think we can safely conclude that F.T. Bradley was not buried in a farmer's field because he was denied admittance to the local cemetery, and it is doubtful that he committed suicide. But the full story has yet to be told.

SOURCES

"Bradley," *Emerson International*, 13 February 1879, page 4.

[Bradley farm], *Manitoba Free Press*, 26 April 1879, page 1.

[Bradley marriage licenses], *Manitoba Free Press*, 19 July 1879, page 1.

"Emerson news," *Winnipeg Daily Times*, 13 February 1884, page 1.

"The Emerson customs house," *Winnipeg Daily Times*, 16 February 1884, page 4.

"The customs shortage," *Winnipeg Daily Times*, 23 February 1884, page 4.

"Bradley arrested," *Winnipeg Daily Times*, 25 February 1884, page 8.

"Sudden death," *Winnipeg Daily Times*, 28 February 1884, page 8.

"The customhouse trouble," *Emerson International*, 28 February 1884, page 3.

"Demise of Mr. Bradley," *Manitoba Free Press*, 29 February 1884, page 4.

"In memorium," *Manitoba Free Press*, 6 March 1884, page 3.

"Frank McGinley," *Manitoba Free Press*, 19 March 1884, page 4.

Probate Will [Frederick Thomas Bradley], Winnipeg Estate File 327, ATG0025A, GR0170, Archives of Manitoba.

"Bankrupt!," *Emerson International*, 19 June 1884, page 3.

[Phillips], *Emerson International*, 3 July 1884, page 3.

[Royal Commission], *Emerson International*, 17 July 1884, page 3.

Town of Emerson tax assessment rolls, 1883-1884, Archives of Manitoba.

"All in the family," *Marquette [Rapid City] Reporter*, 7 March 1895, page 2.

British Columbia death registrations, http://search-collections.royalbcmuseum.bc.ca/Genealogy

"The rise and fall of Emerson" by Marjorie Forrester, *Manitoba Pageant*, April 1957.

Economic history, MeasuringWorth.com

ACKNOWLEDGEMENTS

Keen local historian Wayne Arseny first alerted me to the Bradley grave site and toured me through the Emerson Masonic Lodge. I thank Karen Prytula, a distant Bradley relative, for providing details about his early life and Stan Barclay for providing information about Bradley's involvement with the Masons. Efficient as ever, Monica Ball at the Manitoba Legislative Library located several stories about the Bradley embezzlement case in the *Emerson International* newspaper.

Copley Anglican Church

I had heard that Copley Anglican was sometimes called the "Bootleggers' Church." What had earned it this moniker, I wondered, as I drove to its site in the extreme southwestern corner of Manitoba? The name of the local municipality, Two Borders, was my first clue. Copley was close to two borders: five miles from Saskatchewan and two miles from North Dakota. And what about the isolation? I could not see a house for miles in any direction. It was just the sort of place that would appeal to someone wanting to escape the attention of the law. Arriving at the churchyard, I found a small cemetery with a handful of crumbling stone markers and the fieldstone walls of a building that looked like it had been abandoned for a very, very long time.

Copley Anglican Church, soon after construction in 1892. PHIL RIPPIN

Throughout the late 19th and early 20th centuries, the Canadian government did its utmost to entice settlers to take up farming in southern Manitoba. Immigration agents were dispatched all over Europe where the best farmers were thought to reside, hoping to convince them to move to Canada. Racist notions of who would make the best farmers meant that people from Britain—and northern Europe more generally—were especially favoured. In the mid-1880s, a cohort of Britons arrived in Manitoba, intending to settle the southwestern area of the province. No one thought to ask if the land there was fertile, or the climate congenial, or if the Britons were experienced farmers. Everyone seems to have assumed naively that success was guaranteed. History would prove otherwise.

Among the settlers was Goddard Gale, an artist from London. His father was a prominent barrister and cricket player; his mother was the socialite daughter of a diplomat. In the fall of 1884, after spending several years as an engineer and surveyor for the Canadian Pacific Railway, and reportedly being the first white man to set eyes on Lake Louise in the Rockies, Gale took up residence in the Copley district of Manitoba (then known as Butterfield, after the local post office). He became a community leader, serving on the council of the Rural

Municipality of Arthur, before its partition into three smaller municipalities, two of which reunified in 2015 to form Two Borders. Being a staunch Anglican, it was inevitable that Gale would take a leading role in construction of the first Anglican church west of the Souris River. He wrote letters to friends back home, seeking donations, and appealed to British church societies for help in fundraising. Volunteers began to build a church on 4.6 acres of land in the autumn of 1890 and it was completed by the spring of 1892. In a letter written to relatives back home, Gale's visiting father reported:

> "The building, which is fifty-six feet long, twenty wide and twenty high, is built of stone quarried by the farmers last year and hauled to the site of the building. It consists

From Residential Schools to Bank Vaults to Grain Elevators 59

almost entirely of grey and red granite and sandstone found in the sloughs—dried up watercourses—all over the prairie. The sidewalls are ten feet high and two feet thick and the east and west walls twenty feet in height. The church is pure Gothic, and the roof of wood, covered with shingles—wooden "slates," which look much nicer than slate and are almost imperishable in this climate."

Known formally as St. George's Anglican Church, local names included Butterfield Church or, more commonly, Copley Church in commemoration of a local settler. On 4 September 1892, the building was consecrated

The interior of the former Copley Anglican Church, 1967. ARCHIVES OF MANITOBA

by Bishop Robert Machray and Canon Samuel Matheson, both visiting from Winnipeg, and assisted by itinerant Anglican clerics Charles Wood and Frank Mercer. The official opening had been preceded by the first burial in its cemetery, a year earlier, of Goddard's brother Arthur, who had drowned in a well. Soon after the consecration, Goddard's first-born child joined his uncle in the cemetery. In addition to the church, the community boasted a post office and one-room schoolhouse.

But the true nature of the Copley area soon became clear. Its general aridity made the soil prone to wind and water erosion. Below-average rainfall combined with crop losses due to gophers, fungus, and freak hailstorms doomed the community nearly from the start. Most settlers began to leave for greener pastures elsewhere. Gale and his wife moved to Winnipeg, where in 1894 he operated the Winnipeg School of Art and Design on Main Street before moving to San Francisco, California. There, he took several famous panoramic photographs of the devastated city following a 1906 earthquake. Other Copley settlers moved to nearby Lyleton, where growing conditions were better, but others returned to England or went to Saskatchewan, the United States, or Australia. By 1903, St. George's had almost no parishioners. In June 1913, the impressive stone building was deconsecrated, after being used for just 20 years. The communion vessel, wall hangings, and service books were taken to a newly opened Anglican church at Pierson, ten miles to the north, while the organ and pictures were given to Eunola School, seven miles farther north of Pierson, where services were held in the absence of a formal church building. The isolated building at Copley was abandoned.

The old church may have enjoyed a renewed, if illicit, life during experimental bans on the sale of intoxicating liquor, widely viewed by moralists as the primary cause of social decay. Local lore holds that, during the formal years of Prohibition in Manitoba (1916-1923), Saskatchewan (1917-1925), and the United States (1920-1933), the isolated location of the Copley building and its close proximity to the American and Saskatchewan borders made it an attractive warehouse for contraband. It is a great story—especially the juxtaposition of criminal booze sales in a church—but it is a tale for which I could find little corroborating evidence.

Even if bootleggers never visited Copley, it is clear that vandals did. Efforts in 1932 to protect the building's interior from damage, by boarding its doors and windows, would ultimately prove futile. The walls and roof were still intact by the mid-1960s but the doors and window coverings had been removed. By the time that I visited in the autumn of 2011, only remnants of the walls were still standing. The wooden roof and floor were gone, probably lost to a fire. Although the cemetery was well tended, the site appears to have few, if any, visitors. In the end, Copley Anglican Church bears quiet testament to the ambition and ultimate failure of many would-be farmers to make a life for themselves in the harsh prairie climate. Only those who were tough and experienced managed to prevail.

Views of the Copley church and cemetery, October 2011. GOLDSBOROUGH

SOURCES

"Obiter dicta," *Manitoba Free Press*, 21 April 1894, page 10.

Harvests of Time: History of the R.M. of Edward by Edward History Book Committee, 1983, pages 146-148.

ACKNOWLEDGEMENTS

I thank Phil Rippin (Penticton, BC) for providing a wonderful early photo of the Copley Anglican Church and Felix Kuehn for his detailed research on Goddard Gale.

Transcona Cordite Plant

It is hard to imagine that a ditch could have historical significance. But a ditch running through Transcona on its way to the Red River was once the conduit for the disposal of waste water from one of the largest weapons factories on the prairies during the Second World War.

OPPOSITE Concrete foundations for buildings at The Ranges area of the Cordite Plant, June 2016. GOLDSBOROUGH

Soon after the war was declared, the Manitoba government began to lobby the federal government to locate some of its munitions manufacturing capability here. Government officials touted several advantages. Electricity, which would be needed for any manufacturing process, was readily and cheaply available from hydroelectric power plants on the Winnipeg River. As a province well-endowed with lakes and rivers, a manufacturing plant here could be assured of ample supplies of fresh water. The fact that Winnipeg was a major railway hub for the Canadian Pacific and Canadian National, meant that transportation of raw materials and finished products could be arranged easily. Manitoba had an abundant labour force and, perhaps most significantly for those worried about the possibility of sabotage by enemy agents, a munitions plant in western Canada, far from the European battlefields, had a distinct safety advantage.

In 1940, the federal government announced that it would build a plant to make cordite in Manitoba. A propellant resembling brown-coloured twine, cordite was invented in 1889 as a smokeless replacement for gunpowder. Used by British forces during the First World War for rifle shells, tank guns, artillery, and naval guns, its formulation was refined before the Second World War where its numerous applications included the detonation system of the atomic bomb dropped on Hiroshima, Japan in 1945.

A site for the Cordite Plant was selected in the Rural Municipality of Springfield, east of what was at that time the City of Transcona, roughly nine miles from downtown Winnipeg. Construction began in 1941 and was completed for a total of $20 million. Roughly a square mile in area, a perimeter fence patrolled by armed guards enclosed the site and its 230 buildings, including offices, machine shops, hospital, hotel, residences, telephone exchange building,

View of the Cordite Plant, no date, shows widely spaced buildings to minimize the damage from an accidental explosion. TRANSCONA HISTORICAL MUSEUM

Square-mile area of the Cordite Plant, bisected by the Cordite Ditch running, 2006. DENIS SABOURIN GEOMATICS

and laundry. Buildings were spaced widely to minimize the extent of damage in the event of accidental explosions. At the core of the facility was a three-storey factory and twin-stack power plant that produced about two-thirds of the electricity used in manufacturing. A network of rail tracks shuttled materials around the site. Each day, the Greater Winnipeg Water District delivered up to 10 million gallons of water while waste water was carried to the Red River in the Cordite Ditch. The plant opened in June 1941, operated by Defence Industries Limited, a Crown Corporation.

The basic ingredients for making cordite are nitroglycerin and guncotton, made by mixing nitric acid with glycerine and cellulose, respectively. What little we know about the manufacturing process

at the Transcona plant, we owe to Ray Gill (1915-2009), who helped to build the facility, and left a brief memoir of his later work there. To make cordite, acid from lead-lined vats was transported to the Gun Cotton Area where it was added slowly to wood pulp—or, in later years, a material made from sea gull dung—in porcelain-lined basins. This produced a material that looked like heavy whipped cream. The acid was removed and the material was pressed into blocks of guncotton. These blocks were then moved to The Ranges where the guncotton was blended with a stabilizer and petroleum jelly, then kneaded into a soft, pliable dough. Finally, the dough was pressed through dies into strands, cut into short lengths, dried, packed, and shipped.

The Cordite Plant worked 24 hours a day, seven days a week, with three shifts of workers each day. It was a major source of local employment, of both women and men, with levels peaking at 4,200 people. The abundance of explosives necessitated

Wooden buildings used in the manufacture of cordite during the Second World War were so thoroughly impregnated with explosives that they put to the torch rather than attempt to decontaminate them in late 1945. *MANITOBA INDUSTRIAL TOPICS*

strict safety protocols and a "zero tolerance policy." In July 1942, a worker caught smoking on the premises was sentenced to three months in jail while those caught with matches paid stiff fines. Surprisingly, there was only one fatality during the five-year lifespan of the facility: a truck driver was killed when cordite was stacked too high, causing a spark and a massive explosion.

Over the course of its operational life, the Cordite Plant churned out 30,000 tons of guncotton, 14,500 tons of nitroglycerin, 75,000 tons of nitric acid, and 167,000 tons of sulphuric acid, and packed 65,300 tons of cordite. Production ended on 23 August 1945, eight days after Japan's surrender. The following day, staff layoffs began. Local municipal officials hoped the large manufacturing plant—and its associated tax revenue—could be maintained. Many of the buildings had not been designed for longevity but it was hoped the administration building, power station, laboratories, and other service buildings could be reused. Other buildings were thought to be so thoroughly impregnated with nitroglycerin that they were not possible to salvage.

In November 1945, several buildings were blown up using 500 pounds of cordite. During 1946, wooden buildings were disassembled. Some 1,460 windows, 800 doors, 350,000 feet of electrical writing, lumber, and asbestos siding were re-used in housing projects around Winnipeg, including 72 bungalows built for married veterans, known as "Veteran's Village," on the University of Manitoba's campus in Fort Garry. For a few months in mid-1946, one

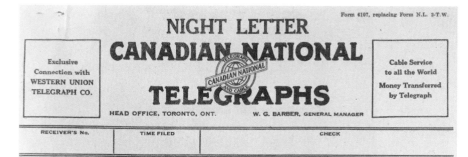

Telegram from Manitoba Minister of Mines and Natural Resources to C.D. Howe, federal Minister of Munitions of Supply, advocated the advantages of building a cordite plant in Manitoba, August 1940. ARCHIVES OF MANITOBA

Warning sign from the perimeter of the Cordite Plant. TRANSCONA HISTORICAL MUSEUM

of the residential buildings at the former plant was used to accommodate Japanese-Canadians who had been detained as "enemy aliens" during the war. By 1947, the power plant, administration building, and machine shop remained standing. Finally, by mid-June 1948, they too were demolished.

Today, very little remains at the site. The most conspicuous remnant is the Cordite Ditch that bisects the former plant. A short stretch of wire from the perimeter fence, labeled with threatening signs about trespassing, can be seen along the highway north of the Dugald Road.

Railway tracks that once crisscrossed the site can be seen in aerial photographs and concrete foundations for The Ranges are still present. Yet, it is hard to believe a vast military complex that employed thousands of people once stood here. In 2010, the City of Winnipeg erected commemorative signage along the Cordite Ditch, over two miles from the actual plant site. Were they worried about residual explosives?

SOURCES

"Cordite Plant," Deputy Minister of Natural Resources Files, 1940-1946, Archives of Manitoba, GR1600, G4512.

"Cordite Plant," Premier's Office Files, 1940-1941, Archives of Manitoba, GR0043, G63.

"Cordite Plant smoker jailed," *Winnipeg Tribune*, 30 July 1942, page 13.

"Two go to jail for smoking in Cordite Plant," *Winnipeg Tribune*, 5 March 1943, page 1.

"Cordite building reduced to ashes," *Manitoba Industrial Topics*, Volume 5, Number 4, November-December 1945, pages 16-17. [Manitoba Legislative Library]

"Cordite Plant lumber aids veterans' homes," *Winnipeg Tribune*, 5 September 1946, page 7.

"Cordite Plant – Dugald Road (Highway No. 15)," Transcona Heritage Resources Inventory, December 1999, pages 124-131. [Transcona Historical Museum]

Memoir of Ray Allison Gill. [TH99.24.1, Transcona Historical Museum]

Obituary [Ray Gill], *Winnipeg Free Press*, 21 February 2009.

ACKNOWLEDGEMENTS

I am grateful to Alanna Horejda, Curator at the Transcona Historical Museum, for providing access to the museum's files on the former Cordite Plant. Many of the details about the plant and its construction were found by Nathan Kramer, historical researcher extraordinaire.

Remaining remnant of the fence that once surrounded the entire perimeter of the Cordite Plant, June 2016. GOLDSBOROUGH

Aerial view of the Cordite Plant site showing the Cordite Ditch at left, building foundations of The Ranges in the centre, and lines marking the railway tracks that once criss-crossed the site, June 2016. GOLDSBOROUGH

Fort Daer

As I drove up to the American border, I wondered what the customs officer was going to think about my motive for wanting to enter his country. When he asked how long I intended to stay, he seemed surprised that I would visit only about 20 minutes. I was heading to a spot a little over two miles south of the Emerson border crossing. My destination was the south bank of the Pembina River where it discharges into the Red River, to the now-abandoned site of Fort Daer.

Thomas Douglas, the Fifth
Earl of Selkirk—Lord Selkirk—
was an investor in the Hudson's Bay
Company (HBC). But he also had a
social conscience and felt strongly
that the people displaced from the
Scottish Highlands through the 18th
and 19th centuries, in a notorious act
known as The Clearances, should
have a home in the New World. In
1811, he received from the HBC a grant
of 116,000 square miles in the Red
River Valley where he planned to
settle the Scots. To prepare for their
arrival at the junction of the Red
and Assiniboine Rivers, Selkirk dispatched an advance work party led by
Miles Macdonell (as first Governor
of the Selkirk Settlement, for whom
a Winnipeg collegiate would later
be named). They arrived at York
Factory, the HBC post on Hudson

Bay, on 24 September 1811, too late
in the year to head inland. They
were forced to over-winter there so,
as a result, they were late to arrive
at The Forks. On 4 September 1812,
Macdonell formally took possession
of the Selkirk Settlement and,
about a month later, he and his men
planted a bushel and a half of wheat
in hopes of having a crop the following year.

Meanwhile, a party of Scottish
settlers, including women and children, left Stornoway, Scotland on
24 June 1812 and arrived at York
Factory on 28 August 1812. After
resting for a week, they continued
inland in eleven York boats and three
canoes, arriving at The Forks on
27 October 1812, not far behind the
Macdonell work party. Macdonell
realized they did not have enough

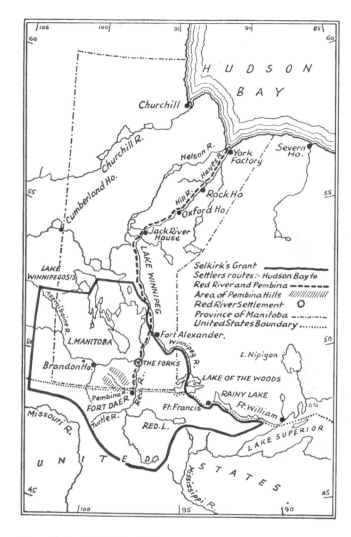

Map of the Selkirk Land Grant
"The Lord Selkirk Settlement at
Red River, Part 1" by Anne Matheson
Henderson MANITOBA PAGEANT, MANITOBA
HISTORICAL SOCIETY

Fort Daer monument in a public park at Pembina, Northa Dakota, May 2011.
GOLDSBOROUGH

supplies at the Selkirk Settlement to sustain all the settlers through the winter and that better conditions were available farther south, at the junction of the Pembina and Red Rivers, the traditional winter headquarters of Métis bison hunters. So the settlers continued upstream (south) to Pembina. On the north bank of the Pembina stood Fort Pembina, a fur-trading post of the North West Company, an HBC rival.

The Selkirk Settlers occupied the south bank of the Pembina and there set up makeshift huts. The young men from the group went out in search of bison while the women, children, and older men remained behind. On 24 December 1812, they hoisted a flag over the partially constructed fort and named it Fort Daer in honour of Dunbar James Douglas, the eldest son of Lord Selkirk, who also went by the name of Lord Daer. In the spring of 1813, after the ice had left the Red River, the settlers returned to The Forks to build homes and plant more crops. The results were less than encouraging so they returned to Fort Daer to spend the following winter. In fact, the settlers would spend the next three winters there. The only image we have of Fort Daer comes from several years later. In 1822, a 16-year-old artistic prodigy named Peter Rindisbacher—whose Swiss parents had immigrated to the Selkirk Settlement in hopes of establishing their home there—sketched Fort Daer and Fort Pembina from the east bank of the Red River. It shows a modest wooden palisade surrounding a large U-shaped wooden building that presumably was used by the HBC for its fur-trading. Whether or not the building stood when the Selkirk Settlers were in residence is unknown.

The year 1812 was noteworthy for more than just the arrival of the Selkirk Settlers; it was the year that Great Britain battled the newly established United States of America. Six years after the battle, a treaty between the combatants defined the American border west of Lake of the Woods as being the 49th line of latitude. As a result, Fort Daer was now in American territory. In 1822, the HBC ordered the fort to be abandoned.

Many years later, in 1948, a monument at the former Fort Daer site (now a state park and recreation area) was erected. It was one of the first projects of the Pembina County Pioneer Daughters, a group founded in 1941 by local women to preserve the history of the region. They understood the significance of the spot. But a wary Canadian customs officer, on my return home after a brief visit to the monument, did not understand, at least not until I gave him an abbreviated version of this story. I told him that, were it not for the protection afforded by Fort Daer at a critical time, the Selkirk Settlement might have failed. The settlers would have died or moved elsewhere. Without them, a small European outpost—now Winnipeg—would not have become the first permanent agricultural settlement in prairie Canada.

SOURCES

"The Lord Selkirk Settlement at Red River" [three parts] by Anne Matheson Henderson, *Manitoba Pageant*, 1967-1968.

Pembina County Pioneer Daughters Collection, Chester Fritz Library, University of North Dakota.

Lord Selkirk: A Life by J.M. Bumsted, University of Manitoba Press, 2008.

ACKNOWLEDGEMENTS

I am indebted to the indefatigable Ed Ledohowski for making me aware of the Rindisbacher image of Fort Daer, and members of the Bicentenary of the Red River Selkirk Settlement Committee for helpful conversations in the lead-up to the scandalously under-celebrated two-hundredth anniversary of the arrival of the Selkirk Settlers, in 2012.

Gervais Bowstring Bridge

I am frequently asked how I find historic sites like the ones described in this book, especially obscure structures in out-of-the-way places. In the case of the Gervais Bowstring Bridge, about a mile south of the Trans-Canada Highway near Newton Siding in the Rural Municipality of Portage la Prairie, I learned of its existence from my friend Neil Christoffersen. Neil has an abiding interest in Manitoba's past and, as the Reeve of a Rural Municipality, is prone to travel back roads. He knew that I would be keenly interested in this bridge because it is a well-preserved example of a once-common, now-rare bowstring arch. Tracking down the story of this lonely bridge led me to find its cousin, another abandoned bowstring, seven miles away as the crow flies.

The bowstring arch bridge built near the railway siding of Gervais, in the Rural Municipality of Portage la Prairie, in 1919.
GOLDSBOROUGH

Bridges are an important part of Manitoba's transportation history. As farmers spread across the prairies in the late 1800s, they encountered the myriad, meandering rivers and streams that punctuate an otherwise vast landscape. Crossings at shallow places had been used for eons by bison, Indigenous people, and fur traders but these were not always located at convenient spots for farmers. Later, ferries provided a means to cross these rivers. But as trains and, later, automobiles became the primary means of travel, bridges provided better access to once isolated places. They were an essential ingredient of the extensive provincial road network that we enjoy today. Highways and their bridges contributed to the demise of railways as the primary means of carrying people and goods around the province, and also to the waning of many small, rural communities.

The earliest bridges in Manitoba were built with local materials, usually wood. They were often short-lived, as they tended to float away during floods, were distorted by shifting of the earth and spring ice, or rotted over time. The demand for more robust, permanent bridges grew in the early 20th century as steam- and gas-powered machines began to replace horses as the engines of agriculture. Municipalities began to vigorously improve the primitive trails on "road allowances" that had been surveyed on one-mile grids across the prairies in the 1870s. In February 1914, the Manitoba government passed The Good Roads Act to foster development of rural roads. It mandated the formation of a three-man Good Roads Board led by Manitoba's first Highway Commissioner, Archibald McGillivray

(for whom Winnipeg's McGillivray Boulevard is named), along with former Winnipeg Mayor Thomas Deacon and Virden-area farmer and municipal Reeve Charles Ivens. One of the Board's first actions was to appoint Manson Lyons as its Chief Engineer. A native Nova Scotian, Lyons came to Manitoba in 1912 to design drainage works and bridges for the provincial government.

Lyons, or one of three bridge engineers under his supervision, undoubtedly designed the Gervais Bowstring Bridge. Known locally as "The Rainbow Bridge," probably because its graceful twin arches look vaguely like a rainbow, a bowstring resembles a curved bow facing upward with a string spanning the river. Engineers see

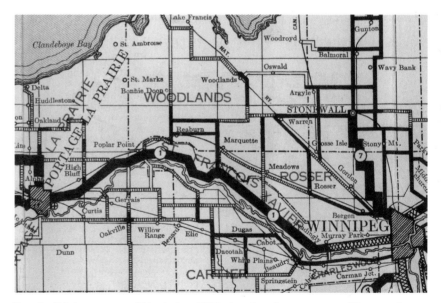

Detail of highway map of Manitoba, 1930, showing the area around Portage la Prairie, including the railway siding of Gervais north of the bowstring arch bridge.

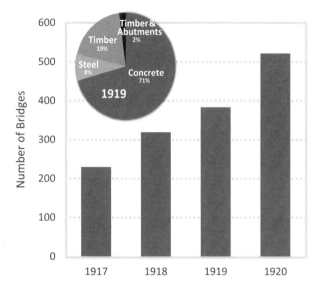

Graph of bridge construction in Manitoba, 1917 to 1920. GOOD ROADS BOARD ANNUAL REPORTS, MANITOBA LEGISLATIVE LIBRARY

the bowstring as an efficient way to carry the weight of the bridge deck on which vehicles cross the river. Made of concrete—a mixture of Portland cement, gravel, and water—strengthened with steel rods embedded inside, on wood or concrete piles and footings, the bridge decks were usually just wide enough for a single vehicle. If two drivers approached opposite ends of the bridge at the same time, one had to yield until the other had crossed.

So far, I have found six intact bowstring bridges in my travels. (A seventh near the village of Roseisle is no longer identifiable as a bowstring because its arches were removed to enable farm equipment and other wide vehicles to cross.) They were complex, time-consuming bridges to build so they were typically found on crossings of larger rivers by major roads where the traffic volume was sufficiently high to warrant the trouble and expense. That's the confusing thing about the Gervais bowstring. It straddles the relatively modest La Salle River. It is situated on a dirt road at least a mile from a major highway and is probably used only by the occasional farm truck or tractor. Why was such an elaborate bridge built at such an obscure spot?

Obsessively, I searched for an answer to this question. Had there been a major road here in the past? Provincial maps from the 1920s did not show any in this vicinity. Had there been unfulfilled plans to build a major road here? Certainly, around the time this bridge was built, the

network of provincial trunk highways was starting to form, led by pioneering automobile enthusiast Arthur "Ace" Emmett. The "Portage Highway" that followed the Assiniboine River from Winnipeg to Portage la Prairie, for example, would eventually become a component of the Trans-Canada Highway. But that road (today's Provincial Trunk Highway #26) ran north of the Assiniboine, many miles from the Gervais bowstring. The answer finally came when I visited the public library in Portage la Prairie. There, I pored through fragile, old books containing hand-written minutes of the municipal council. I learned that, in October 1917, the council had asked the Good Roads Board to contribute half of the cost to construct no fewer than nineteen bridges around the municipality. The council proposed to issue debentures, at an interest rate of 6%, to raise the $32,350 needed to pay the municipality's half-share of the construction costs. To gauge the support of local residents for the plan, a referendum was held in

December 1917 and, by a vote of 295 to 63, the bridge project was approved.

Despite the favourable reception by Portage taxpayers, it was not a foregone conclusion that the bridges would be constructed. The Good Roads Board had to be convinced the bridges were a wise investment of public funds, and had to be situated on one of two types of roads: a provincial highway or a market road. Provincial highways were defined as ones that were useful over a large geographic region whereas market roads provided local benefit, mostly for farmers to transport their produce to the nearest town or railway station. The application to the Good Roads Board had to include a statement of the municipality's assessed tax base (so the Board could be assured of the municipality's ability to cover its share of the costs), a map showing the location of the proposed work relative to major roads, and an estimate of its cost. The Board assisted the municipality in determining this cost by having its engineers visit the site and later prepare detailed construction blueprints.

How did the Portage municipal council and Good Roads engineers justify building a bowstring bridge on a dirt road in the middle of nowhere? It turned out that, in 1917, the bridge site was just a mile away from the railway station of Gervais on the Grand Trunk Pacific Railway (later part of the Canadian National Railway)—continuing an alphabetical series of stops that included Beaudry, Cabot, Dugas, Elie, and Fortier. Although flow in the La Salle River hardly trickles most of the time, it can increase

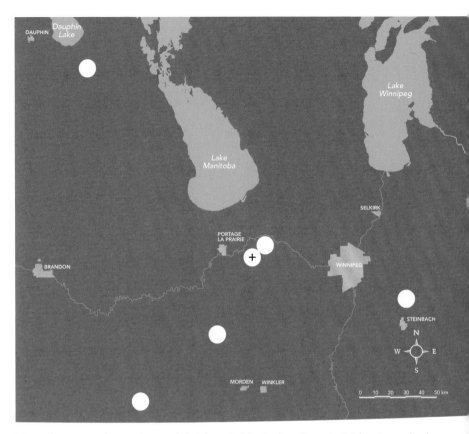

Map of surviving bowstring arch bridges in Manitoba. Gervais Bridge is marked with +. GOLDSBOROUGH

dramatically in wet years, especially when it receives overflow from the Assiniboine. At such times, a small, low-level bridge would be submerged. To assure local farmers of access to the Gervais station, even during floods, Good Roads engineers decided a substantial bridge was needed. Why was it to be made of concrete? By late 1917, the First World War had been raging for three years. Supplies of structural steel were scarce, and therefore costly, and the labour to construct bridges was likewise scarce as able-bodied men were enlisted for military duty overseas.

Concrete was an ideal material for bridge construction when resources were limited; plentiful and relatively inexpensive to produce, it was durable and required little or no ongoing maintenance.

Mill Creek bowstring arch bridge, July 2014.
GOLDSBOROUGH

Public tenders for the Portage bridges were issued and the lowest bid for the Gervais bowstring came from Winnipeg contractor William Newman. In fact, Newman's firm won the contract for three bowstrings in the municipality: the one over the La Salle River, as well as ones over Rat Creek in the western part of the

municipality and Mill Creek in the eastern part. This made me wonder if either of the other two bridges had survived. The Rat Creek site is near the present-day Yellowhead Highway so it was probably replaced long ago as traffic volume had increased. But the Mill Creek bridge site seemed remote, on an unremarkable dirt road not unlike the one by the Gervais bridge, although it too had been justified in 1917 as being on a locally-important market road. Peering at a fuzzy satellite photograph of the Mill Creek area, it seemed to me there might be vestiges of a bridge there. The next time I was in the area, I drove to the spot and, sure enough, there was another remarkably intact bowstring. Like the one over the La Salle River, locals called it a "Rainbow Bridge" too.

Construction of the fifty-foot-long bowstring bridge over the La Salle River began in June of 1918. Foundation piles were driven and footings had been built by the time that cold weather forced the workers to stop for the winter. Construction resumed in the following spring and,

by the time the bridge was finished in October 1919, the total cost of construction was $7,003, shared equally by the municipal and provincial governments. (Meanwhile, the Mill Creek bridge was finished a few months earlier at a cost of $6,681.) By the end of that year, the Good Roads Board had overseen the construction of 64 bridges around the province, all but six of them made of concrete, bringing the total to 384 bridges in the five years since it was established.

When the First World War ended, prosperity returned to the prairies. As grain prices rose and farmers delivered increasing bounty to market, the demand grew for all-weather, graded and graveled roads, along with bridges. Arguably, the "Golden Age" of bridge-building in Manitoba started in the 1910s with the establishment of the Good Roads Board, and continued through the Depression years of the 1930s, when the federal government put unemployed people to work by contributing half the cost of building projects. By 1936, Manitoba had 1,578 new bridges.

With the new-found freedom provided by the burgeoning road network, and fostered by growing numbers of automobiles, Manitobans began venturing farther afield. Ace Emmett introduced the system of road numbering and signage that would be embraced around the continent, and maps from his Manitoba Motor League (today's CAA Manitoba) provided guidance. Through the 1950s and '60s, an increasing proportion of the early gravelled highways were paved with concrete or asphalt.

The future traffic envisioned by Good Roads engineers and Portage municipal officials on the roads leading up to the two bowstring bridges never developed. The Mill Creek bridge served only local traffic, as there was no nearby bridge over the Assiniboine River to enable access to the Trans-Canada Highway north of the river. When the Trans-Canada was re-routed to its present course, five miles south of Mill Creek, the old bowstring bridge was even more isolated. As for the Gervais bridge, there was never really a need for it. Another bridge over the La Salle built at the same time, one mile due west, provided an adequate means of travelling between Newton and Portage la Prairie. And the Gervais railway station was never anything but a minor stop on the low-traffic Cabot Subdivision of the Canadian National Railway. When the line was finally abandoned by the railway in April 1965, its land was used by the provincial government to twin the Trans-Canada Highway. Today, Gervais is an inconspicuous bluff of trees alongside the Trans-Canada Highway east of its crossing of the Assiniboine River.

Most early bridges in rural Manitoba are long gone because they were inadequate for our modern traffic needs. But two fine old specimens in the Rural Municipality of Portage la Prairie survived because they never met their full potential. They serve to remind us of the heady, early days of highway travel, when anything was possible, and plans were not fulfilled by reality.

SOURCES

"A.C. Emmett and the development of good roads in Manitoba" by Karen Nicholson, *Manitoba History*, Number 27, Spring 1994.

Public Accounts, Good Roads Board, 1917, Manitoba Legislative Library.

Manitoba Department of Public Works, Good Roads Board Annual Reports, 1916, 1917, 1919. Manitoba Legislative Library. [paper-bound pamphlets in envelope]

Cummin's Rural Directory Map for Manitoba, published by the Cummins Map Company, 404 Chambers of Commerce Building, Winnipeg, 1923.

"Hearing set on CNR bid to abandon rail line," *Winnipeg Free Press*, 2 December 1964, page 3.

"Abandoning of line approved," *Brandon Sun*, 22 April 1965, page 3.

Geographic Names of Manitoba, Manitoba Conservation, 2000.

Mill Creek Memoirs by Mill Creek Book Committee, 2006.

ACKNOWLEDGEMENTS

Thanks to Neil Christoffersen for finding the Gervais bowstring in the first place, the kind folks of the Portage la Prairie Regional Library for giving me access to municipal records, and Monica Ball of the Manitoba Legislative Library for guiding me through the arcane world of government documents.

Loyal Orange Lodge #1514, Graysville

Laughing out loud. That is what I thought as I drove up to a small, white building in the village of Graysville, west of Carman in the Rural Municipality of Dufferin. Emblazoned on its false façade, intended to make the unassuming building look larger than it was, were the letters LOL, familiar in our acronym-crazy age as an expression of mirth. Below the letters was the number 1514.

The lawn around the building appeared well-tended but its peeling paint and badly degraded shingles made it clear this building had not been the home of a Loyal Orange Lodge in many years. I had passed this innocuous little building many times in the past, paying it no attention, and therefore not suspecting its significance to my family.

In 1688, Dutch Prince William of Orange became King William III of England, Scotland, and Ireland and, two years later, he battled forces loyal to King James II at the Battle of the Boyne, leading to the ascendancy of Protestantism in what is now Northern Ireland. In 1795, Protestants wanting to perpetuate William III's memory, and promote loyalty to the Protestant monarchy, formed a fraternal organization called the Orange Order. Eventually, Orangemen made their way to the "New World" and established the Grand Orange Lodge of British America. Its members spread across Canada and were especially numerous in Protestant-dominated Ontario. All levels of society were represented, including politicians (no fewer than four Prime Ministers of Canada were Orangemen), businessmen, and, especially here in agrarian Manitoba, farmers. While many Orangemen had Irish ancestry, there was no restriction based on ethnicity and members included those with English, Scottish, and German roots.

The purpose of the Orange Order was to provide a venue for social interaction and mutual support between its members, to help them achieve "a high level of Christian, moral and ethical conduct in their personal lives." At meetings held at monthly intervals near the full moon, members would don cloaks and brightly-coloured, elaborately-braided sashes to which various metal badges were pinned. They administered pledges of initiation to new members, conferred degrees on those who had achieved deeper understanding of arcane Orange rituals, and carried on secret

A banner inside the Graysville Lodge, dedicated to "The Glorious Pious & Immortal Memory of Wm III [King William III]," reminded Orangemen of the "Deeds of Our Forefathers" – the battles with Catholic forces at Derry, Aughrim, Enniskillen, and Boyne. GOLDSBOROUGH

proceedings and lessons. Each year, the Grand Orange Lodge mailed a password to each "primary lodge" in communities within its jurisdiction and, to ensure it was not revealed to outsiders, the password was written in code. Orangemen had secret signs by which they could identify each other in public and gain admittance to a lodge during its closed meetings. They pledged to help brothers in need—financially or spiritually as circumstances warranted—and to

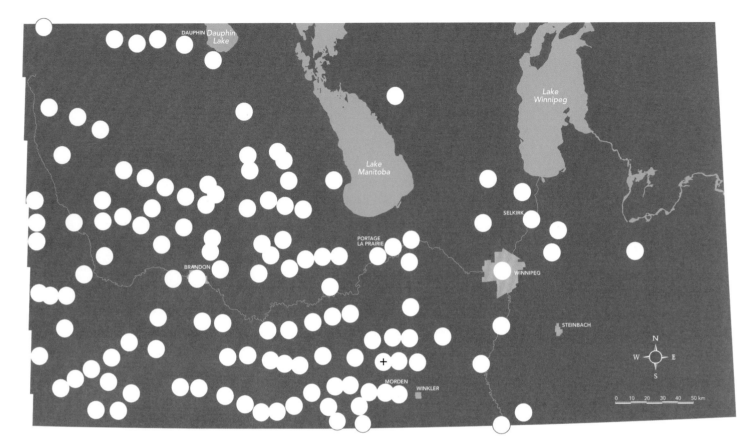

Map of Manitoba communities that, at one time or another, had an Orange Lodge. Graysville Lodge is marked with +.
LOYAL ORANGE ASSOCIATION FONDS, ARCHIVES OF MANITOBA

visit them during hospital convalescence. Funeral benefits were available to the families of deceased Orangemen, and insurance for living ones. Like most fraternal organizations that flourished in the 20th century—Masons, Odd Fellows, Foresters, Eagles, Hoo Hoos, Knights Templar, United Workmen, Knights of Columbus, and others—members of the Orange Order supported public charities and fundraised for hospitals and medical research against cancer, muscular dystrophy, and other ailments.

The Orange Order played a significant role in the founding of Manitoba. During a tumultuous period in 1870, when Louis Riel and the largely Catholic Red River Métis fought to gain entry for Manitoba into Confederation, a vocal Orangeman named Thomas Scott was captured and later executed. Inflamed passions among Ontario Protestants led the Canadian government to dispatch a military force to the Red River Settlement (now Winnipeg) under the command of British officer Garnet Wolseley. One of Wolseley's soldiers, Thomas Hickey, carried a charter authorizing him to establish the settlement's first Orange Lodge, which occurred in September

1870 aboard a steamboat anchored in the Red River by Upper Fort Garry. Lingering hostilities about separate schools for the education of Catholic and Protestant children—a plank consistent with Orange philosophy—led the provincial government, in 1890, to abolish separate schools, make English the default language, and undermine French rights in Manitoba for decades. Thomas Scott's corpse was never found but he was commemorated by the Scott Memorial Lodge in Winnipeg. A central co-ordinating body, the Grand Orange Lodge of Manitoba, formed in 1872.

At one time, there were over 180 primary lodges in Manitoba. Virtually all large towns had one—metropolitan Winnipeg had at least 22 over the years—along with most smaller towns. There were geographic patterns to Orange popularity. Most lodges were in the areas of province settled predominantly by Anglophones: around Winnipeg, in southwestern Manitoba, and the Swan River Valley. There were

few in areas settled by Ukrainians, Icelanders, Mennonites, and Francophones. At least during the early 20th century, Orangemen in Manitoba had a clearly articulated political agenda. Its major tenets were an absolute separation of Church and State; a non-sectarian national school system; use of English as the only official language throughout Canada; compulsory education of all children; encouragement of immigration from the British Isles, United States, and northern Europe; public inspections of educational and charitable institutions to ensure compliance with standards; suppression of vice and the prohibition of marriage under the age of 18; prohibition of liquor sales; and the elimination of patronage from governmental activities. And the Orange Lodge was unabashedly Protestant when it called for "… the total suppression and abolition of all convents, monasteries, nunneries, asylums, hospitals, houses of detention or correction, or any other institutions where any or

all of the inmates have not free and unrestricted communication with the world and to which the relatives and friends of such inmates have not free access and full and unrestricted opportunities and facilities of conversing freely and privately with them without obstacle or interference in any way of any kind whatever from any person or persons." In the Orange world view, Catholics failed to meet this standard because they owed primary allegiance to the Pope rather than the reigning monarch.

Like most towns in southern Manitoba, Graysville was a product of the railway. The Canadian Northern Railway arrived here in 1902, building a station that became the nucleus of a community on land once belonging to farmer George Gray. But local Orangemen preceded Graysville, having established Lodge #1514 (numbered sequentially from the first lodge in Canada) at Campbellville, a long-since-abandoned "town" roughly half-way between Graysville and Carman, and named for the abundance of

Campbells who settled there. Graysville holds a special place in Orange symbolism, sitting less than a quarter mile from the Boyne River, named for the battle at which William III prevailed. In 1908, an Orange Hall was built in the village, on the south side of the newly constructed All Saints Anglican Church, now gone. Before local Presbyterians began building their St. Paul's Church

A cabinet contained Orange paraphernalia, including robes, sashes, and badges. GOLDSBOROUGH

on the south side of the hall, in early 1912, they paid the Lodge $2 per month to rent the Orange Hall for Sunday services. (St. Paul's would become a United Church following the 1925 unification of Methodist, Presbyterian, and Congregational faiths in Canada.)

On a chilly day in early 2016, I visited the former Graysville Orange Lodge along with two members of the St. Paul's congregation, which owns it now. The old wooden building, now more than 100 years old, is used mostly for storage of church materials but the power is still turned on and I was told the furnace would work if its tank had fuel. The hall had several surprises in store as we unlocked the door and stepped inside. On its walls was a pair of remarkably intact banners exhorting Orangemen to "Remember the deeds of our forefathers" and "No surrender." I had seen one of them before, in an historical photograph of Graysville Orangemen marching in a parade. On a raised platform at one end of the main room was a white, wooden arch emblazoned with the words Union, Truth, Love, and Loyalty. In a corner, a large wooden cabinet contained ceremonial Orange regalia and a khaki-coloured metal box that had once contained land mines. Inside it was a jumbled collection of dusty, old papers. I was permitted to borrow them for more careful perusal in the warmth of my home office. There, a bundle of documents, mostly from the 1940s to 1960s, yielded clues to the lodge's membership and fate.

The documents reveal that, in the late 1940s, over half of Grayville lodge members came from the local area, with the bulk of the rest from Carman to the east or Stephenfield to the west. Members from farther afield—such as Winnipeg, Winnipeg Beach, Vancouver, or the United States—probably had family ties linking them with Graysville. Each new member had to be vouched for by two existing members and disclose their occupation, religious denomination of themselves and their wife (if married), age, and place of birth. Of 23 men applying for admission between 1946 and 1948, all but two were farmers. Only three were born outside of Manitoba and the average age of applicants was 30 years. Eight were married and 19 belonged to the United Church; the other four were Presbyterian, Anglican, or Lutheran.

One of those Graysville Orangemen was my maternal grandfather. However, the records showed that he stopped paying membership dues in 1953. Wanting to know more, I spoke with his son—my uncle—who reminded me that 1953 was the year my mother attended grade 12. She had taken grade 11 at Graysville but, because the school did not provide grade 12 instruction—which she needed to fulfill her aspiration to become a teacher—she was obliged to take her final year elsewhere. She chose to go to St. Claude, a Francophone community with a school run by Catholic nuns—allegedly the first Protestant student they had ever accepted. My mom's memoirs talk about how nervous she and my grandparents were when they met the Mother Superior for the first time. I was reminded of a clause in the initiation pledge made by new Orangemen: "That I am not now,

nor ever will be a Roman Catholic, nor am I married to, nor will I ever marry a Roman Catholic, nor educate, nor permit my children to be educated in that faith, or in any Roman Catholic School or Institution, except where no Protestant or Public School exists."

How did grandpa reconcile his Orange pledge with his daughter's education? Did he quit the Lodge voluntarily to avoid formal censure? Was he kicked out? Or was he merely conserving money to pay her tuition? (My grandparents' farm never provided them with much more than a subsistence living.) I will probably never know. But it adds a poignant footnote to an otherwise mundane statistic, and leads me to wonder how many other Orangemen had to make difficult choices when their personal lives conflicted with Orange philosophy. Certainly, my grandfather was not the only one to leave the Graysville Orange Lodge in the early 1950s. In 1948, the Lodge boasted 75 members, probably most of the eligible men in the area. The total fell to 25 men through the 1960s, including some who transferred their membership from closed lodges nearby, before declining to 13 members by 1974. When Lodge #1514 closed permanently in 1983—one of the last primary lodges to do so—and ownership of the old hall and its contents transferred to St. Paul's, there were just nine members.

With the benefit of hindsight, it is clear the Graysville Orange Lodge, along with its brethren in other Manitoba towns, was doomed by demographics. Its members became elderly, its world view was increasingly out of step

A booklet in the former Graysville Lodge containing instructions for the initiation of new members was encoded to prevent knowledge of Orange rituals from falling into the hands of non-members. GOLDSBOROUGH

INSTRUCTIONS TO CANDIDATE

Orange or Initiatory Degree

BY THE

LECTURER

———

Lecturer.—Bro.———I will now instruct you in the secrets of the Orange or First Degree of our Association. There are Four Signs and Three Passwords, viz.:

The 317 or Salutation Sign.

The Prayer Sign or Sign of Fidelity.

The Recognition Sign and Answer.

The Voting Sign.

The Annual Password.

The Inside Password.

The Retiring Password.

And the Honors of the Association.

The 3 1 7 or Salutation Sign is given in this manner: Follow me—Extend the 6 6 3 9 n 6 9 5 7 5 9 1 of the 9 9 7 8 2 e 8 1 5 4, place the 2 8 3 4 2 on the 6 9 9 1 2 t 6 9 n 9 5 4 5 6 0 6 9 5 7 5 9, forming the 8 1 5 4 in the shape of a 3 3 7, then draw the 8 1 5 4 back in a line from the 2 6 4 7, and at the same time 1 2 6 6 7 over and raise the 8 1 5 4 to the 4 6 3 2 8 once as if 3 1 7 7 9 5 7 e 5 1 2 5 9. The significance of this sign is a representation of the 2 8 9 5 5 e 8 3 5 4 9 5 4 n 3 8 6 1 5 5 a 9 1 9 1 5 3 9 2 5 1 who 3 1 7 7 5 4 but did not 2 5 5 5 3.

with progressive society, and its rituals were seen as irrelevant by a new generation. The Grand Lodge of Manitoba underwent similar decline, as its collection of primary lodges grew smaller with each successive year: 39 in 1970 dropped to 10 by 1989. Through the 1970s, Grand Lodge representatives vigorously denied they were anti-Catholic, arguing that their pro-Protestant views did not mean they hated those of other faiths. There were internal calls for reform, but they were too little, too late. A 1974 motion to admit women as members (rather than to an auxiliary called the Ladies' Orange Benevolent Association)—interestingly, proposed by the Graysville Lodge—had a catch, that female members should not be able to achieve the highest degrees of membership. Indeed, the lodge seemed resolutely stuck in the past, as evidenced by its insistence in 1979 that the national holiday on the first of July should remain Dominion Day. No one seemed to appreciate the symbolism when, in 1989, a trophy that had been presented annually since 1933 to the Manitoba lodge having the greater membership increase, went missing and was retired quietly. The Grand Orange Lodge of Manitoba followed the trophy into oblivion. Winnipeg's Scott Memorial Hall, which had been retrofitted to enable wheelchair access for its handicapped members, was sold in 1994. The Orange Order still exists, albeit in a much diminished state, and there are now just two lodges in Manitoba: at Winnipeg and Neepawa.

Many organizations, clubs, associations, and congregations of long standing are seeing the same sorts of wane as the Orange Lodge. We seem no longer to be enticed by formal memberships. Instead, we define ourselves in ways that are more individualistic and anonymous, and less personally demanding. We are members of vaguely defined "clubs" and online communities that do not require a long-term commitment and strict adherence to dogma. But at least small vestiges of the past survive in places like Graysville; buildings that provide us with personal surprises. And that's no laughing matter.

SOURCES

Grand Orange Lodge of Western Canada, http://grandorangelodgeofwesterncanada.com, accessed 24 January 2016.

Graysville: A Manitoba School and its Community by Graysville School Reunion Planning Committee (Carrol Bruce, Judie Owen, and Ethel Hook), June 2011.

Loyal Orange Association Fonds, Archives of Manitoba.

Loyal Orange Lodge History in Western Canada, http://www.orangelodge1654.com, accessed 24 January 2016.

The Orange Order in Canada, edited by David A. Wilson, Ireland: Four Courts Press, 2007.

The Rural Municipality of Dufferin, 1880-1980, by the Council of the Rural Municipality of Dufferin, 1982.

The Sash Canada Wore: A Historical Geography of the Orange Order in Canada by Cecil J. Houston and William J. Smyth, Toronto: University of Toronto Press, 1980.

ACKNOWLEDGEMENTS

I thank Jim MacNair and Beverly Stow of the St. Paul's United Church (Graysville) for their kind support, and my uncle George Hodgson for insightful conversation.

Harrison Flour Mill

Grain has been a part of my family for over a century. Both sides of my family were grain farmers. One of my early memories is of sitting beside my uncle aboard a combine as he threshed wheat and being shrouded in billowing clouds of grain dust. Later, my parents would gift my young family with bags of whole wheat flour made in a small counter-top grinder using wheat grown on their farm. We gave up farming several years ago but, even today, as I fight off a bout of spring flu, I am reminded of my family's heritage when I drape a soothing, cloth bag around my neck. It is filled with our wheat that had been heated in a microwave oven.

The Harrison Flour Mill, August 2016. GOLDSBOROUGH

For more than 200 years, western Canada has been an important grain-growing region. To use grain to make bread and other products, however, you cannot start with the whole grain kernel. It becomes much more versatile when it has been crushed to a fine powder, making flour. For centuries, grist millers have been an important part of the flour supply chain. At the Red River Settlement established in 1812 by the Selkirk Settlers, there was wheat milling capability. Robert Logan, who arrived in 1819, operated a wind-powered mill on his property along the Red River. Between 1829 and 1832, Métis leader Cuthbert Grant operated a water-powered grist mill on Sturgeon Creek at the site of a working re-creation built in 1974. In the early 1880s, Ontario settler John Gregory built a three-storey stone mill building that used water next to it in the Souris River, southwest of Wawanesa, to mill grain brought by farmers from as far away as the United States. (Today, only a few stones of the Gregory mill's

foundation, and the half-mile-long millrace are still visible at the site.) Through the 20th century, numerous large-scale commercial mills operated in Winnipeg and St. Boniface. The vast majority of these mills are gone, replaced by a few huge mills in strategic places across Canada, but the oldest flour mill in western Canada still stands in excellent condition, in the village of Holmfield, about nine miles southeast of Killarney.

Brothers William, George, and Matthew Harrison arrived in southwestern Manitoba in 1878 and built a flour mill and sawmill at the now-deserted town of Wakopa, on the edge of the Turtle Mountains. When the settlement was bypassed by the newly arrived railway, in 1885, the Harrisons left their sawmill and moved to the western end of the Turtle Mountains, and built a grist mill and elevator at Killarney. William and George Harrison built a grain elevator at Holmfield in 1892 and, four years later, sold their Killarney holdings and consolidated their business there, building a grist

The original milling machinery inside the Harrison Hill, August 2016. GOLDSBOROUGH

mill to process grain for local farmers. A large warehouse to store grain that awaited milling was built next to the mill in 1898. By this time, there were nearly 100 similar mills operating around Manitoba.

In the "long run" grain milling process used at the Harrison Mill, the first step was to remove impurities such as small stones, sticks, and seeds of weeds and other plants. The grain was crushed by steel rollers into coarse particles then bran (the hard, outer layer of the grain) was sifted out. The bran was sprinkled with a bit of water to remove the maximum amount of flour adhering to it. The remainder was crushed again and sifted to remove the germ (embryo). At flour mills elsewhere, the flour could be made whiter by treating it with chlorine or peroxide but the Harrisons did not bleach

A 1200-pound mill stone is all that remains of a water-powered grist mill operated near Lockport by Donald Gunn and his family as of 1854. Broken into three pieces, it was found discarded in 2003 and incorporated into a display on Red River milling by the local Heritage Advisory Committee. GOLDSBOROUGH

their flour in this way. Instead, they used a "sparker" to electrically burn the oxygen out of the air and bleach the flour by exposure to the remaining nitrogen. Whole wheat flour included the bran, germ, and the starchy inner layer, called endosperm, whereas white flour (which preserved for much longer than whole wheat flour) included only the endosperm. In payment for his services, the miller kept a proportion of the grain. At the Harrison Mill, a farmer traded 3.8 bushels of wheat for 100 pounds of flour and the grain acquired by the mill in this way was milled for sale. The Harrisons sold their flour under the name "Turtle Mountain Maid."

Originally powered by a steam engine brought from California, the Harrison Mill was converted to diesel power in 1932 then to electricity in 1947. An associated workshop enabled the Harrisons to make repairs on site, and they did mechanical work for their neighbours until dismantling the shop in 1955. Peak production occurred during the Second World War when, working

24 hours a day, seven days a week, they produced about 50,000 hundred-pound sacks per year, or about a half million pounds of flour. Sacks of Harrison flour were shipped around the world, each proudly stamped "Made in Canada."

In 1926, the Harrisons replaced the original grain elevator with a larger one, then in 1959 added a second, smaller elevator built at Holmfield, but not at this site, by Federal Grain Limited. During this same period, the family also purchased a lumber business, and built a lumber yard adjacent to the mill in 1962. The Harrisons closed their lumber business in 1972 but continued to mill grain.

Demand for the Harrison's milling service dropped over time, for at least two reasons. First, improved local roads meant it was more lucrative for farmers to export their grain for cash sale rather than mill it locally. Second, as farm families grew smaller and more wealthy, the need for flour obtained by barter was reduced. In increasing numbers, wheat farmers bought their flour—possibly made hundreds of miles away in a large, efficient mill—from the local grocer rather than the local miller. Annual production at the Holmfield mill in the late 1970s was about 2,200 bags and the mill operated only about forty days a year. It no longer shipped grain for export. The mill finally closed at its 100th anniversary, in November 1997.

Three generations of Harrisons have operated the mill at Holmfield. The last two operators were a pair of brothers, William "Bill" Harrison and Errick Harrison, whose father Abram Harrison—son of founder William Harrison—served as a Progressive Conservative MLA (1943-1966), Speaker (1958-1963), and Minister Without Portfolio (1963-1966) in the Manitoba Legislature, in addition to running the mill. The Harrison brothers worked in the mill through childhood and put themselves through university and, later, law school while working there. They practised law at Killarney for several years, while working at the mill on weekends. Before passing away in 2007, Bill Harrison taught his three daughters how to mill so they could keep the family tradition alive.

Although the Harrison Mill has not operated since 1997, it is still operable using the original milling equipment from 1898. The mill building is kept maintained, and its stonework was restored with new cement-based mortar in 2007. And it is opened periodically for tours, most recently for a sunny August day in 2016. Grain will always be an important symbol of the prairies. As I sit with a warm, wheat-filled bag around my neck, I find it comforting to know that, even as the nature of modern milling has favoured a few enormous mills (most of them in eastern Canada), a small, 120-year-old mill at Holmfield stands ready to turn grain into flour on a moment's notice.

SOURCES

[Advertisement, Harrison Milling & Grain Co.], *Belmont News*, 12 October 1961, page 8.

"Mill of the century," *Baldur Gazette*, 6 October 1976, page 9.

"Flour-milling tradition kept in Harrison family," *Winnipeg Free Press*, 6 November 1976, page 30.

By the Old Mill Stream: A History of the Village of Holmfield & District by Holmfield History Book Committee, 1982.

"Holmfield mill old but it's no museum," *Winnipeg Free Press*, 28 Sept 1990, page 3.

"Trivia challenge," *Winnipeg Free Press*, 6 January 1992, page 11.

"A history of flour milling in Manitoba" by Karen Nicholson, Neil Otto, and Ed Ledohowski, Manitoba Historic Resources Branch, May 1992.

"Holmfield Flour Mill" by Kateylyn Harrison, 1998. [http://www.tivy.com/JimTTree/NTivy_AHarrisonMore.htm]

"Phantoms of the past," *Winnipeg Free Press*, 4 September 1999, page 430.

"Their hearts are in Holmfield," *Winnipeg Free Press*, 3 July 2001, page 12.

"Restoration," *Baldur Gazette*, 21 August 2007, page 2.

Obituary [William Edward Harrison], *Brandon Sun*, 15 December 2007, page 21.

Canadian National Millers Association [http://www.canadianmillers.ca]

ACKNOWLEDGEMENTS

I thank Glen Suggett for providing photos from his 1992 tour of the Harrison Hill. Errick Harrison gave an excellent and informative tour during an open house in August 2016.

Hartney Town Hall

I have visited nearly 2,000 commemorative monuments around Manitoba. Nearly half of them are for schools, most in rural parts of the province. A common refrain on many of their inscriptions is that the school was the "centre of the community." The schoolhouse was the location of local education, certainly, but it was often also used for local recreation (sporting events), legislation (polling stations for elections), and salvation (religious services).

The former Hartney Town Hall, April 2016. GOLDSBOROUGH

In urban communities of the early 20th century, the school was a beehive of activities but it was not always the community centre. The municipal office might fit the bill, insofar as it was where one called with a question, complaint, or emergency, and where local decisions about community services were made. But public meetings were usually held in the Town Hall, which typically had a large, open room and a stage. Any town with aspirations of greatness could be counted on to have a splendid Town Hall. Hartney, 35 miles southwest of Brandon as the crow flies, was no exception.

Like many communities on the prairies, Hartney owes its existence to a railway, but farmers from Ontario beat the Canadian Pacific there. Among them was James Hartney, who arrived in 1882, bought two sections of land, and hired men to break the virgin prairie. In his first year of farming, Hartney sowed 160 acres of wheat and reaped a sufficiently encouraging crop that, in the fall, he imported a railway car of seed wheat to Brandon, reserving a portion for himself and selling the remainder to his neighbours. Two years later, most land parcels in the area had been taken up and homesteaders began clamouring for postal service so they would not have to travel to Brandon to get their mail. Hartney petitioned the federal government to establish a post office on his farm and it was duly named in his honour. Hartney later moved to Souris with his family, and represented the area in the Manitoba Legislature in the early 1890s, but he retained ownership of his original farm, renting it to James

The Hartney Town Hall, with firefighting equipment and crews in front, circa 1906. GRASSLAND MUNICIPALITY PHOTO COLLECTION

Beynon, whose two daughters, Francis and Lillian, would find fame as journalists and feminists. In 1888, when the Canadian Pacific began constructing a line into this region, running from Brandon to Estevan, Saskatchewan, a site just north of the "Hartney Farm" was the logical place for a station. The Beynons organized a party to celebrate the arrival of the first train, on Christmas Day 1890.

A town blossomed beside the newly established railway station at Hartney. Two grain elevators were constructed immediately, each with a capacity of 30,000 bushels, and there were seven by 1905. Roads on either side of the tracks were given the unimaginative names of East Railway Street and West Railway Street, with the former becoming the main street of commerce. By the time of the 1901 federal census, Hartney boasted a population of 504 people—142 men, 120 women, and 242 children—in 103 households. They included bakers, bankers, barbers, blacksmiths, brickmakers, butchers, carpenters, clerics (Anglican, Methodist, and Presbyterian),

A practice room for the Hartney Brass Band and Orchestra on the second floor of the Town Hall now contains discarded theatre chairs and a candy dispenser festooned liberally with pigeon feces, April 2016. GOLDSBOROUGH

confectioners, domestic servants, dressmakers, farmers, farm implement dealers, furniture dealers, grain buyers, hoteliers, insurance agents, laundrymen (Chinese, of course), lawyers, liverymen, machinists, merchants, millers, pharmacists, photographers, physicians, publishers, railwaymen, salesmen, shoemakers, stone masons, store clerks, tailors, teachers, tinsmiths, veterinarians, and wagon makers. There was a weekly newspaper, *The Hartney Star*, and as of 1900, a second railway, the Canadian Northern. By 1906, Hartney was home to 653 people.

Part of the Rural Municipality of Cameron when it was founded, Hartney skipped the usual protocol of becoming a Village and jumped right to Town status when, in February 1905, it was incorporated by an act of the provincial legislature. The new council was optimistic for their town's future. One of their first acts was to approve the expenditure of $7,000 to build a town hall, to be used for public meetings and to house Hartney's firefighting equipment: a gasoline-powered fire truck and water storage tanks. A site was selected at the intersection of West Railway Street and River Avenue. Owned by a town councillor who was prevented by law from selling it to the town, he resigned, sold the land for $900, and was re-elected by acclamation the following month. When estimates of the cost were $4,500 over budget, a war of words erupted in the local newspaper between an advocate for expanding the scope of the project and an equally vocal opponent who felt the town should live within its means with a smaller hall. Ultimately, the council went back to local taxpayers and the additional expenditure was approved. A proposal from local contractor Arthur Vaughan was accepted and construction of a two-storey brick structure began in 1906. In addition to providing space for the fire hall, the main floor contained an auditorium with seating for 425 people, a stage, two dressing rooms, and a kitchen. The upper floor was subdivided into rooms that could be rented to groups as meeting space. The two largest rooms were occupied by local fraternal organizations, including the Masons and Odd Fellows. A rehearsal hall for the Hartney Brass Band and Orchestra was sandwiched between the lodges.

In the end, construction of the Hartney Town Hall cost $9,895. It opened officially on 15 October 1906 with speeches by the Mayor and members of the town council along with "a concert of readings and vocal and instrumental solos by the Palmatier sisters that was so much enjoyed that this concert group

returned for several succeeding winters to give concerts." Events during its first year of operation included a dinner by local Presbyterians, an address by Premier John Bracken, a temperance meeting, a literary debate, a church bazaar, a lecture by a local cleric on "Birds, Bees, and Butterflies," a meeting to discuss the new provincial telephone network, an annual meeting of the local Grain Growers' Association, and a gathering of the Hartney Agricultural Society. The new Hall hosted concerts, plays and operettas, balls and dances, banquets and fowl suppers, flower shows, school assemblies, games, displays of agricultural produce, talent shows, military enlistment drives and drills, corporate shareholder meetings, farewells, and memorial services. It provided a tangible unifying force for the region by bringing people from the surrounding rural districts together with those from Hartney during its sundry social functions. As former resident Hazel Parkinson noted in her 1957 memoir:

A door peephole allowed Masons to identify those wishing to enter their secret chambers on the second floor of the Hartney Town Hall. Masonic items were found among the debris during a visit in April 2016. GOLDSBOROUGH

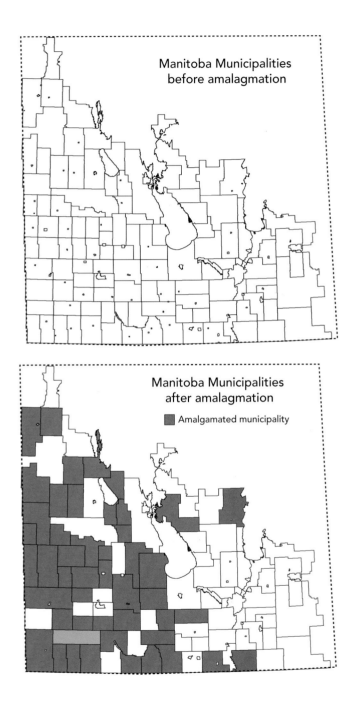

Manitoba Municipalities before amalagmation

Manitoba Municipalities after amalagmation

■ Amalgamated municipality

"Standing strong and sturdy on its corner, surmounted by its square bell tower, the town hall is a monument to the foresight of the council and citizens who erected it and is still the centre of Hartney's public life."

The federal census reveals the waxes and wanes that Hartney has undergone through its 110-year period of incorporation. From a height of 659 people in 1916, it declined to 468 people by the middle years of the Great Depression. Through the Second World War and into the early 1960s, it grew at a steady pace, peaking at 621 people in 1966. From the 1970s onwards, however, it has declined fairly consistently. By 2011, Hartney had 415 people. Over the years, the range of services eroded so that most of the once-busy commercial buildings along East Railway Street are now vacant. The Town Hall of West Railway is likewise empty, having lost most of its users when a new hall was constructed in 1982. (The fire hall moved next door and, in the 1960s, the bell tower on the northeast corner of the Town Hall, where fire hoses had been hung to dry, was removed.) The Hartney band disbanded years ago. In 1985, the Masons and Odd Fellows abandoned the second floor and moved across the tracks into the former Woodhull Pharmacy building (operated at one time by Margaret Woodhull, who I mentioned in another chapter as one of the first graduates of Winnipeg's Pharmacy

Map of municipality before (TOP) and after (BOTTOM) amalgamation in January 2015, showing the Municipality of Grassland in blue. GOLDSBOROUGH

College). Now that building is closed too and, having been determined to be structurally unsound, is slated for demolition. The main floor of the Town Hall, used to show movies on weekends, closed in 2007.

In January 2013, the Manitoba government announced that it would enforce the Municipal Act that requires municipalities to have a population of at least 1,000 people. Existing municipalities with a smaller population would be forced to amalgamate with neighbouring municipalities until they achieved this threshold. It was the single-most significant change in Manitoba's municipal landscape since the 1880s when the county system was abolished in favour of our present system of municipalities. In the aftermath of the sweeping amalgamations that occurred in January 2015, when 198 municipalities were winnowed down to 137, one of the most difficult decisions was the location of the municipal office. Any community losing its municipal office saw itself as being demoted in local importance, while those keeping their offices breathed a sigh of relief, at least until the next round of amalgamations. In 2015, the Town of Hartney ceased to exist when it joined the new Municipality of Grassland, along with the Rural Municipalities of Cameron and Whitewater. Hartney had previously also hosted the Cameron municipal office and now is the office for Grassland. The former municipal office for Whitewater, in Minto, is now relegated to the status of satellite office for the new municipality. In a game of "municipal musical chairs" that followed the amalgamation, long-time

A pair of antique movie projectors, used until the theatre in the Town Hall was closed in 2007, remained in the building as of early 2016. GOLDSBOROUGH

municipal employees had to compete for fewer jobs. In the case of the new Grassland municipality, the former Chief Administrative Office (CAO) for Hartney and Cameron became the CAO for Grassland, based in Hartney, while the former CAO for Whitewater became the Chief Financial Officer for Grassland, based in Minto.

On a sunny, spring day in April 2016, the Grassland CAO, Brad Coe, a keen local historian, invited me to tour inside the old Town Hall. As we walked toward the building, I noticed there did not appear to be any major structural issues. The locally-made, amber-yellow bricks of its exterior were mostly intact, other than a crack on the second floor of the north side. Most of the windows on the main floor were boarded up, but several of the ones on the second floor were open. The front view of the building was essentially unchanged since construction, except that the doorway into the fire hall is now boarded up and guarded

The former municipal office in the village of St. Laurent, in the Rural Municipality of St. Laurent, was built in 1902. It was made a municipally-designated historic site in 2002. GOLDSBOROUGH

by a large bell that once adorned the Hartney Public School. Stepping inside the building, I noticed that the electricity was still turned on and the lights were working. Peering into what had once been the cavernous theatre on the first floor, the renovations made in the name of energy conservation were evident. I had been told the building was notoriously cold in the winter. Sometime in the 1960s, judging from the profusion of faux-wood paneling popular at that time, someone had built an insulated "box within a box" by constructing two partition walls, each insulated with fiberglass bats, running the length of the room, with an insulated ceiling between them. A third wall sealed off the former stage at the front and provided a flat surface on which movies could be projected. The enclosed space was less than half the size of the original, and it was heated by its own nearby furnace. Two large film projectors from the 1940s or '50s stood in the former fire hall above the main entrance and projected through holes knocked in an interior brick wall. The local Elks showed movies on Friday and Saturday evenings until 2007 when it was deemed too costly to upgrade the projectors to the now-ubiquitous digital format.

There were no lights on the second floor, as power there had been disconnected when the Masons and Odd Fellows moved out in 1985. It was probably just as well that we could only see with the aid of flashlights, and light from open windows, for it seemed that legions of pigeons had taken up residence through the years. I saw no live pigeons during my visit but virtually every flat surface had been anointed with their feces and there were skeletal remains here and there. Pigeon poop with fallen ceiling plaster covered the floors in a squishy, gravelly mixture. One of the rooms was clearly the former Masonic meeting place, as its entry doors had peepholes so the Masons could identify those wishing to enter. In the old band rehearsal room were several rows of the original seats from the theatre downstairs, a pair of ancient film projectors (possibly the ones used to project the town's first movie, in 1910), and an art-deco candy dispenser from the 1930s. Metal ducts running through several of the rooms and hallways all terminated in a small room whose floor was covered with bricks. It had probably once enclosed a furnace used in a futile attempt to keep the second floor rooms warm. The whole place needed a thorough cleaning but it seemed basically sound.

A century ago, Hartney was a thriving town offering a full range of commercial, professional, and social services. Today, with the amenities of Brandon available within a 45-minute drive, there is little reason to duplicate them at Hartney. Like other communities in rural Manitoba facing municipal downsizing and amalgamation, it seems unlikely that Hartney's declining population over the past 50 years will reverse any time soon. The old Town Hall shows the effects of that decline, whereby an attractive building sits empty because the space it provides is not needed and it dates from a time when building insulation and energy conservation were not in the general mindset. Old Town Halls elsewhere in Manitoba—such as at Boissevain, Dauphin, Manitou, and Virden—are still in active use but, in Hartney, there are newer, more cost- and energy-efficient alternatives. I truly wish there was a basis for optimism but I fear that pigeons will be the only users of the 110-year-old "community centre" into the foreseeable future.

SOURCES

The Canadian Album: Men of Canada or Success by Example, Vol. III [James Harvey Hartney], Bradley, Garretson & Co., Brantford, Ontario, 1894.

1901 Canada census [Arthur Vaughan], Automated Genealogy.

Henderson's Manitoba and the North West Territories Gazetteer, 1905. [Peel's Prairie Provinces]

The Mere Living: A Biography of the Hartney District by Hazel McDonald Parkinson, 1957. [Manitoba Legislative Library, F5649.H37.par]

A Historical Directory of Manitoba Newspapers, 1859-1978 by D.M. Loveridge, University of Manitoba Press, pages 66-67.

A Century of Living: Hartney and District, 1882-1982 by Hartney and District Hostorical Committee, 1982.

ACKNOWLEDGEMENTS

I thank Brad Coe (Municipality of Grassland) for his enthusiasm on all facets of Hartney history, and especially his willingness to tour me through the former Town Hall, along with local historian Jack Van Dusen. Brandon-based historian Ken Storie has done exceptional work in documenting the history of towns and municipalities in southwestern Manitoba, including Hartney. This chapter benefitted from Barry Flett's voluminous knowledge of antiques and collectibles.

There is no building that symbolizes prairie Canada better than the grain elevator. Most people have romantic notions that several stand in every small town around Manitoba but the truth is markedly different. From a maximum of over 700 elevators in the 1940s, fewer than 200 remain today, and they are disappearing at a rapid rate.

Helston Co-Operative Pool Elevator #160

They may all be gone within a decade, replaced by massive concrete structures in a few key spots. Finding an old wooden grain elevator still standing at its original site is a rare treat.

In July 2012, I discovered such an elevator in the little village of Helston but I did not find it as a result of some systematic search. I had been exploring Ayr School, an abandoned one-room schoolhouse several miles southwest of Gladstone. It was late in the evening and the sun was setting. As I headed home on a dusty country road, I saw on the horizon the top of an elevator poking above the trees. My curiosity piqued, I drove toward it. Arriving at Helston—which today consists of just a few scattered houses and, to be honest, not much more than it had in its heyday—I could find no road or rails leading to the elevator. After some searching, I found that the road was almost completely hidden by trees and tall grass. As I walked along the long-abandoned path, the old elevator slowly came into view. Both of its large wooden doors—which for decades had beckoned farmers to bring their wagons and trucks into the elevator for sorting and

shipment to the larger world—were wide open. Looking up at the west side facing the setting sun, I saw a large gaping wound—a hole several feet across. It had probably formed because forgotten moist grain somewhere in the elevator's bowels had rotted its way out. Such holes are a clear sign of neglect and do not bode well for the elevator's future. They accelerate the rate of decay, as they permit birds and other creatures, as well as rain and snow that cause further rotting, easier access to the interior.

The story of the Helson grain elevator starts in 1901 when the Canadian Northern Railway (predecessor to

View of the abandoned grain elevator and annex at Helston, showing the weigh scale and dump pit. GOLDSBOROUGH

today's CNR) built a branch off its line between Portage la Prairie and Gladstone to head west then north up to Neepawa. Along the way, it created a siding that it named Mekiwin, a Cree word meaning "gift." Initial confusion with a post office of the same name, near the aforementioned Ayr School, soon led railway officials to rename it Berton then, in 1924, to Helston to avoid further confusion with the town of Benton in Alberta. Once a railway line was built, Gladstone farmer Peter Broadfoot saw a business opportunity and, in 1901, he constructed a grain elevator at Berton/Helston. Four years later, it

was joined by a second elevator belonging to the Western Canada Flour Mills, one of the largest grain-handling firms on the prairies, started in the 1880s by Brandon miller Andrew Kelly. To one or another of these elevators (it is unclear how long there were two elevators in Helston but archival records indicate there was only one by 1917), farmers from the surrounding country came with their horse-drawn wagons, loaded with grain. Driving up an earthen ramp into the elevator, a powered hoist would lift one end of the wagon, causing the grain to pour through a grate in the floor, down a chute to a pit at the bottom of the elevator. There, a vertically-oriented loop of heavy canvas to which hundreds of scoops were attached—known as the leg—would elevate the grain (hence the name, elevator) from the pit to the top of the building, from which the operator could then route it into one of several storage bins depending on the grain type and quality.

By the 1920s, Manitoba farmers had become dissatisfied with the service they were receiving from the big grain companies, who they felt were making excessive profits at their expense. In response, in January 1924 they formed the Manitoba Co-operative Wheat Producers Limited and, in April 1925, Manitoba Pool Elevators (MPE) as a subsidiary to build and operate grain elevators around the province. The idea was that this company, owned by farmers themselves, would charge only

what it cost to provide the service, and return profits to the farmers. To remind people of this fundamental philosophical difference with other grain companies, MPE elevators often had the motto "Service At Cost" painted prominently on their exteriors. (I must admit that, as a kid, I didn't understood what "at cost" meant so I thought the motto was confusing; why would a business brag about something so obvious that it charged for its service, I wondered?) Another way in which MPE elevators were different from those of other companies is that most of them were not, in fact, owned by MPE. Instead, the elevator was the property of a local co-operative association. Unlike elevators operated by for-profit businesses, with corporate headquarters in a city far away, the headquarters for the company who owned an MPE elevator were right in community and the affairs of the corporation were overseen by a local group of shareholders. The local association took care of purchasing grain, storing it temporarily in their elevator, and

View of the abandoned grain elevator at Helston, July 2010. BERNIE FREEMAN

delivering it by rail to a terminal elevator, usually at a shipping point like Vancouver, Thunder Bay, or sometimes Churchill. Annually, members of the association met to elect representatives to serve on a board of directors and to hear reports from the MPE officers on matters affecting the association. The board made most of the routine decisions on elevator operations, including the hiring of an agent (sometimes called the buyer or manager) who was the main liaison between the shareholders and the

The door into the leg of the one of two surviving Pool elevators at Barnsley, mid-way between Carman and Elm Creek, reveals the scoops attached to a flexible, circular belt that elevated the grain to the top of the elevator. Most parts of the leg, and the elevator itself, were made of wood to avoid sparks (and the resulting fires) that could occur when two metal parts came into contact.

MANITOBA HISTORIC RESOURCES BRANCH

elevator. The agent made the day-to-day decisions about grain buying and only sought input from the board as needed. Profits could go into an equity fund from which an individual member could be paid a share when they died, reached 65 years of age, or quit farming. Members could also be given an allocation from annual profits in years of surplus.

In May 1940, the Western Canada Flour Mills elevator at Helston was sold for $5,000 to MPE and, three months later, MPE sold it for $6,650 (presumably, the principal plus 33% accumulated interest) to the newly incorporated Helson Co-operative Elevator Association No. 160. The Helston Association, represented by 11 farmers voted to its inaugural board, agreed to re-pay the debt to MPE in twenty annual payments of $332.50. The idea was that MPE had the financial means to build (or in the case of Helston, buy from a corporate owner) an elevator, alleviating the prohibitively high up-front cost that would otherwise be incurred by an association. In return,

farmers of the association pledged to deliver grain to "their" elevator and would share in the profits in doing so.

One of the first acts by the new Helston Association was to hire 47-year-old Grover Lobb, who had worked for Western Canada Flour Mills since 1927 and was generally thought to be efficient and knowledgeable, as its agent. It was a demanding job with long work hours that required the agent to live nearby. (In Grobb's case, his home sat right next to the road into the elevator.) Farmers could arrive with grain deliveries most days of the week and all hours of the day. The board appears to have recognized the burden this imposed on Lobb and, in 1944, its advised members that they should "refrain from delivering grain to the elevator after 6 PM during the winter months." (Deliveries could still occur around the clock during the busy harvest time in the fall.) In 1947, the board approved the closure of the elevator on Saturday afternoon during May, June, and July "to give our agent a half holiday each week" and, in 1952, the agent was authorized to take six days of holiday, presumably his only prolonged vacation time during the year, "during deer hunting season to be taken at his discretion." Lobb purchased grain delivered by shareholders and, in later years, also sold pesticides and fertilizer, and scheduled the use of specialized farm equipment bought by the Helston Association. A generator outside the elevator, usually powered by gasoline, provided electricity for lights inside the elevator, where open flames were strictly forbidden due to the risk of fire in a mostly wood building filled with highly flammable wood and grain dust. The only part of the elevator that was heated in winter, usually by woodstove, was a small office building next to the elevator, and this was typically where locals congregated for morning chats over coffee. Here the agent would complete business transactions and maintain records required by MPE and the local board. Only in 1962 was the agent authorized to buy an adding machine to aid in accounting.

By most accounts, the Helston Association was a commercial success, with shareholders from Helston and the surrounding communities of Arden, Edrans, Gladstone, Keyes, Mayfeld, Mekiwin, and Neepawa. Within six years, the growing demand and deteriorating condition of the 40-year-old wooden structure led the Association to ask MPE to build them a new one. (Its foundation was apparently so bad that Lobb could not fully fill the storage bins on one side of the elevator, or risk a collapse.) During the summer of 1946, the original

A grain elevator at Elva, in southwestern Manitoba, was constructed in 1897 by the Lake of the Woods Milling Company. Closed and sold to private ownership in 1968, it became the oldest of its kind in Canada when an elevator at Fleming, Saskatchewan that was two years older was destroyed by an arson fire in 2010. GOLDSBOROUGH

elevator, capable of holding 25,000 bushels of grain, was demolished and its lumber was recycled to construct the present 40,000-bushel structure. Although the board hoped they could connect their elevator to the provincial power grid—a service that was just starting to reach this area of rural Manitoba—the cost was found to be prohibitive, forcing them to stick with the generator for operating the hoist and leg. Despite the modest increase in capacity of the new elevator, it was not enough to satisfy local demand, which had grown from 139,151 bushels delivered in 1941 to 405,121 bushels in 1952. By the mid-1950s, the elevator was full before the entire harvest had been delivered to it so the board approved plans to construct a 54,000-bushel wooden annex—essentially, additional storage bins standing immediately adjacent to the main elevator to which the operator could re-direct flow from the leg—during the winter of 1956-1957.

The Helston Association's board embraced the social responsibility implied by the MPE approach. In 1946, they asked to participate in the MPE's lending library program, which made books available on a wide range of topics to the local community otherwise having no access to such material. Most years, as part of the annual meeting of the shareholders, the board hosted a dinner for the members and their wives, which probably represented the social event of the year for the community. In 1960, the board responded to members of a local sewing club who had asked for a sewing machine that "we would donate up to $100.00 for this machine. If their club ceased to operate the machine was to be returned to the Association." (It is hard to fathom what use the Association would make of a sewing machine should the club follow through on its obligation.) But the board did not approve all such requests. A proposal to donate money to Brandon College was declined because "our board were of the opinion that the farmers were paying their share of education locally." And the board's decisions sometimes seemed downright miserly. It decided in 1961 to re-hire Grover Lobb, who by this time had served the Helston Association faithfully for 20 years and, in fact, had 34 years of cumulative service at the elevator, for "one more year at 275.00 per month with the understanding that if he finds that due to ill health he cannot carry on he will be automatically retired." There was no word of a pension. When Lobb finally stepped down the following year, he was presented with an engraved watch, despite not having served the 25 years demanded by company policy for such a prize.

For most of the railway lines in the agricultural belt of Manitoba, grain deliveries to the local elevators were the primary economic benefit for the companies who operated those lines. Given the enormous cost to the railway companies of operating a vast network of lines across the prairies, especially on lines with only a few, poorly used elevators, it was inevitable that the companies would seek to eliminate money-losing lines. An internal memo written for the executives of MPE in early 1970 stated that "it is the writer's opinion both railways [CPR, CNR] will be successful in abandoning nearly all of the lines in Manitoba that are: a) short spurs and have a light tonnage mile, b) are within reasonable distance from other existing lines, c) are too costly to maintain due to bridges, terrain or weight of steel, [or] d) have been purposely neglected by the railways to hasten their departure." This prediction would largely come to pass over the next decade.

Inklings that the days were numbered for the rail line through Helston came as early as December 1966 when the CNR filed an abandonment application with the federal government. Local farmers were relieved when the application was rejected and service was assured until at least 1975 by a new federal *Transportation Act*.

Unfortunately, it was a temporary reprieve. Continuing rumours that the line would be abandoned prompted the Helton Association, in March 1976, to appeal to the federal Grain Handling and Transportation Commission. Their brief stated that the track was in good repair and had carried some 81 carloads of grain in 1975. The five-year average annual

A grain elevator at the former railway siding of Cameron (named for Melita implements dealer A.E. Cameron, who owned the land where the siding was established), in what is now the Rural Municipality of Two Borders, was built by the Lake of the Woods Milling Company sometime between 1902 and 1910. Known for its "Five Roses" brand of flour, the elevator was closed in the late 1960s and sold into private hands. The rail line is long gone and the elevator is now abandoned in the middle of farmland. GOLDSBOROUGH grain intake at Helston was 236,077 bushels, over twice the capacity of the elevator, and there were 64 farmers delivering grain to it, who would presumably be inconvenienced if the line was abandoned. The nearest alternative to the Helston elevator was at Firdale, 13 miles away, but it was not considered an acceptable choice because that elevator was "practically inaccessible … due to poor access roads and hilly terrain." On the other hand, by this time Manitoba Pool was advising farmers that elevators were only viable if they handled over 400,000 bushels per year, and Helston did not make the grade.

Despite uncertainty over the status of its rail line, the Helston Association seemed to be doing well financially. In 1967, it reported income of $29,049 and expenses of $21,603, producing a surplus of $7,445 from which $4,968 was dispensed to members. But there were worrying signs of things to come. Maintenance of the elevator had been postponed so that, by 1975, the agent reported that "Fertilizer shed needs new ridge cap. Car loading dock needs to be replaced. Planks need to be replaced on the in-drive. Office needs re-siding and painting." More significantly, "he also stated that the gangway is too low to handle semi-trailer trucks so he will not be able to load rape seed [canola] in trucks." In other words, the elevator could not accommodate the larger farm trucks that were becoming more common at this time. And the long, faithful service of men like Grover Lobb would not be seen again. In the last decade of its life, the Helston Association hired no fewer than six agents, some of whom stayed less than a year

and were criticized by shareholders for their questionable "personality and grain buying habits."

In 1978, the CNR finally received approval to abandon the line through Helston and the elevator closed that December. It was used for a time to store corn and members of the Helston Association asked MPE to consider moving the annex to nearby Golden Stream, which remained on an active rail line. Evidently, the economics of moving the annex did not warrant the expense and the annex stayed put. With no prospects for continued operation, the board of directors held a meeting on 18 March 1980 and voted to disband. With no prospects for use by local farmers, the elevator fell into disrepair and the road to it grew over.

Meanwhile, a similar story was playing out in other communities around southern Manitoba. Abandonment of unprofitable railway lines began in the 1960s. In some cases, elevators were sold to farmers for local grain storage. Others, in the absence of periodic maintenance, were damaged by the effects of wind and rain, animals, and vandals, and were torn down or burned to avoid liability. In their place, grain companies began to build vastly larger elevators made of concrete or steel in a few strategic spots. This obligated farmers to purchase larger vehicles to transport grain greater distances to these facilities and it forced municipal and provincial governments to upgrade roads to sustain the increased traffic.

The trend is sobering. In 1960, there were 699 licensed "primary elevators" in Manitoba, with an average capacity of 68,531 bushels. By 2014, there were 85 elevators with an average capacity of 582,859 bushels, nearly ten times as large as those 50 years earlier. But elevators were not the only things getting bigger; the companies that operated them also grew. Facing competition in an increasingly globalized marketplace, in 1998 MPE merged with the Alberta Wheat Pool, its counterpart in Alberta, to form a new company called Agricore. Three years later, Agricore merged with United Grain Growers (another old Manitoba-based grain company founded on the principle of farmer ownership) to form Agricore United. Then, six years later, Agricore United was bought by the Saskatchewan Wheat Pool and the whole entity was renamed Viterra. Finally, in 2013, Viterra was purchased by the multinational Anglo-Swiss company, Glencore International. In the aftermath of this corporate snowballing, a vast number of country elevators—some less than a couple of decades old—were declared surplus and were demolished or sold. My friend Jean McManus, who has made it her mission to photograph every one of the wooden survivors, believes there are just 165 of them as of late 2015. And, of course, the MPE mantra of "Service At Cost" is an increasingly foggy memory.

So what does the future hold for the decaying, 70-year-old elevator at Helston? Unfortunately, nothing good. Sooner or later—I predict sooner—it will be gone. If rotting timber does not bring about its demise, a vandal with a match will. Clearly, the elevator serves no useful purpose for its community. But it does remind us of a time when Helston was part of something much bigger, of a nation connected by a network of rails, where the bounty of the annual harvest was stored in these neighbourhood prairie giants, awaiting delivery to a hungry world aboard trains that will never come again.

SOURCES

Manitoba Pool Fonds, S. J. McKee Archives, Brandon University.

"A History of Grain Elevators in Manitoba. Part 1: A History. Part 2: The Architecture of Grain Elevators. Part 3: A Selected Inventory" by John C. Everitt, Economic History Theme Study, Manitoba Historic Resources Branch, 1992.

"Grain Elevators in Canada," compiled by Board of Grain Commissioners for Canada, Winnipeg, 1912-1930, 1930-1953, 1953-1998. [Peel's Prairie Provinces, University of Alberta Libraries]

Legacies of Lansdowne, A Sequel by RM of Lansdowne History Committee, 1984, pages 46-48.

"After Rail Line Abandonment: The Brandon Area Revisited" by Arthur G. Wilson, University of Manitoba Transport Institute, 1989, 100 pages.

Status of Prairie Railway Lines, December 1994, National Transportation Agency of Canada. [Manitoba Legislative Library]

ACKNOWLEDGEMENTS

I thank Ed Ledohowski (Manitoba Historic Resources Branch) for making available a collection of historical photographs of Manitoba grain elevators. Christy "Mo" Henry, the archivist at the S.J. McKee Archives (Brandon University) provided full access to the voluminous records of the now-defunct Manitoba Pool Elevators, which provided invaluable insight into the operation of the elevator at Helston. Archival records of United Grain Growers at the University of Manitoba Archives & Special Collections were also most helpful. Photos of the old elevator were kindly provided by Jean McManus, Bernie Freeman, and Shaun Cameron. Jean also very generously provided a copy of her thorough inventory of surviving elevators.

La Riviere Ski Slopes

I have never been much of a downhill skier. My wife and I tried it many years ago; she had a bad accident that left her with a bum knee, and I never saw the appeal of whistling down a mountain at high speed, with two boards strapped to my feet, narrowly averting life-threatening obstacles. But I certainly appreciate that, starting in the early 1930s, many Manitobans began to embrace winter in a way they had not done before when they started skiing in the Pembina Hills, near the village of La Riviere, at the province's first downhill ski resort.

View from the top of one of the former ski runs at La Riviere, May 2015. GOLDSBOROUGH

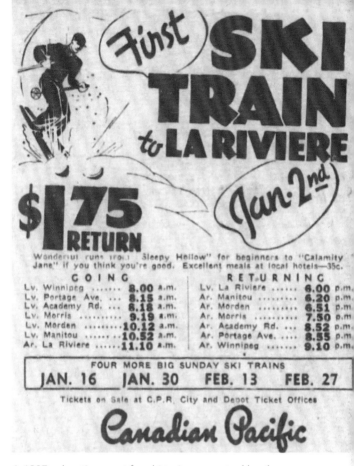

A 1937 advertisement for ski trains operated by the Canadian Pacific Railway between Winnipeg and La Riviere from 1935 to 1953. WINNIPEG TRIBUNE

Our story starts in 1914 when Ida Barclay left her farmer husband Alexander and moved with their four children to nearby La Riviere. There, she took over the Valley Hotel, renamed it the Barclay House, and operated it until her death, providing rooms and meals for visitors as well as a confectionary for locals. La Riviere is nestled in the valley carved thousands of years ago by the Pembina River, where it meets the smaller Mary Jane Creek, about 110 miles by rail southwest of Winnipeg. At the time that Ida was setting up her business, La Riviere had daily (except Sunday) rail service, mostly to pick up grain at the village's three elevators, and to deliver mail, merchandise, travelling salesmen, and residents returning from visits to the outside world.

Today, if we want a downhill skiing holiday, we typically jet or drive to the mountains in Alberta, British Columbia, or farther afield. But this was not a feasible option for local skiers 85 years ago. Winnipeggers keen to hone their skills had to make do with the banks of the Red

and Assiniboine rivers. In early December 1933, four die-hard skiers led by Winnipegger Bob Guthrie, seeing the potential of the Pembina Hills near La Riviere, approached Ida with the idea of establishing a skiing run there. She recognized the business opportunity represented by a bunch of skiers, so she agreed to finance the cutting of the first ski runs on the hill overlooking the railway station, on land owned by the Canadian Pacific Railway. As a further incentive, Ida offered special rates to skiers, including beds for 50 cents a night and all-you-can-eat meals for 35 cents a day.

In late December 1933, nine skiers spent a long weekend at La Riviere and "swore that it was the best way they had ever brought in the New Year." The slopes were described as "very similar to those of Eastern Canada, lightly wooded, which tends to keep the snow light and fluffy." The following winter, a busload of 25 skiers arrived in town and spent a "thrilling day." Returning to Winnipeg, they successfully

lobbied the CPR to arrange a special ski train for 160 skiers on Sunday, 3 February 1935, at a return fare of $1.75 per person. The railway delivered them to the bottom of the new ski hill, adjacent to Mary Jane Creek, and they climbed to the top on foot. (A rope tow line was not installed until 1941.) By cutting underbrush

The original nine skiers who pioneered the ski hill at La Riviere in December 1933, shown in front of Ida Barclay's restaurant and hotel. LEFT TO RIGHT: Stan Rothwell, Les Speechly, Ernie Hanford, Burt Robinson, Doug Groff, Bob Bruce, Hugh Johnston, Charlie Brenan, and Bert Sammons. UNIVERSITY OF MANITOBA ARCHIVES & SPECIAL COLLECTIONS, WINNIPEG TRIBUNE COLLECTION

from Ida's initial runs, they were able to attain speeds of up to 45 miles per hour, with hopes to up it to 60 with further grooming. The word of this successful, day-long ski trip spread and, before long, many more skiers were clamouring for a chance to "hit the powder" at La Riviere.

The CPR ski train ran every second Sunday during the winter. It left Winnipeg at 8:00 AM, picking up passengers at several stations in the city, before heading on to La Riviere. The one-way trip took about three hours. After some six hours of great skiing, the train departed for home at 6:00 PM. It was a huge success, with several hundred skiers making the trip on any given Sunday. Unfortunately, Ida Barclay did not live to see the growth of what she had started. She suffered a fatal stroke at the Morden Hospital on 26 December 1935, mere months after the first ski train arrived. A couple of weeks after her death, skiing

enthusiasts in Winnipeg formed the La Riviere Ski Club to "properly develop the excellent skiing possibilities at La Riviere." In 1937, Ida's contributions to skiing in Manitoba were commemorated by the Ida V. Barclay Memorial Trophy, donated by William Mather of the CPR.

Barclay House continued to operate under two of Ida's daughters. As the provincial road network improved, however, the greater flexibility afforded by driving to La Riviere, combined with the development of Snow Valley near Roseisle, spelled an end for the La Riviere ski trains. The last one ran in 1953 after the railway declared them unprofitable. Buses were pressed into service to transport the skiers. When the CPR would not sell the La Riviere runs to the Barclay family, Ida's grandson Noel Later, himself a champion skier, created new ones, on the opposite side of highway #3. Holiday Mountain Ski Resort opened in 1959 and remains in operation today.

In early 2015, knowing nothing about the early ski history of the La Riviere area, I had a chance to cruise up and down the old ski slopes on a quad. The original runs are now overgrown, so you have to look carefully to see them, but rope tow frames and a sign labelling one of the more challenging runs as "Calamity Jane" were still visible amidst the foliage. At the bottom of the hill was the right-of-way for the railway line, abandoned in 2008, now used by snowmobilers. It is an interesting reflection of our times that the area is still used actively for winter recreation, but now as much by noisy vehicles burning fossil fuels as by skiers powered by muscles and gravity.

The now-abandoned right-of-way for the railway line where ski trains from Winnipeg disgorged hordes of downhill skiers intent on a day of winter fun, May 2015. GOLDSBOROUGH

SOURCES

"Ski-ing at La Riviere," *Winnipeg Tribune Magazine*, 2 February 1935, page 41.

"This ski-er doesn't like snowshoes," *Winnipeg Tribune Magazine*, 30 March 1935, page 44.

"Les Speechly heads La Riviere Ski Club," *Winnipeg Free Press*, 8 Jan 1936, page 12.

"First ski train will go to La Riviere on Sunday," *Winnipeg Tribune*, 6 Jan 1937, page 2.

"Slalom race draws large entry," *Winnipeg Tribune*, 11 February 1937, page 14.

"First ski train in Manitoba tried only two years ago," *Winnipeg Tribune*, 9 January 1937, page 31.

"Skiers to travel by bus to provincial resort areas," *Winnipeg Free Press*, 7 November 1953, page 3.

Turning Leaves: A History of La Riviere and District by La Riviere Historical Book Society, 1979.

The Creation of Holiday Mountain, Holiday Mountain Resort [http://holidaymountain.com/history]

ACKNOWLEDGEMENTS

If it was not for La Riviere native Chris Thompson, I would never have known about the old ski slopes there. He kindly spent an entire day touring me around the area and, with the benefit of a pair of all-wheel-drive quads, we were able to tour the abandoned ski hill. I am grateful to Lewis Stubbs (University of Manitoba Archives & Special Collections) for finding the fabulous photo of the skiers in front of the Barclay House.

An aerial view of the former ski slopes at La Riviere shows Mary Jane Creek and the abandoned railway line at the left, the mostly treeless area in the centre (with barely perceptible runs cut between the trees in a few places), and the present ski slopes in the right background, July 2016. GOLDSBOROUGH

From Residential Schools to Bank Vaults to Grain Elevators   111

Lakeside Fresh Air Camp

In May 2011, I parked my car on the shoulder of highway 222 some four miles north of Gimli and walked through a decrepit chain-link gate, bounded by rusty barbed wire, and along an overgrown path toward Lake Winnipeg. Arriving at the shoreline at the mouth of a small creek, it became clear to me that something substantial had been here.

Large conifer trees looked like they had been planted in a row. Wood and metal rubble was strewn about, along with the twisted and broken remains of concrete foundations for several buildings. Medium-sized trees growing amongst the ruins indicated the buildings were long gone. I was standing at the long-abandoned site of the Lakeside Fresh Air Camp for Children.

Visits to the lakeshore are a well-established facet of life in Manitoba. As early as the 1890s, weary urbanites could climb aboard a horse-drawn wagon to travel to Lake Winnipeg or Lake Manitoba. There, they could escape the sweltering summer heat and enjoy the fresh breezes and inspirational vistas of our vast, inland seas. In the early 20th century, railway lines that snaked up the east and west sides of Lake Winnipeg enabled scores of people to take day-long excursions to resorts that offered entertainment, relaxation, and pampering. Those wanting more prolonged periods of rest and recreation built modest cottages that, in time, grew in size and appointment until they rivaled the features of homes back in the city. Today, there are cottage developments around many of our lakes and memories of life at the lake are treasured by generations of Manitobans. But in those early days, such luxury was far beyond the means of urban children who lived below the poverty line in single-parent families.

The practice of providing an outdoor experience to orphaned and disabled children, to children whose fathers had died or deserted them, or to families devastated by alcohol abuse started in England and the United States in the 1890s. The first "fresh air camp" in Winnipeg was established in 1900 on the Norwood flats. It later moved to Sturgeon Creek near the present-day Grace Hospital

Excited young campers rode the train up the west side of Lake Winnipeg to the fresh air camps in this undated photo. UNITED CHURCH OF CANADA ARCHIVES

then, in 1911, to a site on the west side of Lake Winnipeg. Among the fresh air camps established around Gimli, by various organizations, were Camp Sparling (1911, Methodists), Camp Robertson (1913, Presbyterians), B'Nai Brith Camp (1917, Jews), Camp Morton (1920, Roman Catholics), Sandy Hook Camp (1921, Salvation Army), and Camp Gilwell (1934, Boy Scouts).

The Lakeside Fresh Air Camp may owe its existence to a golf ball. In 1890, Norman Leslie moved to Winnipeg to become manager of the Imperial Bank of Canada's downtown branch. As a member of the city's business elite, Leslie built a cottage on a 15-acre wooded estate on Lake Winnipeg. In early 1916, Leslie's only child, a 15-year-old son, cut into a golf ball with a knife, causing its pressurized, acidic contents to spray into his face. Despondent that his son would be blinded for life, Leslie was speaking with Lieutenant Governor Douglas Cameron at the Manitoba Club when he suffered a massive seizure and was carried

home. Within 48 hours, he was dead. (Fortunately, the young Leslie kept his eyesight and went on to a long career in banking and service.) In May 1921, five years after Leslie's death, a group of his friends led by banker Harold Shaw formed the Lakeside Fresh Air Camp Association. Incorporated "for a benevolent and provident purpose, not connected with trade or commerce, that is to say, for the purpose of establishing, maintaining and operating as a camp for the health and recreation of children," the Association purchased the Leslie lakeside property (including the cottage with its furnishings) from his estate, at a cost of $8,500. In time, dormitories were constructed, along with a dining hall, kitchen, and indoor play area for use during wet weather. The plan was to provide an opportunity for fifty underprivileged

Given their proximity to Lake Winnipeg, it was no surprise that swimming would rank highly among activities available to campers. UNITED CHURCH OF CANADA ARCHIVES

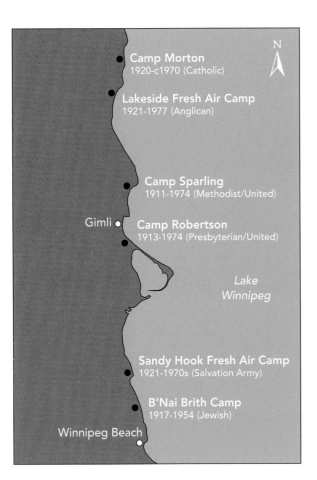

Map of the fresh air camps on Lake Winnipeg. GOLDSBOROUGH

Camp Morton
1920-c1970 (Catholic)

Lakeside Fresh Air Camp
1921-1977 (Anglican)

Camp Sparling
1911-1974 (Methodist/United)

Gimli

Camp Robertson
1913-1974 (Presbyterian/United)

Lake Winnipeg

Sandy Hook Fresh Air Camp
1921-1970s (Salvation Army)

B'Nai Brith Camp
1917-1954 (Jewish)

Winnipeg Beach

N

The Lakeside Fresh Air Camp war memorial at nearby Camp Morton, September 2010. GOLDSBOROUGH

girls and boys between the ages of seven and eleven (and sometimes their mothers) to visit the camp for several days where it was hoped they would receive "the maximum of fresh air, wholesome food, and healthy recreation." Although other camps in the vicinity were operated by religious faiths, the Lakeside Camp had no restrictions as to race or creed—although the camp seems to have had a loose affiliation with the Anglican Church, and was known initially as Camp M'Elheran in commemoration of Anglican cleric Robert McElheran. Lucky campers were chosen on the basis of need by social workers from such institutions as the Margaret Scott Nursing Mission and Victorian Order of Nurses. Children would be supervised by a "thoroughly experienced matron, one of strong motherly instincts, who will see to the comfort, cleanliness, security and feeding of children" along with a trained nurse, salaried staff including "captains" responsible for ten children each, and volunteer helpers. The first campers arrived at Lakeside in late June 1921.

Funds to operate the Camp came from a variety of sources, including members of the management committee (made up of powerful and wealthy Winnipeggers, many with connections to the banking or grain-trading industries), public campaigns by school children and service clubs (notably, the Gyro Club of Winnipeg and Gimli Kinsmen), and Tag Days where men would purchase lapel pins from women or girls, sometimes with an optional kiss.

Initially, the Camp received no government grants. One of its early donors was The Winnipeg Foundation, coincidentally also established in 1921 with an initial endowment from banker William Alloway. Food to feed the campers was mostly donated by local farmers.

In 1922, the Camp had a prestigious visitor when Lieutenant Governor James Aikins unveiled a monument on its grounds, commemorating 120 employees of the Union Bank of Canada who were killed during the First World War. During the ceremony, bank officials presented the deed for the property to the Association as a tribute to their fallen employees. In time, Camp buildings were named for other long-standing donors and supporters, including the 11-bunkbed "Pentland House" for banker Charles Pentland, 11-bunkbed "Shaw House" for camp founder Harold Shaw, the "Kneeland Hall" dining room and kitchen for grain merchant Elbert Kneeland, and the 6-bed "Brown Hospital" for long-time Camp matron Ethel Brown. "Gyro Hall," named for the Gyro Club, was for indoor recreation and, by the 1960s, it contained a player piano, television, soft drink machine, ping pong table, tables and benches. A bridge over the small creek led to office and staff quarters as well as a playground and ballfield. All buildings were of simple, wood frame construction that typically did not stand up well to the ravages of time. By the 1970s, several cottages were described in a management report as "very new" while the Sellers Cottage (probably the original Leslie Cottage, renamed for grain merchant Harry Sellers) was "ancient."

Penniless waifs dreamed of joyful times on Lake Winnipeg, in this 1937 sketch by editorial cartoonist Arch Dale aimed at convincing Winnipeggers to support the camps financially. WINNIPEG FREE PRESS

Records on Camp operations during the 1960s and 1970s have survived at the provincial archives. From them, we get a general sense of its activities. In 1967, a total of 503 campers attended Lakeside for stays ranging from 11 to 18 days. Day-to-day administration was the job of a Camp Director and meals were prepared by a Head Cook and Assistant Cook, assisted by seven Kitchen Helpers. Maintenance of the grounds and buildings was

Manitoba Lieutenant Governor James Aikins attended the 1922 unveiling of a war memorial, shown here covered by a sheet, at the Lakeside Fresh Air Camp for employees of the Union Bank of Canada killed in the First World War.

WESTERN CANADA PICTORIAL INDEX, UNIVERSITY OF WINNIPEG ARCHIVES

the responsibility of a Groundskeeper and Assistant Groundskeeper. Indoor and outdoor programming for campers was designed and delivered by a Camp Program Director and Assistant Camp Program Director, along with 12 counsellors. Unfortunately, the records also reveal the gradual financial strangling that the Camp suffered through this period. It ran a deficit for several successive years amid rising costs. Whereas a two-week stay in 1958 had cost $36 per camper, the total had risen to $46 by 1969, and $60 in 1973. Where once public and private donations had sustained the Camp, now two-thirds of its operating revenue came from government grants. In 1967, the Rural Municipality of Gimli began to impose municipal taxes on the property that had previously enjoyed an exemption. In return, the municipality offered to "pick up dry garbage at the odd times, and possibly spend some money to prepare the road base better." The change undoubtedly imposed a severe burden and it might have been the last straw. The following year, the Association sold its property to the provincial government for $65,000 and the government promptly leased it back to the Association for $1 per year. But it was a temporary reprieve. In 1975, the entire site was leased to the Society for Crippled Children and Adults (today's Society for Manitobans with Disabilities, which had been using the site for some years). Finally, in November 1977, the Lakeside Fresh Air Camp ceased operation. Its buildings were demolished or moved away, a truncated version of the war memorial was moved to nearby Camp

Morton (and was still there as of my visit in 2011), and the site began to be reclaimed by the forest from which it was carved more than 50 years earlier.

SOURCES

"Norman Leslie of Imperial Bank dead," *Manitoba Free Press*, 26 February 1916, page 4.

"Fresh air for kiddies at Camp M'Elheran," *Manitoba Free Press*, 18 June 1921, page 2.

"Off for Gimli camp," *Manitoba Free Press*, 22 June 1921, page 5.

"500 visitors attend unveiling of Union Bank war memorial," *Winnipeg Tribune*, 12 July 1922, page 3.

"$100,000 aid for camp," *Winnipeg Free Press*, 15 May 1975, page 16.

Gimli Saga: The History of Gimli, Manitoba by Gimli Women's Institute, 1979, pages 384-385.

Lakeside Fresh Air Camp Fonds, Archives of Manitoba, P4853.

The United Church of Canada Archives (Conference of Manitoba and Northwestern Ontario), University of Winnipeg.

"Fresh air for kiddies": The fresh air camps of Lake Winnipeg" by James Burns and Gordon Goldsborough, *Manitoba History*, Number 66, Spring 2011.

ACKNOWLEDGEMENTS

I thank Diane Haglund, former archivist at the United Church of Canada Archives at the University of Winnipeg, for her help in locating information on the Lakeside Fresh Air Camp. Brett Lougheed and his staff at the University of Winnipeg Archives provided photos of the unveiling ceremony for the Lakeside war memorial. Editor extraordinaire Jim Burns was my co-author on a *Manitoba History* article on which this chapter is based.

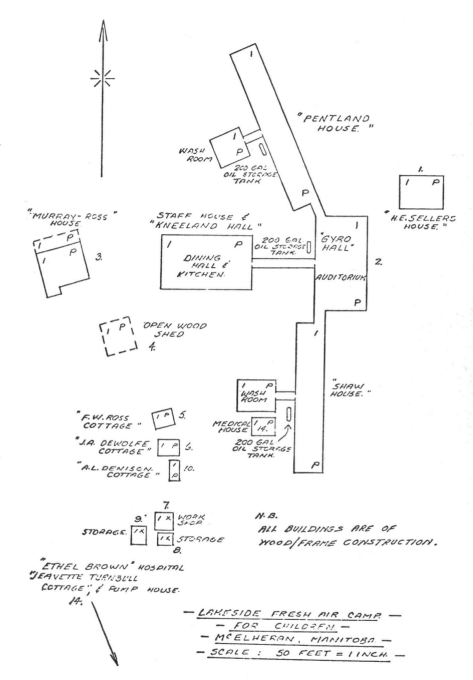

Long-standing donors and supporters of the Lakeside Fresh Air Camp were commemorated by the names of buildings in this site map from the 1970s. ARCHIVES OF MANITOBA

Leacock House

One of my all-time favourite books is *Sunshine Sketches of a Little Town* by Stephen Leacock, with its humorous and affectionate depictions of the foibles of life in small-town Ontario. Leacock contended the situations and characters of the book were fictional but, if so, the fictional veneer was very thin. Its personalities ring so true to me because I met people just like them as a youngster in small-town Manitoba during the 1960s.

Edward Phillip "E.P." Leacock
(1853-1927), at the time of his
election to the Manitoba Legislature,
August 1882. ARCHIVES OF MANITOBA

In another of Leacock's works, an essay published in 1942 entitled "My Remarkable Uncle," he describes a person from his own family, his father's brother, Edward Phillip Leacock, known widely as "E.P." People often remark that Canadian history lacks the colourful characters and scoundrels with which American history seems so replete. Yet, E.P. Leacock amply challenges this assertion. A flamboyant name-dropper with a "marvelous talent for flattery and make-believe," who conferred ersatz honorifics and claimed fictitious friendships at the drop of a hat, E.P. Leacock cut a wide swath through Manitoba while living here from the 1870s to 1890s. He leaves us with at least two tangible reminders, both houses, one of which sits on a hill overlooking the town of Birtle in western Manitoba.

Born on the Isle of Wight on 28 December 1853, Leacock claimed to have been educated in Switzerland before he arrived in Canada in 1878, and in Manitoba in June 1879. Here, he was involved with several companies, including the Westbourne and North West Railway Company, Manitoba Drainage Company, Birtle Farming Company, and Canadian Pacific Express Company. He was president of an imaginary railway to the Arctic Ocean, although other railways all over North America provided him the courtesy of free passes. Supposedly, he made a fortune in the land boom that followed the arrival in Winnipeg of the Canadian Pacific Railway, then lost it, but managed to carry on with "hotel credit, borrowed loans and unpaid bills." One of Leacock's scams, when asked by a hotelier to pay a $76 tab, was to

advise the man to give him $24 in cash, so he could send an even $100 on his return home. Yet, Stephen Leacock hastened to point out that:

"This does not mean that E.P. was in any sense a crook, in any degree dishonest. His bills to him were just "deferred pay," like the British debts to the United States. He never did, never contemplated, a crooked deal in his life. All his grand schemes were as open as sunlight – and as empty."

A view of the Leacock House at Birtle, circa 1886. Shown in the photo, standing at left, was Capt. Harry Arnold, killed in South Africa during the Boer War, and right, unknown. E.P. Leacock is seated with his son on his lap, along with Dr. David Harrison, MP for Neepawa, William Pentland of the Land Titles Office at Birtle, and Mrs. Leacock with her daughter. The little girl in front is not identified. BIRTLE EYE-WITNESS

When Manitoba joined Confederation in 1870, its western boundary was only about 80 miles west of Winnipeg, just slightly past Portage la Prairie. In 1880, the scuttlebutt was that the line would be extended the following year, to its present-day location. This would bring the village of Birtle—100 people, two general stores, and a sawmill nestled in a picturesque valley beside the Birdtail River—into Manitoba. Birtle boosters envisioned numerous opportunities that would ensue so it was probably inevitable that a man like E.P. Leacock would be drawn there. In December 1880, he showed up in Birtle and dispensed liberally of his hospitality, including a "good supply of oysters, cigars, and Walker's best" stout. He was

supposedly engaged in farming and lumbering, promised to build a bridge across the river, and bought three acres of land on which to build "a summer residence on the rustic style, to be carpeted with furs and skins." It was one of the few of Leacock's grandiose claims to be fulfilled, as construction of the house began in 1881. The building—known locally as "The Castle" due to its prominent turret—stood to the north of the town. Built of wood and stone, it would come as no surprise that corners were cut during its construction but these would not be revealed for decades. A road from the town in the valley below wound its way up a steep ravine that had been used for generations as part of the Fort Ellice Trail. The Castle was not completed by the time that Leacock moved into it with his new wife, Georgina Eliza Vickers, who he had married in Toronto on 6 August. (Georgina had an impressive pedigree, her grandmother being Susanna Moodie whose 1852 memoir *Roughing it in the Bush* is a modern-day classic of the pioneer experience in early Canada.) Over the next five years, the Leacocks had three children, all born in Manitoba: Thomas Murdoch (Kildonan, 1882), Ela Mary Moodie (Winnipeg, 1884), and Agnes Mary (Birtle, 1886).

When the area around Birtle joined Manitoba, a by-election was called to elect a representative in the provincial legislature. Four men ran for the office, including Leacock, and on 2 November 1881, he came in dead last, garnering just 18 percent of the 465 votes to be cast. He was beaten by Stephen Clement, a farmer from Shoal Lake. In a fit of pique, Leacock abandoned the unfinished

A view of the Leacock House in the 1890s, in a portfolio of Birtle images commissioned by Mayor Charles Flower. BIRDTAIL COUNTRY MUSEUM

Castle and moved back to Winnipeg. Completion of the house was left to its next occupant, John Crawford, who would later serve as Birtle's first mayor.

Back in Winnipeg, Leacock built an even grander 2½ storey, 23-room house on the bank of the Red River on Scotia Street. According to his nephew, E.P. Leacock "filled it with pictures that he said were his ancestors and carried on in it a roaring hospitality that never stopped."

Meanwhile, Birtle's newly occupied seat in the legislature was quickly vacated when Clement resigned to become Sheriff of the Western Judicial District, based at Brandon. Leacock ran in the subsequent by-election, on behalf of the Conservative party, and won by a margin

The Castle, March 2016 GOLDSBOROUGH

Structural problems in its foundation have caused large cracks and missing stones in its exterior walls, March 2016. GOLDSBOROUGH

of 179 votes over his sole opponent, John Crawford. But Crawford did not go down without a fight, promising to reporters after the election to disclose "some startling revelations as to the manner in which the campaign was conducted." Perhaps it was just sour grapes on Crawford's part. I could find no further reports of his revelations, but whatever they were, the election's outcome was unchanged and Leacock assumed his seat in the legislature.

A member of the John Norquay government, Leacock completed the rest of Clement's term, then was re-elected twice, but neither time decisively. In the general election of 1883, he won by just 9 votes, out of 493 votes cast. In 1886, his majority was 8 out of 448 votes. He seems to have taken a spirited part in legislative debates but he gradually grew disillusioned. In late 1887, Leacock broke ranks with his caucus over the awarding of a contract to build a railway to the American border. He chose not to stand for re-election in 1888 although there were rumours that he

was courted for other constituencies. He considered running for Sir John A. Macdonald's Conservatives in an 1889 federal by-election (Leacock often claimed to be Macdonald's close confidant) but bowed out in favour of fellow Conservative Alphonse LaRivière, for whom he campaigned. Two years later, Leacock attended Macdonald's funeral, afterwards running into his nephew on the streets of Toronto, who described him as looking "a trifle shabby."

Georgina Leacock died at Toronto in October 1893, at the age of 37. Leacock's dubious past had caught up with him and he could get little work. Finally, in 1894, he left his three young children in Canada and returned to England where he lived quietly as "Colonel Leacock of the North West Mounted Police" among maple trees grown from Canadian seed to remind him of his adopted home. He represented a monastery that was down on its luck in a claim against the British government that brought a substantial payoff. The brothers were so grateful that they appointed Leacock their permanent manager. He died at the monastery in April 1927.

Leacock's Winnipeg house was purchased by lawyer Nathaniel Hagel, and in 1911 by the Sisters of Our Lady of Charity of the Good Shepherd who came to Winnipeg to care for girls who had passed through the city's juvenile court system. The house became the basis of today's Marymound. Meanwhile, the Leacock House in Birtle was occupied by a long succession of owners. Its turret was removed in 1943. The last occupants, the Blackhall family, moved in in 1951. Mrs. Eliza Blackhall, who had served as a nurse on the battlefields of the First World War, died in 1988 at the age of 91, and the house has been vacant ever since.

I visited the Castle in the summer of 2015 and again in early 2016. Unlike stone buildings elsewhere around Birtle, whose walls remain straight and true despite the passage of a century or more, its exterior stone walls have shifted and broken in numerous places, probably due to construction deficiencies in its foundation. Stones have come tumbling out and are lying in the grass around the building. Windows and doors will not open due to extreme shifting, all of which renders the place uninhabitable. The present owner thinks that, if it does not fall of its own accord, the Castle may have to be demolished in the near term. It seems a shame that a building with a link to a character like E.P. Leacock should end in such a way. If he were to return to Birtle to see it, perhaps Leacock would be wistful, in a way like his nephew's nostalgic memory of the fictional Mariposa:

"But of course "home" would hardly be the word you would apply to the little town, unless perhaps, late at night, when you'd been sitting reading in a quiet corner somewhere such a book as the present one."

SOURCES

"Birtle, N.W.T., Matters and things in that vicinity – An election boomlet," *Manitoba Free Press*, 16 December 1880, page 1.

Marriage registration [Edward Phillip Leacock], death registration [Georgina Leacock], Ancestry.

"City and provincial," *Manitoba Free Press*, 4 September 1882, page 16; 14 September 1882, page 8.

Birth notice, *Birtle Observer*, 18 June 1886.

A Political Manual of the Province of Manitoba and the North-west Territories by J.P. Robertson, 1887, page 73. [searchable copy at https://books.google.ca/books?id=hVUvAAAAYAAJ]

"An indictment," *Manitoba Free Press*, 29 November 1887, page 4.

"Early pioneer of Manitoba is dead in Britain," *Winnipeg Tribune*, 3 May 1927, page 5.

A View of the Birdtail: A History of the Municipality, 1878-1974 by Marion Alba, 1974.

Obituary [Eliza Blackhall], *Birtle Eye-Witness*, 23 November 1988, page 14.

ACKNOWLEDGEMENTS

The people of Birtle are rightfully proud of their community's rich history, in which E.P. Leacock was a conspicuous early participant. I was first alerted to The Castle by long-time friend Ron Bell, who owns the building and its property today. Keen historian and Birtle native Nathan Hasselstrom, now at the University of Ottawa, shared his research on Leacock. Brenda Samchuk of the Birdtail Country Museum was most generous with her time and collections.

Leary Brickworks

In April 2012, fire destroyed an old building on Albert Street in Winnipeg's Exchange District. The next day, I was at the site, digging through the smoldering rubble. Although the façade of the building had been nondescript, it concealed what was believed to be the city's oldest remaining building made of bricks, constructed in 1877. I wanted a sample. Fortunately, I got there ahead of the bulldozers and was able to scrounge several battered, yellow bricks. To most anyone else, they were garbage. For me, they were a treasure from a time when Winnipeg was becoming a city.

Turning a brick over in my hands, I saw it was irregularly shaped, suggesting it had been individually formed rather than mass-produced, and baked in the heat of the sun rather than with a kiln. I wondered about the person who had made it. Unfortunately, unlike many of the early brickmakers, he had not seen fit to stamp his name in the brick's "frog"—the indentation on one or both sides that provides a place for mortar to adhere. So his identity will be forever unknown. But the brick holds pride of place in my collection, as one of the oldest native-made specimens of what is arguably our most ubiquitous building material. Name most any historic building around the province and it probably contains at least a few bricks, if only in its chimney. Made from locally quarried clay (or shale, a rock made of consolidated clay), mixed with water to make a sticky slurry and pressed into shape, "green" bricks reach maximum hardness when exposed to temperatures over 900 °C. A range of colours reflects their specific chemistry and firing temperature. Bricks are fire-resistant, pest-resistant, strong, durable, and easily portable. That's why the now-abandoned Leary Brickworks near the village of Roseisle is so important as the last example of its kind in the province. Truly, history was made there.

No other site in Manitoba matches the intactness of the Leary facility but I have visited several other former brickworks in the course of my travels. Just west of the village of Sidney, in sight of the Trans-Canada Highway midway between Portage la Prairie and Brandon, is a large, shallow pit where clay was quarried by the Sidney

George Leary and a brick-pressing machine at Winnipeg, February 1899.
INA BRAMADAT

An idealized sketch of the Leary Brickworks, from the company letterhead, when it was in operation between 1910 and 1917. ED LEDOHOWSKI

Brick and Tile Company. Established in 1909, and bankrolled by English investors, the plant consisted of brick presses, eight (and possibly as many as twelve) "beehive" kilns, warehouses, and underground tunnels. The tunnels connected the presses with the kilns, to enable green bricks to be transported by narrow-gauge railway in all weather. The plant had a staff of 50 men, producing about 25,000 bricks per day. Sidney bricks had a characteristic red colour, and were used in the construction of numerous prominent buildings around Manitoba, including several schools in Brandon. In Winnipeg, the former Eaton's Mail Order Building, Minto Armoury, St. Edward's Roman Catholic Church on Arlington, the Merchants Bank at Main and Bannerman, and the Manitoba Sports Hall of Fame Building on Pacific Avenue are all made from Sidney bricks. A shortage of

A view of the Leary Brickworks, late 1940s. Today, only the kiln, chimney, press building, and a portion of the drying shed remain. INA BRAMADAT

Interior of the beehive kiln at the Leary Brickworks, showing the vented floor through which hot air rose to cure the green bricks inside, October 2012. A wheelbarrow used to move bricks stands at right. GOLDSBOROUGH

labour during the First World War led to its closure in the spring of 1915. After the war, the company's assets were sold to the Sidney Brick and Clay Works Limited which operated the plant until 1927. Winnipeg's Alsip Brick, Tile and Lumber Company bought it the following year, and operated Sidney as a branch of its main Winnipeg brickworks until closing it in late 1933. Alsip demolished the brickworks but continued to quarry clay for its Winnipeg plant, removing some 75 railway cars a year from the ground,

leaving a sizable pit that I mentioned earlier. The foundations of several buildings are still visible, as are the remnants of five kilns, water wells, and a railway loading ramp. I was even able to climb down into one of its tunnels, now mostly collapsed and filled with rubble.

There was once an extensive brickmaking facility at La Riviere. Today, nothing remains above ground. But mounds of soil excavated by ground squirrels making burrows at the site contain numerous small pieces of red-orange bricks.

Likewise, I have found brick fragments scattered throughout farm fields where brickworks once operated in the Rural Municipalities of Pembina and Whitemouth. There were many other brickworks, large and small, situated all over the southern part of the province where clay was available: Altamont, Asessippi, Balmoral, Beausejour, Brandon, Brookdale, Carberry, Carman, Clearwater, Crystal City, Cypress River, Darlingford, Deleau, Deloraine, Dominion City, Douglas, Eden, Edrans, Emerson, Gilbert Plains, Gladstone, Glossop, Grand Valley, Grandview, Hamiota, Hartney, Holland, Kenville, Killarney, La Broquerie, Lac du Bonnet, Lavenham, Lockport, MacGregor, Manigotagan, Melita, Millwood, Minnedosa, Morden, Morris, Neepawa, Newdale, Ninga, Oak Lake, Pilot Mound, Portage la Prairie, Rapid City, Russell, St. Alphonse, St. Boniface, St. James, Selkirk, Somerset, Souris, Stony Mountain, Swan River, Virden, Wawanesa, and Winnipeg. But, as

The massive pressing machine used to form green bricks into shape, October 2012. GOLDSBOROUGH

A drier/conveyor machine used in an unsuccessful attempt by Winnipeg contractor Erven Tallman to resume operation at Leary in 1962 now stands on the partially-collapsed riverbank, May 2015. GOLDSBOROUGH

I said, the best place in Manitoba to see how bricks were made is near Roseisle.

The Leary Brickworks nestles in the scenic hills about 20 miles west of Carman and 65 miles southwest of Winnipeg. There, a small, curiously domed building—a beehive kiln—stands next to a tall, square chimney and a two-storey wood frame building near the South Boyne River. I had vague recollections of it from childhood trips with my grandparents, who lived in the area. At the time, I knew nothing about the former brickworks. Fortunately, as I grew older and became more interested in it, I was able to speak with members of the Leary family, who still live near the site and guard it faithfully. From them, I learned about George Leary and his pioneering efforts for the Manitoba brickmaking industry.

Leary was born in Kilkenny County, Ireland in 1849. While still a young boy, he and his family moved to Jamaica and then to the West Indies, where his father was a mailman. By 1861, they had relocated to the cooler climes of Ontario where George taught school for a time before seeking adventure and opportunity in Manitoba. Arriving at Winnipeg in 1874 aboard a Red River steamboat, George and brother John joined a party of homesteaders headed to the boomtown of Nelsonville, six miles northwest of present-day Morden. There, Leary helped to build Presbyterian and Methodist churches, though he himself was an Anglican, and was an active member of the local Orange Lodge. In 1880, he caught of the eye of Armintha "Mint" Ager, who had arrived in Manitoba with her family a couple of years after the Learys. They married in 1880 and operated a general store and post office at Nelsonville. When the town was bypassed by the railway, most everyone packed up and moved to Morden. Leary joined them briefly before returning to Winnipeg around 1890. There, he worked as an accountant in a government office and later as a partner in a grain-buying business with Rodmond Roblin, a future premier of Manitoba and grandfather of another premier, Duff Roblin. During the mid-1890s, Leary spent a couple of years in Ireland as an immigration agent on behalf of the Canadian government before coming back to Manitoba as an auditor for the provincial government and an active participant in Conservative politics.

By 1899, Leary had somehow acquired an interest in brick-making technology, joining two years later with four other men in forming the Kelzer Brick Machine and Manufacturing Company to make and sell brick-making equipment invented by partner and civil engineer D.A. Kelzer. Around the same time, Leary joined in forming the Boyne Valley Brick Works Company to exploit clay deposits on land he had bought in 1900 near Roseisle, in the valley of the South Boyne River. One of his partners in the venture was Hugh John Macdonald (only son of Prime Minister Sir John A. Macdonald) who worked as a lawyer in Winnipeg. The company built a brickworks on Leary's Roseisle property and, under Leary's supervision, they produced bricks at a rate of up to 12,000 a day, obtaining a distinctive salmon-red colour when the grey

shale was fired. In 1905, the firm became the Dominion Pressed Brick Company, with Leary's old business partner Rodmond Roblin as one of its directors.

In 1910, the Leary family assumed sole proprietorship, under the name of Learys Brick Company, and made and shipped bricks throughout the province. Winnipeg buildings constructed of red Leary bricks during this period included the Brooklands School and the first Kelvin High School—both now demolished—and the older parts of the Fort Osborne Barracks (now the Asper Jewish Campus). There are probably many others but it is only possible to tell with certainty when the distinctive "Learys" stamp can be seen in exposed frogs, usually when a brick building is renovated or demolished.

In 1917, two years after George Leary retired from active involvement, the brickworks was forced to close due to the scarcity of labour and business, both conditions arising from the First World War. His son Bill, a decorated war veteran, returned after his military discharge and took up farming while refurbishing the old brickworks with the intention of reopening it someday. The refurbishment took nearly 20 years to complete. In 1947, after sitting idle for 30 years (during which time George Leary had died, in 1939), the Leary Brickworks reopened and operated successfully for six years. Unfortunately, Bill Leary's grand plans were cut short when he died of complications following an injury in March 1953. The facility again sat dormant until Winnipeg contractor Erven Tallman attempted to resume operation in 1962

An abandoned tunnel at the Sidney Brickworks through which a narrow-gauge railway once transferred green bricks from the press building to the kilns, September 2012. GOLDSBOROUGH

the towering brick chimney, the bee-hive kiln and three-storey-tall drying shed, and a wooden frame building housing a shale crusher and brick press. All are in an advanced state of deterioration, having sat unused for more than 50 years. The buildings are shaky. The chimney sports a large crack down its length. The roof of the kiln looks like it may collapse inward at any moment. Visitors are welcome to view the buildings from the nearby public road but, not surprisingly, the Learys have had recurring problems with trespassers. Family members, who still live in a distinctive brick house built by Bill Leary—made, of course, using Leary bricks—told me that while most visitors are respect-ful, a few flaunt the conspicuous "No trespassing" sign. A few years ago, a trespasser with a history of

with bricks made under the Leary name. Tallman had little experience in brickmaking so he was unable to produce bricks with satisfactory hardness. According to Leary family members, numerous specimens of the last failed batch, which crumble when pressure is applied, survive today, tarnishing the good reputation

that George and Bill Leary enjoyed during their tenure. Ownership of the facility reverted to the Learys but it was never used again.

I have visited the Leary Brickworks several times. It is a pic-turesque site and the decaying build-ings are evocative of the pioneer era. Remaining from the glory days are

mental illness was found dead beside the crusher building and his bag was found on its roof; whether he fell while trying to scale it, or jumped, is unknown. Fortunately, I was able to get a close look when the Learys accompanied me on a visit in October 2012. Subsequently, I met Bill Leary's daughter, who lives nearby, and she provided historical photos and voluminous details about her brickmaking forebears. Most significantly, she presented me with a Leary brick—one of the good ones, not a crumbly Tallman brick—that she and her son salvaged when the Brooklands "Red School" in Winnipeg was demolished in 2009. That brick now sits alongside its yellow kin from the old Albert Street building in my growing collection.

A sample brick from the former Leary Brickworks, made circa 1953. GOLDSBOROUGH

SOURCES

"Manitoba Gazette," *Winnipeg Morning Telegram*, 1 April 1901.

"Boyne Valley Brick Works" by Hugh J. Borthwick, *The Chronicle*, 1901.

"Re-opening of Leary's brick plant re-establishes district industry," *Dufferin Leader*, 8 January 1948.

"Bricks from the Roseisle Hills," *Dufferin Leader*, 9 July 1948, page 2.

"Leary Brickworks, Learys, Manitoba" by David Neufeld, *Manitoba History*, Number 20, Autumn 1990.

Manitoba Brickmakers by Hugh Henry, Manitoba Museum of Man and Nature, 1992.

George Leary, 1849-1939: Glimpses into the Life of an Enterprising Irishman, compiled by Ina (Leary) Bramadat, 2010.

Manitoba Brick Yards by Randy Rostecki, Manitoba Historic Resources Report, May 2010.

ACKNOWLEDGEMENTS

Dr. Ina Bramadat, daughter of brickmaker Bill Leary, lives in the Roseisle Hills near the former brickworks. She provided generous hospitality and a vast amount of genealogical information on her family. Lynette and Murray Stow, present owners of the site (Lynette is a granddaughter of brickmaker Bill Leary), allowed me to visit it several times and shared their sometimes-harrowing experiences with it. Chris Thompson, a descendant of early brickmaker Murdock McLean, showed me the documented and undocumented locations of brickworks in the La Riviere area. Neil Christoffersen (Mayor, Municipality of North Norfolk) has aided and abetted my fascination with bricks, and arranged for me to tour the former brickworks near Sidney. For his comprehensive research on the history of brickmaking in Manitoba, I commend the incomparable Randy Rostecki.

Little Saskatchewan River Hydro Dam

I know that I am speaking with someone from outside Manitoba when I refer to our power service as "Hydro" and they give me a quizzical look. We take for granted that electricity is generated with flowing water but, of course, this is not the case everywhere. In Manitoba, we have an abundance of fresh water, in myriad streams and rivers, lakes, and wetlands.

Much of our water finds its way into mighty rivers that flow into Lake Winnipeg. From there, the water heads toward Hudson Bay. On the Winnipeg, Burntwood, and Nelson Rivers, we have constructed enormous dams to impound the water temporarily so it can be rerouted through turbines to generate electricity that is then transmitted through lines all over the province. Our abundance allows us to enjoy power rates among the lowest on the continent, and to be a net exporter to neighbouring provinces and states. If we think about the history of our power network, we might think of how it came to be, with the very first hydro dam. Perhaps you might have visited the remains of a now-abandoned dam on the Winnipeg River near Pinawa, built between 1903 and 1906, and think it was the first. You would be wrong. That distinction belongs to a structure, very modest

Aerial view of the Little Saskatchewan Hydro Dam and its reservoir on 19 May 1947, a year before it was destroyed by flood waters that rushed down the Little Saskatchewan River. MANITOBA AIR PHOTO LIBRARY

by modern standards, on the Little Saskatchewan River northwest of Brandon, built in 1900.

When Manitoba's first dam was built, the technology behind hydroelectric power production was new, having been introduced to the world by American inventor George Westinghouse in 1891. The firm responsible for the dam near Brandon was the Brandon Electric Light Company, incorporated in January 1889 by a group of Brandonites led by Isaiah Strome, George Paterson, and Ernest Christie. With the demand for electrical power growing in Brandon, they built a steam-powered generating plant. The facility on the Little Saskatchewan, built eleven years later, was intended to bolster the steam plant, generating electricity at a lower cost because its fuel was essentially free. The company chose a site 1½ miles by water from the spot where the Little Saskatchewan flows into the Assiniboine River. Work by Brandon contractors Charles and Henry Koester began in September

1900. They drove tamarack piles 12 to 16 feet into the ground to support a palisade of vertical wooden timbers, about 175 feet wide, erected across the river valley. Then, the wooden dam was reinforced with stones. The new dam impounded the river about one-half mile behind it with a hydraulic head of 12 to 16 feet. The plant's two generators, installed in a 1,200-square-foot, wood-frame building next to the dam, could produce up to 1,000 horsepower, or 0.75 megawatts, of power. (Compare that

OPPPOSITE Stumps of the wooden piles that formed part of the hydro dam on the Little Saskatchewan river were visible when river levels were low in October 2012. GLEN COOK

with the 1,340 megawatts generated by the Limestone station today.) The electricity was then conveyed to Brandon by a nine-mile-long heavy copper wire supported by wooden poles. Completed in August 1901 at a cost of some $150,000, Brandon made history when, on the evening of 4 October 1901, it became the first place in Manitoba to power its lights entirely by water. However, there were limits; the plant could only operate during ice-free months, from April to November, so the steam plant was used during the winter. Together, the two plants generated the majority of power for Brandon, so much so that when, in February 1913, a generator at the steam plant broke down, businesses all over the city—including all three daily newspapers—were paralyzed.

In 1913, a second hydro dam was constructed on the Little Saskatchewan, at Minnedosa. Six years later, the Manitoba Power

Postcard view of the Little Saskatchewan Generating Station in operation, circa 1910. GOLDSBOROUGH

Commission, predecessor to today's Manitoba Hydro, began supplying electricity to Brandon year-round from its dams on the Winnipeg River, backed up by crude-oil-burning plants at Minnedosa and Virden. The original plant on the Little Saskatchewan was decommissioned in 1924, never having met its full potential because the river did not have enough water to generate power on a reliable basis. In 1930, when the Power Commission took over the Brandon Electric Light Company facilities, it was estimated the former hydro plant had contributed only about six percent of total annual power consumption in Brandon. In early May 1948, the first hydro dam on the Little Saskatchewan was washed away when the second one, at Minnedosa, could not withstand the pressure of floodwater backed up behind it and broke, sending a spate of water downstream.

I did not know what to expect as I walked along the bank of the Little Saskatchewan River in August 2014. A group of professional engineers interested in the engineering history of Manitoba had visited the site two years earlier and had told me they found stumps of the wooden piles that once anchored the dam and a concrete foundation for the powerhouse. At the time of my visit, water levels in the Little Saskatchewan were higher than when the engineers had been there, so I could see no sign of the piles. But several large chunks of concrete peeked out of the vegetation on the north bank. Across the river, a pile of stones marked where the dam had reached the south bank. As I gazed at the meandering little river, and the remains of Manitoba's first hydro dam, I thought about how important hydroelectricity is to our lifestyle today. At that moment, my pockets contained three devices that would have astounded those visionary early Brandonites—a cell phone, a digital camera, and a GPS receiver—all of them utterly dependent on Hydro. How far we have come in a little over a century.

SOURCES

"Water power for Brandon," *Manitoba Free Press*, 27 September 1900, page 6.

"Electric Light Co.'s power dam complete," *Brandon Western Sun*, 2 May 1901, page 5.

"Brandon and district, its growth & progress," *Brandon Western Sun*, 25 July 1901, page 16.

"Local and district," *Brandon Western Sun*, 10 October 1901, page 12.

"City of Brandon without power," *Winnipeg Tribune*, 7 February 1913, page 1.

"Harnessing the Little Saskatchewan at Minnedosa," *Manitoba Free Press*, 3 May 1913, page 51.

"Arbitrators' price on Brandon plant $500,000 in excess of real value," *Winnipeg Tribune*, 8 November 1930, page 32.

"G.A. Paterson, 73, dies at Brandon," *Winnipeg Free Press*, 30 October 1941, page 6.

"Minnedosa streets awash," *Winnipeg Tribune*, 5 May 1948, page 1.

A History of Minnedosa: 1878-1948 by Minnedosa Women's Institute, page 14.

"History of the Electrical Industry in Manitoba" by David S.G. Ross, MHS *Transactions*, Series 3, 1963-1964 Season. [http://www.mhs.mb.ca/docs/transactions/3/electricalindustry.shtml]

Powering the Province: Sixty Years of Manitoba Hydro, Winnipeg: Manitoba Hydro, 2011, page 11.

Minnedosa River Hydropower Station, Heritage Committee, Association of Professional Engineers and Geoscientists of Manitoba. [http://heritage.apegm.mb.ca/index.php/Minnedosa_River_Hydropower_Station]

ACKNOWLEDGEMENTS

I thank Glen Cook of Manitoba Hydro for first making me aware of the Little Saskatchewan dam site and for enabling my visit to it in 2014. Ken Storie alerted me to an aerial photo from 1947 that showed the reservoir behind the dam on the Little Saskatchewan River.

Isaac Pitblado was one of Winnipeg's most powerful lawyers. Born in Nova Scotia in 1867, he came to Winnipeg with his family in 1882. There was no law school here at that time so, from 1886 to 1890, he apprenticed in an established law firm. Called to the Bar in 1890, he joined a law firm that is still in operation today. If you were one of Pitblado's clients at the turn of the 20th century and dropped by his office during September or October, there was a good chance that he would be out indulging in his passion for duck hunting.

Mallard Lodge

To see him, you would have to trek to Delta Marsh, on the south shore of Lake Manitoba, north of Portage la Prairie, where Pitblado had a modest "duck shack." Pitblado was not the only avid waterfowler among the professional elites of Winnipeg. Duck hunting was enjoyed by a wide swath of society, including physicians, businessmen, and even members of royal families. Hunting lodges were situated all around the edge of the marsh. By far the grandest of them all, now abandoned, was Mallard Lodge, built by a curmudgeon named Donald Bain who, in addition to being one of Winnipeg's most affluent businessmen, had ties to the Stanley Cup.

Delta Marsh, one of the largest freshwater wetlands in North America, has been a popular destination for millennia. Aboriginal people went there to hunt ducks and geese, and to enjoy the refreshing breezes off the lake. Large numbers of Europeans began arriving in 1900 when a railway line arrived at the lakeshore. In 1901, Brandon lawyer and senator John Kirchhoffer built a hunting lodge there. He named it York Lodge in anticipation of a visit later that year by the Duke of Cornwall and York—the son of King Edward VII who later became King George V—during His Royal Highness' cross-country tour of Canada. On 6 October 1901, the Royal party detrained at Poplar Point, ten miles south of the marsh, and were transported to its edge by wagon, where they

OPPOSITE The abandoned Mallard Lodge overlooking Lake Manitoba, July 2016. WILLIAM PLENTY

Fieldstone fireplace inside Mallard Lodge, circa 1934. UNIVERSITY OF MANITOBA ARCHIVES & SPECIAL COLLECTIONS, BAIN-PIM COLLECTION

transferred into canoes for a paddle to York Lodge. The Duke took up residence in his namesake lodge while other members of his party were accommodated in tents. Over the course of the next three days, several hundred ducks were shot. The future king is said to have enjoyed the experience so much that he vowed to return for another visit. In preparation for that visit, Kirchhoffer built a larger building that became known as Kirchhoffer Lodge. It featured a large fieldstone fireplace and the door from the original York Lodge, signed by His Royal Highness and other members of the 1901 group. After Kirchhoffer died, his lodge and its surrounding land was purchased by American businessman James Ford Bell. The lodge

Mallard Lodge, 1940s. UNIVERSITY OF MANITOBA ARCHIVES & SPECIAL COLLECTIONS, BAIN-PIM COLLECTION

Donald Bain (right) with two unidentified guests in summer attire and one of his beloved curly-coated retrievers, no date. UNIVERSITY OF MANITOBA ARCHIVES & SPECIAL COLLECTIONS, BAIN-PIM COLLECTION

stood empty until February 1950 when it was moved to a more readily accessible site. Its heavy stone chimney was left behind and it still stands at the original lodge site, far from public access on a private road along the lakeshore.

Donald Bain was another noted visitor to Delta Marsh. Born in Belleville, Ontario in 1874, into a well-to-do Scottish family, he moved to Winnipeg when he was six years old. Bain's athletic prowess was quickly recognized when, at the tender age of 13, he won the provincial roller skating championship. He was a natural athlete, competing in numerous sports and winning trophies in gymnastics, cycling, figure skating, and lacrosse. His greatest claim to fame is as a member of the Winnipeg Victorias hockey team. In 1895 and again in 1901, the Victorias captured the Stanley Cup—at the time given to the country's best amateur hockey team—by challenging and beating teams from eastern Canada. Bain retired from the Victorias in 1902, at the height of his fame, apparently to focus on his growing business as a broker in wholesale groceries. But Bain continued to compete in figure skating into his 50s. Like Isaac Pitblado and other professional men of his generation, Bain was a skilled marksman, having won trapshooting competitions as early as the 1890s. In the early 1920s, he visited Delta Marsh to hunt ducks, probably as a guest of one of his business colleagues. Later, he became a member of a private hunting club at the marsh, and in 1929 he purchased a large block of land adjoining the club's property. The existing lodge on Bain's new property was a small

Donald Bain (right) with two unidentified guests hunting in Delta Marsh, no date. UNIVERSITY OF MANITOBA ARCHIVES & SPECIAL COLLECTIONS, BAIN-PIM COLLECTION

one not befitting his growing business wealth so, in 1932, he hired a contractor to build Mallard Lodge. Apparently patterned on a Scottish hunting lodge that he had admired, Mallard Lodge was more elaborate than any of the other "duck shacks" on Delta Marsh. At 2,400 square feet in area, it was far larger, having two storeys plus a full basement. With a coal-fueled furnace in the basement, it was designed for year-round use, something no other hunting lodge was intended to do. Electric lights throughout the building were powered by a bank of batteries in the basement that were charged by a generator housed in a nearby building. A cistern in the basement held water pumped into it from Lake Manitoba or a well, providing running water for the kitchen, sinks in most of its seven bedrooms, and a toilet and huge porcelain tub in its single bathroom on the second storey. The living room on the main floor featured a massive fieldstone fireplace, surrounded by comfy armchairs, with the walls adorned by taxidermic specimens from Bain's various hunting forays.

Mallard Lodge was not simply a place that Bain used for a few weeks in the fall. It was his refuge from the business world of Winnipeg and he relaxed there for long periods of time throughout the year. And he protected his privacy fiercely. He erected a metal fence around the entire property, infuriating scores of hunters (including my grandfather) who had previously taken for granted their ability to hunt wherever they pleased. When the original contractor for Mallard Lodge objected to building it on Bain's chosen site, arguing that sand there would not provide a stable platform, Bain fired him and supervised the work himself. (Over eighty years later, Bain turned out to be right: there is nary a crack in the lodge's concrete basement, and none of its windows and doors have had problems due to shifting.) Bain constructed a road through the marsh so he could drive to his lodge year-round. He tussled with the man hired to build the road, who objected to working on Sundays. When it was finished, Bain refused to let anyone

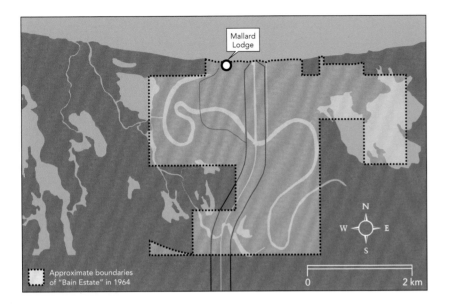

Map of the Bain property at Delta Marsh at the time of its sale to the provincial government in 1964. DRAWN BY GORDON GOLDSBOROUGH

breed known as the curly-coated retriever. Having dense curly black fur that makes them look superficially like a poodle, Bain was supposed to have had as many as 70 curlies at one time, although he usually had one or two as his favourites. A dog cemetery on the grounds of Mallard Lodge had individual graves marked with brass plaques. There was a dock on the shoreline for Bain's boat and, as of the mid-1950s, a row of war-surplus military vehicles parked end to end. Bain had purchased them in an attempt to curb erosion in front of the lodge that was occurring due to high lake levels during this period. Later concealed by beach sand, they were revealed by floods in 2011.

After Donald Bain died in 1962, Mallard Lodge sat vacant. Its contents were sold at an auction attended by scores of people, many of them drawn by curiosity after having been denied access to the famous "Bain estate" for so many years. In 1964, the building and its 2,000 acres of land were sold to the provincial government. The plan was to use the land for the outlet structure of the Portage Diversion, an artificial channel built in the late 1960s to divert water from the Assiniboine River just west of Portage la Prairie into Lake Manitoba, as a counterpart to the Red River Floodway for alleviating flooding in southern Manitoba. There were no plans to use Mallard Lodge until Sterling Lyon, the provincial Minister of Natural Resources and later Premier of Manitoba (and himself a keen Delta waterfowler) met with Dr. Robin Connor of the University of Manitoba. Lyon proposed that the university use the Mallard Lodge as a station to support

else drive on it, not even his neighbours from the hunting club in which he was still a member. And guests invited to Mallard Lodge had to adhere to Bain's strict code of no swearing and no drinking (he was a firm teetotaler). There were several outbuildings around Mallard Lodge. The original lodge served as a home for Bain's resident caretaker. A long, narrow building was a garage for expensive and exotic automobiles from Bain's large collection. Former railway boxcars were used for storage and for hanging game that had been shot in the marsh. And there were dog-houses, lots of them. A life-long bachelor, Bain was a fanatical dog-lover, being especially enamoured with a English

research and university courses in environmental subjects. In 1966, the University of Manitoba Field Station (Delta Marsh)—later renamed the Delta Marsh Field Station—was established with Dr. Jennifer Shay as its founding Director. Shay was tireless in promoting the facility and she was later inducted into the Order of Canada largely on the basis of her work to equip and operate the Field Station during its first twenty years of operation. After she stepped down in 1986, Dr. Phil Isaac and Dr. Gordon Robinson served as the station's Director for the next two and eight years, respectively. Finally, in 1996, I became its fourth, and final, Director. By the time it closed in 2010, the Delta Marsh Field Station had operated continuously for 44 years, supporting four main activities. First, it hosted primary, secondary, post-secondary and adult education, with emphasis on courses in ecology, environmental science, and biology. Second, it was the base of operation for research in a wide range of fields, principally in the

ecological and environmental sciences. Over the course of the station's history, its users published over 370 scientific papers while 132 theses were written by Bachelors, Masters, and Doctoral students. Third, the land around the Field Station was designated by the provincial government as an "ecologically significant area" of natural wetland, forest, and grassland habitats where the Field Station's staff and researchers helped to promote sound and sensitive environmental stewardship practices. Finally, when the station was not being used for teaching and research, it hosted a wide variety of meetings, workshops, conferences, retreats, and other miscellaneous uses by the broader community. Usage of the Field Station was measured in "user-days" (the number of people multiplied by their days in residence) that increased from around 2,000 when the station was established in 1966 to a peak of about 6,500 around 2000.

Mallard Lodge was always the spiritual headquarters of the Delta Marsh Field Station. Even after we

constructed new buildings that featured air-conditioning and other modern amenities, visitors often preferred to stay in the comfortable, historic splendor of the grand, old building. Generations of visitors have come away with stories about their experiences in Mallard Lodge, including a few of a paranormal variety.

One of the many Christmas cards featuring Mallard Lodge that were sent by Donald Bain to relatives, friends, and business acquaintances, 1940s. UNIVERSITY OF MANITOBA ARCHIVES & SPECIAL COLLECTIONS, BAIN-PIM COLLECTION

As a committed skeptic, I never encountered anything that could not be explained by anything but an overactive imagination. But there are those who persist in believing that Mallard Lodge is haunted. These experiences are in wide circulation, having been featured in a book, an episode of a national television program, and several websites.

In 2010, my 14-year term as Director of the Field Station ended and I decided not to seek a renewal. In

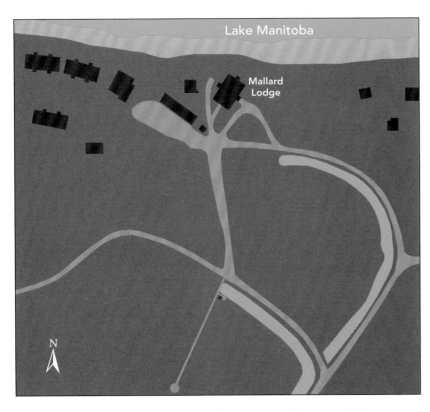

Map of the University of Manitoba's Delta Marsh Field Station, 1986. DRAWN BY GORDON GOLDSBOROUGH WITH INPUT FROM DR. JENNIFER SHAY

retrospect, I regret that decision because the university administrators decided not to replace me and instead gave the responsibilities to someone who was busy with other duties on the main campus in Winnipeg, much less having to assume responsibility for a facility far away. There was no one to advocate on behalf of the Field Station and its unique needs and opportunities. In the fall of that year, the staff was given layoff notices, with assurances they would be recalled in the spring of 2011. The university claimed that it intended to operate the Field Station seasonally, during the spring, summer, and early fall, and close it during the winter, despite evidence that winter was often the busiest time of the year, when visitors paid disproportionately higher fees that helped to offset subsidies provided to students and researchers during the summer.

Unfortunately, the catastrophic flood on Lake Manitoba in 2011 left the station buildings surrounded by water, and three of the buildings nearest to the lake—including a Second World War military barracks for which a fundraising campaign to build a replacement was underway—were severely damaged. Flood waters remained high for much of 2011 and the university decided that it would close the station permanently. It notified the provincial government that it intended to withdraw from a long-term lease that it had held on the property since 1966, and were advised that the province expected the university to return the site to a "state of nature." This entailed removing all of the buildings that the university had moved to or constructed on the site. A local contractor was given

The abandoned Mallard Lodge with armoured military vehicles exposed by beach erosion during the 2011 flood on Lake Manitoba, July 2014. GOLDSBOROUGH

the job with the provision that he could have any buildings he wanted at no cost, but would have to assume all costs to remove them. The two newest buildings, an office/classroom building constructed in 1997, and a residence built in 2003, were picked up and carried away in early 2014. All of the remaining buildings were demolished except Mallard Lodge, the small building beside it that had once housed a power generator (and later occupied by researchers who studied migratory songbirds), and a storage building. By

mid-2014, the site was being reclaimed by tall grass and trees. In the five years since Mallard Lodge was abandoned, it has been broken into several times but, fortunately, no serious vandalism has occurred.

Today, a visitor to Pitblado's former law firm in late fall is unlikely to find many of its partners out hunting in

ABOVE Students, researchers, and staff at the University of Manitoba's Delta Marsh Field Station, June 2002. The author of this book is in the back row at the extreme right. Mallard Lodge stands in the background. DELTA MARSH FIELD STATION COLLECTION, RUSS MEAD

Dr. Robin Connor (LEFT), former Dean of Science, and Sterling Lyon, former Minister of Natural Resources and Manitoba Premier, on the steps of Mallard Lodge at the 40th anniversary of the Delta Marsh Field Station, June 2006. DELTA MARSH FIELD STATION COLLECTION, GOLDSBOROUGH

Manitoba's marshes. Instead, they are more likely to be found on a golf course, a reflection of profound changes over the past century in what people do for relaxation. (I suspect that, as a result, fewer of these modern professionals have a deep understanding of the natural world like Pitblado did.) Some might argue this is a desirable change because they see duck hunting as a barbaric and unnecessarily destructive pastime. Yet, I would point out to such people that the origins of our modern conservation ethic, where we strive to protect endangered natural spaces and wildlife, arose from hunters who realized that they could not overhunt their prey if they wished to enjoy hunting into the future. Indeed, the realization that continued exploitation of natural resources requires

active stewardship was the basis for the founding of Ducks Unlimited Canada, in Manitoba, in 1938. Our modern concept of sustainable wildlife populations is predicated on the necessity of maintaining the habitat that these animals need. A more general concept is that humans are responsible for most of the environmental change that we are now observing and, as such, we must act to counteract those changes or our way of life will be threatened.

Of course, Delta Marsh has not been immune to such changes. Since at least the 1950s, it has undergone dramatic changes including extensive loss of aquatic plants along with the animals that live amongst them. The causes are complex and are believed to be the cumulative result of alterations in the natural pattern of high and low water on Lake Manitoba for the sake of flood prevention, invasion of the marsh by species such as Hybrid Cattail and Common Carp, and contamination of its water by fertilizer, manure, and sewage from the surrounding landscape. This is why

Ducks Unlimited Canada is no longer focused solely on protecting wildlife and their habitat, but is also addressing clean water, climate change adaptation, and other environmental imperatives, something that Canadians can embrace regardless of their views on the merits of duck hunting. Since 2013, I have been part of a group of scientists and managers who are attempting to restore the Delta Marsh. The first step in the multi-year project is to improve water quality by keeping large Common Carp out of the marsh. When carp are abundant, they cause the water to become murky and plants to die for lack of light. Initial results are encouraging but it is too soon to draw conclusions. Several more years of research will be needed to know if we can save this world-famous wetland.

Just as there is a basis for optimism about Delta Marsh, there are grounds to believe that Mallard Lodge can become useful again. I am working with other former Field Station users to establish a not-for-profit organization to move the lodge to a new site, east of the Portage Diversion, and operate it as an ongoing facility for environmental education and research. The encouraging early findings of our marsh restoration project suggest there is life left in the old marsh, and therefore an opportunity to train the next generation of environmental scientists there, in Mallard Lodge. I envision a future in which all visitors to Delta can enjoy and learn about a marsh that abounds with wildlife, in much the same way that John Kirchhoffer, King George V, Isaac Pitblado, and Donald Bain did before them.

SOURCES

Performance metrics of the Delta Marsh Field Station (University of Manitoba), 1966-2010" by Gordon Goldsborough, Faculty of Science, 37 pages.

Delta: A Prairie Marsh and Its People by Glen Suggett, Gordon Goldsborough, and the Delta Marsh History Group, Winnipeg, 2015.

ACKNOWLEDGEMENTS

I have long been interested in the history of duck hunting at Delta Marsh and the various people who engaged in it through the years. This interest culminated in our 2015 book (fourteen years in the making) entitled "Delta: A Prairie Marsh and Its People." I thank the members of the Delta Marsh History Group, most especially Glen Suggett and Shirley Christianson, and the many people who contributed information and photographs. My specific interest in the history of Mallard Lodge was piqued by a chance visit to the Delta Marsh Field Station by Nancy Roberts, a greatniece of Donald Bain. In tracking down other Bain family members, I had the good fortune to meet Donna Smale Pim, another great niece, who donated a large collection of Bain's photographs to the University of Manitoba Archives, a few of which illustrate this chapter. In the course of my research on Bain, I met Jan Taylor, who formerly owned his grand Winnipeg home, and obtained from her a wonderful collection of Bain's photos that successive owners of the home had passed from one to another. They too are now housed at the University of Manitoba Archives. Frank Jankac, formerly at the Manitoba Sports Hall of Fame, drew my attention to a large collection of Bain photos there. Dr. Mark Whitmore, former Dean of Science at the University of Manitoba, provided the opportunity to include Mallard Lodge in this book. Finally, I dedicate this chapter to the many fine people I met through my work at the Delta Marsh Field Station which I hope may one day live again.

Manitoba Glassworks

In May 2003, a fire swept through Delta Marsh, destroying vegetation that had, for decades, concealed an ad hoc garbage dump. There were old car wrecks, metal objects of all sizes and descriptions, and scores of glass bottles. The provincial government arranged to have the garbage carted off to a proper landfill but, before the work was done, collectors swooped in and removed virtually all the bottles which, it turns out, were old and rare enough to be valuable.

View of the former Beausejour glassworks site, March 2012.
GOLDSBOROUGH

I was reminded of this fire recently when I met a fellow who showed me an old bottle from his collection. Made of green-gray glass, it had been used by early Winnipeg brewer Edward Drewry to deliver his product to thirsty customers. Compared to modern bottles, it was curiously irregular in shape with numerous, randomly sized bubbles visible in its sides. An innocuous letter B molded into its bottom revealed it had been made during a span of just a half-dozen years, from 1906 to 1912, at Beausejour. During this period, Beausejour was the epicentre of glass bottle manufacturing in western Canada, as home to the Manitoba Glass Manufacturing Company.

Do you know how many containers are in your home? A quick glance into my refrigerator revealed dozens of containers of all shapes and sizes, and lots more in my cupboards. Many of these containers are made of plastic but a significant number of them are glass. It is a versatile material, in no small part because its clarity makes the contents of whatever it contains readily visible. For millennia, glass has been the material of choice for containers of liquids, with the techniques for making glass being known to the ancient Chinese, Egyptian, Greek, and Roman cultures. All that one needed to make glass was a source of high-quality silica sand and a means to melt it at temperatures over 1000 °C (with crushed glass or "cullet" added to speed up the melting process). Soda ash (sodium carbonate) and limestone (calcium carbonate) were added to the molten glass to increase its later hardness and durability. The age-old process of glass-blowing entailed introducing air into a mass of hot, molten silica in a mold, which determined the shape and embossed text on the resulting bottle. The colour of the glass was a function of impurities in the original sand as well as chemicals added during manufacture, such as chromium (green), cobalt (blue), copper (turquoise), iron (green), manganese (purple), nickel (blue), sulfur (amber), or uranium (yellow or red).

Long before a bottle manufacturing plant was built at Beausejour, glass containers were brought into Manitoba by fur traders of the Hudson's Bay Company and the North West Company, from factories in eastern Canada and, to a lesser extent, from England and other European sources. They contained such trade goods as medicines, inks, preserves, sauces, and wine and liquors. Surviving bottles from these times, often in remarkably good state of preservation, have been found where early garbage pits have been excavated. By the early 20th

The Manitoba Glass Manufacturing Company at Beausejour, circa 1910. ARCHIVES OF MANITOBA, JOHN REIFSCHNEIDER COLLECTION

century, bottles were used for a wide range of commercial applications and the vast majority came from manufacturing plants in eastern Canada or the United States. There was no glass manufacturing capability in western Canada. In 1905, this began to change when German immigrant Joseph Keilbach settled on a farm just outside of Beausejour. He had arrived in Manitoba eight years earlier, along with three of his twelve children, from a farm at Parry Sound, Ontario. On his farm, Keilbach found good quality sand that, after some tests in the forge of local blacksmith John Vass, seemed to have properties suitable for glass-making. He sent samples of the sand to Heidelberg, Germany where analysis confirmed his suspicion. Having no special aptitude for glass-making himself, Keilbach recruited Josef Wenowski, a master glassmaker from Poland, and along with a group of Beausejour men, incorporated as the Manitoba Glass Manufacturing Company Limited. One hundred thousand dollars of capital stock was

issued, divided into one thousand shares of one hundred dollars each.

Keilbach began to build his glassworks in June 1906, assisted by two of his sons and another Beausejour farmer. Built in the Polish-German style and known as the "old barn," the wood-frame, wood-clad building enclosed the furnaces—fueled by local wood and imported coal—where sand was melted, along with areas where skilled glassblowers molded the hot glass into shape. Keilbach had recruited glassworkers from Germany and Poland, aiding several of them in immigrating with their families to Canada and helped them to settle in the Beausejour area. (Some of their descendants remain in the area today.) In the earliest days, the men were assisted by boys and girls as young as 10 to 12 years who performed a range of support tasks. Pre-pubescent boys were found to

The sand quarry near the Beausejour glassworks, circa 1910. ARCHIVES OF MANITOBA, JOHN REIFSCHNEIDER COLLECTION

have higher heat tolerance than older boys so they worked routinely in the hottest parts of the plant. The facility became operational in October 1906. By 1907, it was producing 15,000 to 20,000 bottles per week, operating from September to June, shutting down in the hottest months of July and August. The boom in local population led to incorporation of the Village of Beausejour in 1908.

A distinctive green-gray bottle made for Winnipeg brewer E.L. Drewry at the Beausejour glassworks in 1911. MANITOBA MUSEUM

Keilbach served as a councillor when, the following year, it became an incorporated Town.

The success of the Manitoba Glass Manufacturing Company resulted in a series of ownership changes that led ultimately to its demise. In 1909, Keilbach sold the business to a new group led by Winnipeg entrepreneur (and later Lieutenant Governor of Manitoba) Douglas Cameron, who assumed the role of President. The company's corporate office moved into Winnipeg, near Portage and Main. Cameron had big plans for expansion, as capitalization for the newly enlarged company grew to a cool million dollars. He built a new glass factory next to the "old barn." It was a state-of-the-art facility where, unlike the older building where bottle making was done manually, semi- and fully-automated equipment could mass-produce bottles. It was more spacious and well-ventilated, with an attached workshop and engine room to generate electricity to run the bottle-making machines.

The new plant's workforce was notably different from that of the older plant in two important respects. First, it was staffed by American glassworkers who returned home when the plant shut down in July and August. Consequently, few of them ever set down roots in the way that Europeans had done, preferring instead to live temporarily and exuberantly in Beausejour hotels. Second, the workers were represented by a union, the Glass Bottle Blowers Association of the USA and Canada (GBBA). Working conditions in the new plant were more regulated and one sees few child workers in photographs from this period.

At its peak, the Beausejour glassworks employed around 150 workers, more than double the number that had worked in the original plant. Keilbach's Europeans worked in the "old barn" while the Americans worked in Cameron's new plant. The facility was sending bottles as far away as Victoria, BC, supplying a diverse range of products, including milk bottles, beer bottles, fruit

The derelict glassworks after being thoroughly scavenged, circa 1920. JASON BRAUN, DOMINION GLASS COMPANY ARCHIVES

jars, medicine vials, and ink bottles. No sooner had the plant reached its stride than it drew the attention of the Diamond Flint Glass Company of Montreal. Diamond Flint bought the Beausejour plant in October 1912, ostensibly to expand its manufacturing capability, but more likely to close it and, in so doing, limit competition and drive up prices. In early 1913, Dominion Glass opened a glassworks at Redcliff, Alberta, having been attracted there with municipal offers of free land and free natural gas to fuel its plant. (Around the same time, Diamond Flint reorganized as the Dominion Glass Company, the largest glass producer in Canada, operating after 1976 as Domglas before declaring bankruptcy in 2002.)

The Manitoba Glass plant closed in the spring of 1913, mere months after its sale to Diamond Flint. Wooden crates of finished bottles were stacked outside and were later stolen or vandalized. The automated bottle-making machines from the new plant were disassembled and shipped to Alberta. But the building itself, just a few years old, was simply abandoned. A plan in the late 1910s by Douglas Cameron to get back into the glass business, with a new plant in Winnipeg, was quickly squelched when Dominion Glass caught wind of it. The company reminded Cameron that he had signed a "non-compete clause" as part of the Beausejour sale agreement. A glassworks did eventually operate at Winnipeg under different

management, but only for a brief period, from 1928 to 1930, being nipped in the bud by the Great Depression. That marked the end of glass container manufacturing in Manitoba.

Through the early 1920s, locals scavenged the metal sheeting that covered the exterior of the Beausejour glassworks, then its steel-truss skeleton. Eventually, only the brick and concrete remains of the foundations were left, along with the larger metal mechanical parts. Some of the bricks were taken for new construction projects around Beausejour. The remaining metal was recycled during the Second World War. The only other remaining elements of the glassworks are, therefore, the containers made during its six-year period of operation that exist in collections around the world. In the late 1970s, bottle collector

and historian George Chopping excavated at the site and recovered large numbers of bottles. But he had to be careful in drawing conclusions that bottles he found were made there. They could just as easily have been made all over the world and brought to Beausejour for use as cullet. In the absence of discrete identifying marks such as those on Drewry's beer bottles, collectors sometimes ascribe a Beausejour connection based on the characteristic green-gray colour of the glass. In addition to these bottles, a few rare souvenirs made by glassworkers during periods of downtime, such as glass canes or chains of glass links, have been found.

Garbage dumped in Delta Marsh decades earlier was revealed when a grass fire swept through the area in early 2003. In the aftermath, bottle collectors carted off loads of glass bottles that were revealed in the burned area. GOLDSBOROUGH

I visited the site of the Manitoba Glass Manufacturing Company in March 2012. To be honest, I was underwhelmed when I found only a few nondescript, concrete-lined holes in the ground and a plaque announcing the site as having provincial historic designation. I might have been more impressed had I known that the lake immediately north of the site was also connected to its history. Once the site of Joseph Keilbach's farm, the sand was so thoroughly quarried for bricks and glass that, now filled with water, the pit has become a lake. Named Glass Lake, it is used for local recreation and a watery vista for a row of large homes on its shores. Although the remains were disappointing, the visit did remind me of a heady time when Beausejour was at the forefront of an industry. In my view, it also provides an early case study of what happens when a small company is taken over by a larger one. The small company is digested and its parts are moved to where business conditions are more favourable. The company makes more profit but leaves behind a community that has lost a major source of employment. In this instance, Beausejour went from an unincorporated hamlet to a town during the short-lived boom in its glass-making industry. I am curious to know what sustained the town in the aftermath. Manitoba's loss was Alberta's gain—for a while. The glass plant at Redcliff that benefited from the closure of the Beausejour plant was itself closed in 1989. Today, manufacturing capability in general is being consolidated in a few places around the world—such as China—where the cost of raw materials, labour costs, and workplace safety standards, are low. If the sources of those glass containers in your refrigerator were identified, they are unlikely to be Canadian, much less Manitoban.

SOURCES

"Notice [Manitoba Glass Manufacturing Company Limited]," *Manitoba Gazette*, Volume 36, 1907, page 188.

Manitoba Glass Manufacturing Company listing, *Henderson's Winnipeg City Directory*, 1912, Winnipeg: Henderson Directories Limited, page 1179.

"Bottles! Bottles! Any Old Bottles?" by Stanley S. Silver, *Manitoba Pageant*, Volume 16, Number 3, Spring 1973.

"Recollections of Beausejour and the Manitoba Glass Works 1909-1911" by John Charles Reifschneider, *Manitoba Pageant*, Volume 21, Number 4, Summer 1976.

Bottles of the Canadian Prairies by George C. Chopping, privately published, 1978.

They Stopped at a Good Place: A History of the Beausejour-Brokenhead-Garson-Tyndall Area of Manitoba, 1875-1981 edited by Michael Czuboka, Beausejour-Brokenhead Historical Book Committee, 1982.

Glass in Canada by Thomas B. King, Erin, Ontario: Boston Mills Press, 1987, pages 121-123.

"The Dominion Glass Companies of Montreal, Canada" by Bill Lockhart, Beau Schriever, and Bill Lindsey, Society for Historical Archaeology, Historic Glass Bottle Identification and Information Website. [https://sha.org/bottle/pdffiles/DominionGlass.pdf]

ACKNOWLEDGEMENTS

I thank Monica Ball (Legislative Library of Manitoba) and Barry Flett for their help in locating information. The lion's share of the credit belongs to former Beausejour resident Jason Braun who, since his teens, has been researching the Beausejour glassworks. Jason shared generously with his voluminous research. Until he publishes his work, the full story of this unique Manitoba enterprise will not be told.

Matchettville School

MATCHETTVILLE S.D.
1906-1959

I was astounded. I had found an abandoned one-room schoolhouse as a result of plain, dumb luck. I was driving along a country road, about five miles north of Treherne, in search of a monument that had been erected in commemoration of Matchettville Methodist Church. I knew its approximate location and, as the GPS receiver mounted on my car's dash told me that I was getting close, a stout little building had appeared on the horizon.

Now I was parked beside it, but I quickly discovered that this one was very different from other former schools I had found. Matchettville School was made from home-made concrete blocks that immediately made me keenly interested in it, for reasons that I will explain shortly. But more importantly, it had a huge, gaping hole in its side.

Building shelter on the treeless prairies posed special challenges. Indigenous people who moved in search of food constructed temporary lodgings made from bison hides. The sedentary European settlers who began arriving during the 19th century looked to more durable construction materials. Wood was scarce on the prairies and is prone to burn when your cook stove or furnace throws a spark, or when the surrounding grasslands are set ablaze by lightning or humans. Bricks are great—strong and inflammable, made of locally plentiful clay or shale—but you need to heat them to high temperatures for maximum durability. Field stones deposited all over the landscape during the last glaciation are numerous but they tend to be irregular in size, requiring a skilled mason to cut them into shapes amenable for building. Concrete seems to provide an excellent alternative to all of these.

Concrete has been made since ancient times using three ingredients: water, aggregate (sand, gravel, and stones), and cement. A common mistake is to use the words concrete and cement interchangeably; cement is the adhesive that binds the other ingredients to make concrete. Cement is a caustic powder made from calcium silicates that are relatively abundant in Manitoba, being found traditionally, for example, in the Fort Whyte area of Winnipeg where cement has been manufactured for decades. Wet concrete can be poured into molds to form a variety of block shapes that harden to a strong, rock-like consistency. An advantage of concrete blocks for construction is that they are inherently fire- and vermin-resistant. Furthermore, they can be manufactured with a minimal investment of infrastructure using mostly local, easily transported materials. A void in the centre of the mold minimizes the amount of concrete needed to make a block. On the other hand, concrete blocks have some distinct disadvantages. Although the space inside the block might provide some insulation value, I am told by people who live in concrete-block buildings that they tend to be hot in summer

Photo of Matchettville School taken sometime during its 45-year period of operation. ARCHIVES OF MANITOBA, SCHOOL INSPECTORS PHOTOGRAPHS

and cold in winter. And the finished blocks, being typically much larger than bricks, are exceptionally heavy. In an age where horses and wagons were the standard means of transportation, just a few blocks constituted a full load. Making blocks at the construction site was usually the preferred alternative to moving them.

In 1903, Manitoba newspapers began carrying advertisements touting the benefits of concrete-block machines for local building projects, and salesmen attended country fairs to demonstrate them. A worker shovelled wet concrete into the machine, tamped it to fill the mold completely, let it set for a short time, then removed the mold so the damp block could complete the curing process. The mold often incorporated patterns so the finished product had one or more decorative sides. Blocks varied in size but were generally 24 to 32 inches long, 9 to 12 inches tall, and 3 to 6 inches thick. A Winnipeg contractor estimated that two men mixing ingredients and two men packing wet concrete into molds could make 48 blocks in an hour. An average block weighed more than 50 pounds.

There are two reasons for my fascination with concrete blocks. They are great examples of local ingenuity brought to bear on a basic problem and they express individuality and creativity in their manufacture. Individually made, blocks are as unique as the people who made them, unlike more mass-produced items like bricks. Also, concrete-block buildings are rare in Manitoba compared to those made of other materials, probably because their period of construction was so short.

Local entrepreneurs around Manitoba saw concrete-block manufacturing as a money-making business that required limited investment because blocks did not require high-temperature firing like bricks. In the village of Arden, northeast of Neepawa in the Rural Municipality of Lansdowne, the Arden Cement Block and Building Company was incorporated in early 1904. Its partners included hardware merchant and tinsmith John Gilhuly, merchant and municipal official Maurice Boughton, carpenters George and William Stockdale, and stonemasons Robert Lamb and John Samuel McGorman. They used a block-making machine made by Chicago inventor Harmon Palmer, who had patented it just four years earlier, to construct several buildings around the municipality. Arden was an ideal place for block-making, with the nearby Arden Ridge (a remnant of glacial Lake Agassiz) providing a plentiful supply of sand and gravel. Walking down the main street of Arden today, examples of their work include the Lansdowne municipal office, constructed in 1904 and holding the distinction of being one of the few municipal offices in Manitoba still used for its original purpose. Nearby is the concrete-block post office, formerly a pharmacy and doctor's office, and a two-storey private residence. Several more residences in the surrounding countryside are made from blocks. One of them, now derelict, was salvaged for blocks to build a commemorative monument for the town's former school. South of Arden is the vacant building of Ayr School, built of concrete blocks in 1908 to replace the original log schoolhouse. The new school featured a full concrete basement with such innovative technology as indoor bathrooms for girls and boys, and a coal-fired furnace. The concrete is in fairly decent condition but the wood parts of the building are failing, allowing the rain and snow to enter and rot the building from the inside out. I have visited Ayr School several times and was disturbed to see during a 2015 visit that a name plaque embedded in its exterior blocks had been gouged out.

At Emerson, contractor David Wright championed the use of concrete blocks while also serving as the Receiver and Mayor of the town. Surviving samples of his work include the local Baptist Church and the manse for the Presbyterian Church, as well as the home of pharmacist Ezra Casselman, all built in 1905.

The highest concentration of concrete-block buildings I have found in my travels around Manitoba are close to Austin, and they are likely all the work on one man: local farmer Franklin "Frank" Thomson. Born in Ontario, Thomson came to Austin about 1890 to join his brother, the town's first pharmacist. Three years later, he married a local girl and they had four children. The family lived at Altamont for a few years but returned to farm in the Ravenshoe district. To supplement his farm income, Thomson operated a gravel quarry and concrete block-making business. His own barn was made in 1908 from his concrete blocks. It was pretty shaky when I visited it in 2012. He built Austin's three-storey Argyle Hotel (1908), destroyed by fire in 1947, and Carberry's Gardiner

The one-room Ayr School was built in 1908. Its concrete blocks are largely intact but damage to its roof has allowed water to enter, so the interior is badly degraded, as seen in these views from May 2015. GOLDSBOROUGH

From Residential Schools to Bank Vaults to Grain Elevators   159

Nelson concrete-block house, October 2012.
GOLDSBOROUGH

The two-storey Kilkenny general store at Broomhill, made partly of concrete blocks in 1908. GOLDSBOROUGH

Building, home to a harness-maker for some 48 years and now accommodating the Seton Centre, a museum, art gallery, and gift shop commemorating early Manitoba naturalist Ernest Thompson Seton. Thomson built granaries for his neighbours and he built homes—several of them—in and around Austin. Most are still occupied. A notable exception is the Nelson House northwest of Austin. Its original occupant is unknown but the two-storey building was purchased in the 1940s by returned war veteran Joe Nelson. It served as the Nelson family home for many years but was abandoned when, in 2011, a suspected arson fire destroyed all but its resilient concrete walls.

I have found several concrete-block buildings that are nowhere near any others so their origins are unknown. In the ghost town of Broomhill, in the Municipality of Two Borders, a two-storey building was erected in 1908, partially of concrete blocks, for merchant William Kilkenny and his brother John. In its heyday, the Kilkenny general store was the centre of the community. In front of the building, a hand-operated gasoline pump sat at the south end, by an entrance to the store and post office, with an agency selling Cockshutt Plow and International Harvester implements, and a blacksmith shop at the north end. Three rented residential suites were on the south end of the upper storey, and the north end—reachable by stairs from the outside, now visible only as a pattern on the exterior wall—had a hall used for public functions such as dances and meetings. A full concrete basement offered further space for storage of trade goods. Behind the store were pens where livestock were kept prior to being shipped to market in the Union Stockyards in St. Boniface; sheds for the storage of coal, petroleum products in large metal barrels, and lubricants for farm machinery; and a railway loading platform. The business was operated by a succession of Kilkennys until it closed in September 1964 and the building was sold to a former employee, by whose descendants it is still owned. The roof has collapsed and most of the windows are gone.

In Dauphin, an impressive three-storey concrete-block building was known originally as the Canadian Northern Hotel. Constructed by William Whitmore, who arrived in 1886, the building was purchased around 1911 by rancher and hotelier Daniel Hamilton. He renamed it the Hamilton Hotel and operated it until his death. In 1960, it was purchased by John Kiernicki and renamed the Towers Hotel, operating right up to its fiery death by arson in September 2014. Finally, on Main Street in Altona, we have the fine specimen of the Bergthaler Church Waisenamt. It was built for a mutual aid association introduced by the Mennonites who settled in southern Manitoba in the 1870s, based on a centuries-old tradition in Prussia and Russia to aid widows and orphans and administer estates. The Waisenamt collapsed during the Great Depression and the two-storey building has since had various occupants, now serving as a private home.

For reasons unknown, the "Golden Age" of concrete blocks ended around 1913. That is the year the youngest concrete-block building I have identified so far—the now-demolished school in the village of Lowe Farm— was built. It is possible the outbreak of the First World War put the kibosh on major construction projects. Or perhaps the limitations of concrete blocks became more widely known. For whatever reason, if you discover a

The two-storey, concrete-block building on Altona's Main Street constructed for the Bergthaler Church Waisenamt, a Mennonite mutual aid association, June 2012. GOLDSBOROUGH

Workmen make concrete blocks at the Manitoba Agricultural College, circa 1915. ARCHIVES OF MANITOBA

concrete-block building somewhere in Manitoba, you can safely conclude that it was probably built between 1904 and 1913.

Now let us return to Matchettville School. It lies in an area of the province settled in the late 1880s by Anglophone migrants from Ontario. According to local lore, the district was originally known as Bachelorville due to the scarcity of women and was renamed Matchettville when those bachelors married. In fact, it was almost certainly named for members of the Matchett family who were among the early homesteaders. As land was taken up for farms, the number of school-age children increased so more school districts were needed to educate them. The Matchettville school district was established formally in May 1905 and a school building was constructed the following year. Frank Thomson made the blocks for the school but we do not know if he made them at his farm then hauled them over 18 miles (as the crow flies) to Matchettville or made them at the school site. The inner sides of the concrete walls were covered by lathe and plaster. Only the faux-stone exteriors were visible. Three large windows on its south side permitted maximum sunlight—because it did not have electrical service until probably the 1940s or 1950s—and a small vestibule on its west end was where children entered from outside and left their coats and footwear.

Matchettville School operated for 45 years, with students guided in their studies by a succession of young, mostly unmarried women who would hire on as a teacher, typically for a one-year term, until a better position elsewhere, or matrimony, ended their employment. In 1951, the school closed due to low enrollment and henceforth students from this area were bused to a school in Treherne. In June 1958, following a meeting at the school where School Inspector Richard Moore explained the virtues of consolidation, a vote of local ratepayers approved absorption of the school district into that of Treherne at the beginning of 1959. The little school building was sold to a local farmer for $1. The building was used for decades as a granary, its strong concrete walls capable of holding a large amount of grain. (Wooden school buildings used as granaries typically had to be reinforced to withstand the pressure.)

In August 2003, the south wall of the building was badly damaged when an agricultural combine collided with it, leaving a hole some eight feet in diameter. The concrete blocks themselves were hardly damaged but the mortar holding them together was broken. A good mason could probably have repaired the wall. I am told the combine was badly damaged but its owner did not want to claim insurance because alcohol was involved. Instead, cash quietly changed hands, and the farmer whose granary had been damaged replaced it with a modern steel one. So now the building stands vacant. Unfortunately, this means the little old schoolhouse is more subject to the ravages of weather, animals, and vandals, all of which will contribute to its ultimate demise. A solid building that probably could have stood for a long, long time will meet a premature end. But at least its story has been told. There is something to be said for dumb luck, and a concrete idea.

SOURCES

"Cement block a thing of today," *Winnipeg Tribune*, 4 August 1904, page 7.

"Making cement blocks," *Winnipeg Tribune*, 8 May 1905, page 10.

Tiger Hills to the Assiniboine: A History of Treherne and Surrounding District by Treherne Area History Committee, 1976, pages 60-61.

Through Fields and Dreams: A History of the RM of North Norfolk and MacGregor by History Book Committee of the North Norfolk-MacGregor Archives, 1998.

ACKNOWLEDGEMENTS

I thank Craig Spencer, Reeve for the Municipality of Norfolk-Treherne, who I met coincidentally at a conservation meeting in Brandon, for filling in gaps in the story of Matchettville School. His neighbour Pat Sparling provided additional details. And no story of Manitoba concrete blocks would be complete without a tip-of-the-hat to Neil Christoffersen, Reeve for the Municipality of North Norfolk, who shares my passion for this rare method of prairie construction. Neil has alerted me to numerous historic sites in his vicinity, which was a hotspot of concrete-block manufacture.

McArdle Salt Works

These days, products labeled "artisanal" command high prices. I thought about this the other day at the supermarket when I picked up a package of salt. I pondered how things might have turned out differently for an industrial site along Provincial Highway #10, on the west side of Lake Winnipegosis, about 80 miles south of The Pas. It was a place that I visited in August 2005, the long-abandoned plant of the McArdle Salt Works.

Salt has been used since antiquity as a preservative and flavour enhancer, along with many other applications. Crystalline salt is easily made by evaporating seawater, using the sun or by boiling, although people living far from oceans have had to rely on other sources. Saltwater springs on the west side of Manitoba, along Lakes Manitoba and Winnipegosis, come from deep in the Earth, picking up salt as they pass through deposits laid down millions of years ago when the North American interior was a shallow, inland sea. Cold, salty water bubbling from the ground has been used by generations of Indigenous people, as animals hunted for food were attracted to the springs to fulfill their need for salt. (Even today, farmers provide blocks of salt for their livestock to lick.) Early European explorers of northern Manitoba remarked on natural deposits of dry salt found here and there. Hudson's Bay Company fur trader Charles Isham used salt springs in the vicinity of what is now Swan River when he established a post there in 1790. When Catholic priest Georges Belcourt established a mission at Duck Bay in 1839, he noted that salt production was an important part of the local economy.

One of the most well-known salt-makers in the region was James Monkman, who worked at Duck Bay and the Red Deer Peninsula on Lake Winnipegosis as early as 1818. When geologist Henry Hind visited the area in 1858, he noted that Monkman's facility consisted of "two small log-houses and three evaporating furnaces. The kettles of English construction, are well-made rectangular vessels of iron, five feet long, two feet broad and one foot deep." Thirty gallons of saltwater produced one bushel of salt, and each wood-fired kettle could produce two bushels of salt daily. Monkman and his family

View of the salt factory at Neepawa, 1930s. GOLDSBOROUGH

Ruins of the Monkman Salt Works in 1889, at the time of a visit by federal geologist Joseph Tyrrell. ARCHIVES OF MANITOBA, J.B. TYRRELL COLLECTION

operated seven kettles throughout the summer, giving some indication of the extent of local salt demand. But all good things come to an end, and by the time that federal geologist Joseph Tyrrell visited the region in the 1880s, he found only the ruins of Monkman's operation. Exploitation of Manitoba's salt deposits on a large commercial scale began in the early 20th century when entrepreneurs drilling for oil near Neepawa hit saltwater instead. In 1924, the Neepawa Salt Company was incorporated. By 1932, it was producing 35 tons of salt per day, using water pumped from two deep wells evaporated in a vacuum apparatus.

In 1937, a group of speculators at Swan River, led by Leo McArdle of Tisdale, Saskatchewan and lawyer Edward Crawford of Winnipeg, saw an opportunity to make salt in the region formerly used by the Monkmans. They formed the Northern Salt Syndicate to develop a commercial salt works at a naturally flowing spring that discharged into the Red Deer River on its way into Lake Winnipegosis. They installed a wooden crib at the salt spring to begin extracting water, brought in boiling kettles, and constructed several buildings. The water's salt content was nearly that of seawater and it flowed year-round at a temperature of 5 °C. Unfortunately, the water had one major flaw: it contained a lot of iron. This caused the evaporated salt to take on a distinctly yellow hue which was unacceptable to fussy consumers expecting snow-white salt like the products of eastern Canadian salt-makers. High transportation costs due to the plant's remote location compounded the problem. As a result, the McArdle Salt Works operated for only a short time and it probably produced very little saleable product. The facility was abandoned and, by the time of my visit in 2005, all that remained were the foundations for one of the storage buildings and the crib at the spring itself. Meanwhile, the Neepawa salt factory closed in 1970 and its site is now occupied by a hockey arena. Our salt comes from places far away, and is available in a wide range of colours, including pink, red, blue, gray, and black. I wonder, therefore, if the yellow salt from the McArdle plant in northern Manitoba would be received more favourably by today's trendy consumers?

The cribbing of the salt spring in the foreground is still visible, along with the ruins of a salt storage building in the background, at the former McArdle Salt Works, August 2005. GOLDSBOROUGH

"Northern Salt Syndicate builds plant," *Winnipeg Free Press*, 13 June 1938, page 18.

"Leave for inspection of northern salt," *Winnipeg Free Press*, 9 September 1938, page 15.

Heritage – A History of the Town of Neepawa and District as Told and Recorded by its People 1883-1983 by Neepawa History Book Committee, 1983, pages 125-129.

"Salt-making in Manitoba" by Virginia Petch, *Manitoba History*, Number 51, February 2006.

SOURCES

Narrative on the Canadian Red River Exploring Expedition of 1857 and on the Assiniboine and Saskatchewan Exploring Expedition of 1858 by Henry Youle Hind. Tokyo: Charles E. Tuttle Co., 1971, page 45.

"Mafeking salt well optioned locally," *Swan Valley Star and Times*, 22 July 1937, page 1.

"An explanation," *Swan Valley Star and Times*, 23 September 1937, page 1.

ACKNOWLEDGEMENTS

I thank Kathleen Londry, a former colleague at the University of Manitoba, for giving me the opportunity to visit the McArdle Salt Works during a scientific expedition she led to the region, and Virginia Petch for educating me on the history of local salt manufacture.

Morris Repeater Station

This evening, as my family sat down to dinner, my wife's computer tablet warbled to get her attention. There was an incoming call from her sister who was vacationing in northern Australia. Not only could we talk with her, we could see her lounging on the beach, and as she panned the camera of her computer, we could see the surrounding resort, almost as though we were there.

We exchanged news and made plans for an upcoming family gathering, almost like she was in the room with us, and not on the other side of the planet. As we closed the call, I could not help but think of the telecommunications marvel that this conversation represented, and how amazed and envious my late grandmother would have been about it.

My grandmother loved to have visitors, whether it was a travelling salesman, a friend, or a beloved grandchild. And if she could not chat in person, a telephone call was the next-best alternative. I recall her saying how the telephone was so important to her. Before service came to rural Manitoba, daily life could be lonely, especially for women toiling at homes far from neighbours. The ability to pick up the telephone and talk with someone made all the difference. In grandma's case, she often told the story about speaking to her mother by phone in their native French, and hearing all the Anglophones eavesdropping on the party line hang up in frustration.

And although it was prohibitively expensive and difficult to call relatives living on another continent, it was comparatively easy to seek emergency help from a doctor, police officer, or fireman; negotiate a sale or lodge a complaint; or just share the latest gossip. Simply put, the advent of telephone service made life bearable for many Manitobans.

The first telephone service in Manitoba dates to 1878 when Horace McDougall, the manager of Winnipeg's North West Telegraph Company, installed a line between his home and his office. Others saw the value of the telephone and McDougall's business grew steadily. Two years later, he sold out to the Bell Telephone Company of Canada. By the 1890s, local telephone exchanges began to be installed in rural Manitoba, linking people with their immediate neighbours. In 1900, there were 222 miles of long distance lines. This total more than quadrupled, to 892 miles, within four years. As wires spread across the province, and then into neighbouring provinces and states, the number of people who could be reached by telephone grew exponentially.

But all was not rosy. Bell was just one of many companies seeking to provide service. Systems of rival companies were not interconnected so Bell customers could not call those using a competitor's telephone. Intense competition led to cutthroat tactics. There were allegations that telephone linemen would knock down or saw off the poles of their competitors. In 1906, the provincial government of Rodmond Roblin had had enough. Recognizing the merit of seamless communication to the growth of the province, it created Manitoba Government Telephones as the first government-owned system in Canada. With a monopoly on service, MGT (later renamed Manitoba Telephone System, MTS, precursor to today's publicly traded Manitoba Telecom Services) increased the pace of telephone deployment throughout rural areas.

The challenge in creating these long-distance telephone lines was the inevitable degradation of the electric signal as it passed along a wire.

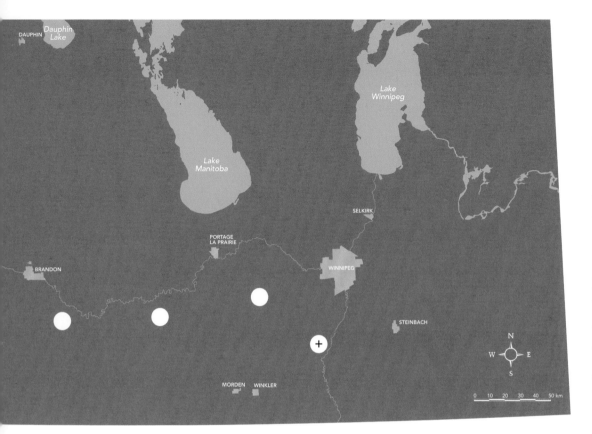

#2, spaced almost exactly 40 miles apart: one between Fannystelle and Elm Creek, one between Treherne and Holland, and one near Wawanesa. They are similar because all four buildings were repeater stations. At one time, most of the long-distance traffic was carried over bare copper wires on wooden poles with wooden cross-arms, each of which had ten wooden pins, with a glass insulator threaded on it, over which the copper wire was passed. Each pair of wires could carry one telephone conversation. In the 1930s, a new system called C-carrier was developed that supported four simultaneous voices. It required a signal amplifier every 200 miles. The later J-carrier system added 12 more channels but, because it operated at higher frequencies, signal losses were greater so it required more frequent amplification, every 40 miles. Sometime between 1950 and 1954, Manitoba Government Telephone constructed J-carrier lines running

Eventually, the noise would exceed the signal and unintelligible static would be all you heard. This was especially problematic for long lines leading out of the province. This is where repeater stations came in. They housed circuitry that amplified the signal before it degraded too much. A network of repeater stations was an integral part of the land-based telecommunications network that connected Manitoba to the world.

A little building that sits alongside Highway #330, about six miles north of Morris, three miles east of Rosenort, is a tangible symbol of this telecommunications revolution. Rectangular in outline, made of red bricks, with a single door on the north end and no windows, it contains one room, now empty. It is one of four identical buildings that I have found in my travels. The other three lie along Provincial Trunk Highway west from Winnipeg to Saskatchewan, with five repeaters along the way. In addition to the three that I had found, a fourth at Kemnay was demolished in the 1960s, after it had become obsolete. The fifth and final repeater on the east-west line was at Virden but, because the amplification circuitry was installed in the local telephone office, there was no need for a separate repeater station. Meanwhile, a second line ran south to the international border, connecting Manitoba lines to those in North Dakota. A single repeater station was needed, the one north of Morris.

Each repeater station was virtually identical inside. From the entrance, several bays ran the length of the building. Each bay was about two feet wide with equipment mounted in racks on either side. With all that electricity running through the circuits, a significant amount of heat was given off. Large fans were used to cool the building's interior as needed, and electric heaters kept it passably warm in winter. The station had no staff and was only visited when service was required. Technicians doing routine maintenance would depart Winnipeg in the morning, visiting each station in turn, returning home by evening.

By the 1960s, advancing technology had made the repeater stations obsolete. Telephone calls began to be carried wirelessly via microwaves, with signals beamed between towers many miles apart. (Eventually, orbiting satellites, cellular towers, and buried fiber-optic cables made these towers obsolete and most have been dismantled.) The little repeater stations were decommissioned. Their electronic equipment was removed and the buildings were sold. One of the stations along Highway #2 is a now snowmobiling warm-up shack and another is a granary. A third is locked up tight but appears to be used as a canvas for local graffiti artists. The one near Morris is used for storage. The service life for these repeaters had already passed by the time that I first noticed them, as a child travelling with my family to visit my grandparents. I wondered why brick buildings that seemed vaguely industrial had been built in farm fields. Little did I know of the key role they had played in improving the quality of my grandmother's life, and that of Manitobans everywhere.

SOURCES

"A History of the Telephone in Manitoba" by Gilbert A. Muir, *Transactions of the Manitoba Historical and Scientific Society*, Series 3, 1964-1965 Season.

People of Service: A Brief History of the Manitoba Telephone System, 3rd edition by Robert H. Drain for MTS Corporate Communications, Winnipeg, 1991. [Manitoba Legislative Library]

ACKNOWLEDGEMENTS

An enjoyable day spent crisscrossing the Rural Municipality of Morris with Reeve Ralph Groening in search of one-room schoolhouse sites led me to discover this innocuous little building. Later, in my attempts to learn more about its history, I connected with Jim Hicks, a now-retired electrical engineer who worked for Manitoba Government Telephones in the early 1950s. He shared his experiences in installing equipment and cabling in this building and its kin, and his anecdote about cooking lunch using the heat given off by the circuitry. I thank Alan Pollard for alerting me to a booklet on the history of MTS.

Ninette Sanatorium

I was near the village of Ninette, inside a 104-year-old, two-storey brick and stone building. It had been closed for several years. Walking down an unlit corridor, I came upon an elevator. Acting on a lark, I pressed the button to summon the elevator. To my consternation, its door opened immediately, beckoning me inside.

What the heck, I wondered; how can an elevator in an abandoned building still be working? Later I learned from the building's owner that, in order to maintain the certification for the elevator, in hopes of one day putting it back into service, she needed to maintain its power. This experience left me feeling that this old medical building, the former Manitoba Sanatorium, was waiting patiently to be resuscitated.

The building owed its existence to tuberculosis (TB), a highly infectious lung disease caused by bacteria whose symptoms include chronic coughing, fever, night sweats, and weight loss. (The weight loss is so marked that, at one time, gaunt sufferers were said to be consumed by the disease, explaining its name by which it was known in the 19th century: consumption.) Although now treatable with antibiotics, early 20th century doctors had few options beyond prescribing rest and relaxation combined with good nutrition or, in severe cases, surgery and exposure to X-rays.

In 1904, a group of concerned Manitobans formed the Sanatorium Board of Manitoba (today's Manitoba Lung Association) to combat TB by building a treatment centre on 103 scenic acres overlooking Pelican Lake. (It was believed the fresh country air and inspiring view would help to restore TB sufferers to good health.) They recruited Dr. David Stewart who became interested in TB treatment after attending an American medical conference in 1908.

OPPOSITE Former main building at the Manitoba Sanatorium, October 2011. GOLDSBOROUGH

Postcard view of the Manitoba Sanatorium by Killarney photographer Percy Edwards, no date. GOLDSBOROUGH

He returned to Manitoba just in time for the opening of the newly constructed Manitoba Sanatorium in May 1909, and over the next 28 years, as its Medical Superintendent, his name would become synonymous with the fight against TB. In 1940, three years after his death, Manitoba's Lieutenant Governor unveiled a monument in his memory on the grounds of the Sanatorium and a TB treatment centre in Winnipeg, now merged into the Health Sciences Centre, was named for him.

The Sanatorium's main building and two smaller pavilions were designed by architect Walter Shillinglaw and constructed by contractor William Bell, both from Brandon. The first patient was admitted on 24 May 1910 and an opening ceremony occurred a month later. The "Ninette San," as it was widely and affectionately known, grew into the largest TB treatment facility in the province, comprising over a dozen buildings. In 1911, noted

Main dining room of the Manitoba Sanatorium, circa 1929. "THE STORY OF THE YEAR 1929-1930," MANITOBA SANATORIUM NINETTE, ELIZABETH DAFOE LIBRARY, UNIVERSITY OF MANITOBA

Winnipeg novelist and cleric Charles Gordon (Ralph Connor) donated funds for a patients' residence, dubbed the Gordon Cottage. The following year, the Imperial Order Daughters of the Empire (IODE) contributed the two-storey King Edward Cottage. Two large infirmary buildings went up between 1914 and 1920, along with three more pavilions, a power house and laundry, carpenter and paint shop, and residences for nurses, doctors, and support staff. A railway line delivered coal for the boilers that provided steam heat throughout the complex. Treatment plants processed sewage and purified drinking water.

In the early years of operation, annual admissions to the Sanatorium climbed rapidly, from 97 people in the first year to a peak of 475 in 1917. A total of 15,248 patients were admitted over the 63-year period of operation. A much larger number of people passed through its doors, as many were examined and found not to have TB. In 1924, for example, 993 people were checked but only 308 were admitted as patients. The rest were diagnosed with bronchitis, asthma, emphysema, and other afflictions. Most of the TB patients were adults—infected children were treated at hospitals around the province—and predominantly Anglophone; in 1923, 81 percent of patients had Canadian, English, Scottish, or Irish roots and the vast majority (97%) were Christian. The three most common occupations of admitted patients were housewives (20%), farmers (16%), and general labourers (11%).

In the early days, X-rays were used extensively in TB diagnosis and treatment, along with exposure to artificial and natural light. Residences at the Sanatorium had large balconies where patients could lounge for hours at a time, soaking up the sun's rays. The average length of stay was described in early medical reports as "considerably over a year" although this figure had decreased to 282 days by 1962. With abundant time on their hands, patients were encouraged to convalesce productively. There was a Sanatorium Orchestra for those with musical aptitude. A school supervised by a part-time teacher offered instruction in grades 1 to 12. Also available were classes in English for non-Anglophones; technical courses by correspondence; remedial work in spelling, grammar, and arithmetic; and lectures in culture, literature, history, and languages. Meanwhile, students from the University of Manitoba's Medical School spent several weeks each year at the Sanatorium to witness the latest techniques for TB treatment.

In the early 1920s, it cost about $2.60 per patient per day to operate the Sanatorium, not including a wide variety of donated items including library books and magazines, floral arrangements, musical instruments and gramophones, fruits and preserves, and kitchen equipment. Operating funds were provided by municipalities from which its patients came, supplemented by a provincial grant and the "Christmas Seals" public fundraising campaign. In 1939, the provincial government assumed all costs, apart from those incurred in the treatment of veterans and Indigenous people who were the responsibility of federal authorities. That same year, the federal government purchased from the Anglican Church the former Dynevor Hospital on the banks of the Red River near Selkirk. It became the Dynevor Indian Hospital,

administered by the Sanatorium Board and devoted to the treatment of TB in Manitoba's Indigenous peoples. Its establishment acknowledged their staggeringly higher rate of TB infection, possibly due to lower levels of natural resistance. Between 1927 and 1947, the average death rate among Indigenous TB victims was thirty times higher than the general population: 1,038 versus 35 per 100,000 people. But with proper care and treatment, the Indigenous TB death rate decreased, as it did for the province as a whole. When the Sanatorium was established, roughly one in a thousand Manitobans died from TB. By the late 1930s, the death rate had decreased to one in two thousand. By 1960, it had decreased further, to one death per 2,500 people.

Many of the San's patients were discharged after successful treatment, although readmission was sometimes required if their symptoms returned, often months or years later. Inevitably, some patients could not be helped. In most cases, the bodies of those who died at

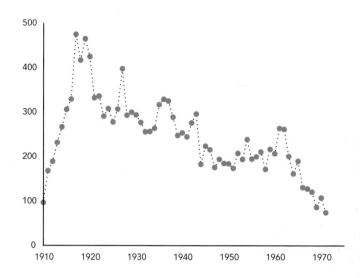

Graph of annual admission totals to the Manitoba Sanatorium. ANNUAL REPORTS OF THE MANITOBA SANATORIUM AT NINETTE, ELIZABETH DAFOE LIBRARY & MANITOBA LEGISLATIVE LIBRARY

The former Dynevor Indian Hospital, a TB treatment facility near Selkirk operated by the Sanatorium Board of Manitoba, 2015. GOLDSBOROUGH

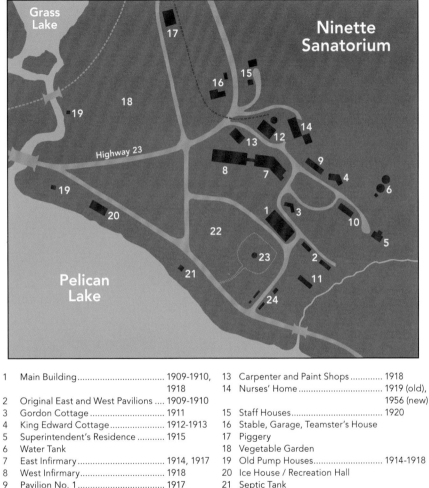

#		Date	#		Date
1	Main Building	1909-1910, 1918	13	Carpenter and Paint Shops	1918
2	Original East and West Pavilions	1909-1910	14	Nurses' Home	1919 (old), 1956 (new)
3	Gordon Cottage	1911	15	Staff Houses	1920
4	King Edward Cottage	1912-1913	16	Stable, Garage, Teamster's House	
5	Superintendent's Residence	1915	17	Piggery	
6	Water Tank		18	Vegetable Garden	
7	East Infirmary	1914, 1917	19	Old Pump Houses	1914-1918
8	West Infirmary	1918	20	Ice House / Recreation Hall	
9	Pavilion No. 1	1917	21	Septic Tank	
10	Pavilion No. 2	1917	22	Nursery / Garden	
11	Pavilion No. 3	1918	23	Formal Lawn / Stewart Memorial	
12	Power House and Laundry	1916-1918	24	Staff Houses	1960s

Sketch map of the Manitoba Sanatorium campus as it appeared in the 1960s.
HOLY GROUND: THE STORY OF THE MANITOBA SANATORIUM AT NINETTE BY DAVID B. STEWART, C1999.

the Sanatorium were returned to their home communities for burial. But those who had no next-of-kin or, more shamefully, Indigenous people, were buried anonymously in the cemetery at nearby Belmont. In 2010, a monument was erected in the Belmont cemetery to commemorate the 318 people who could be identified as having died at the Sanatorium through the years.

By the 1950s, TB treatment facilities around the province included, in addition to the 270-bed facility near Ninette, the 50-bed Central Tuberculosis Clinic, 150-bed King Edward Memorial Hospital, and 280-bed St. Boniface Sanatorium in Winnipeg. For the Indigenous population, there was the 50-bed Dynevor Indian Hospital, 160-bed Clearwater Lake Indian Hospital at The Pas, and 250-bed Brandon Sanatorium. Prevention of TB was fostered by X-ray clinics that travelled to communities around the province and information lectures given to children in public schools. With advances in medical knowledge, and

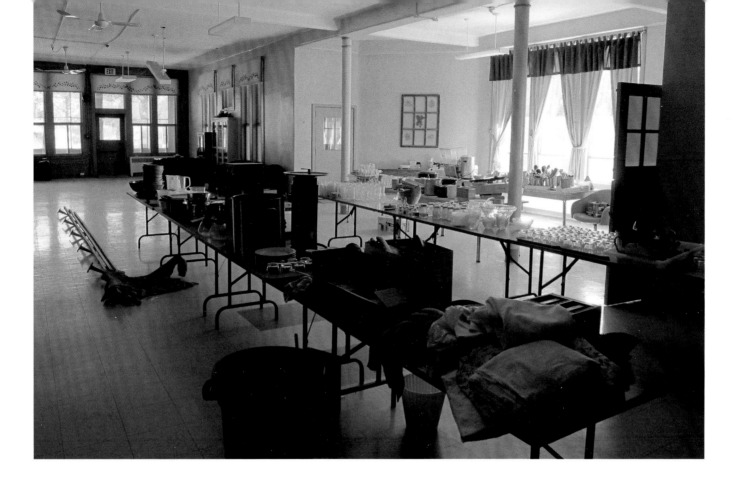

Equipment left in the main dining hall in the former Ninette Sanatorium was still sitting on tables during a September 2012 site visit. GOLDSBOROUGH

particularly the greater use of antibiotic chemotherapy, the annual number of admissions at Ninette dropped, from a peak over 400 in the late 1910s, to half that number through the 1950s. By 1971, with only 75 admissions, it was clear the old San was no longer needed. Most patients could continue their chemotherapy at home. That year, 297 new cases of TB were diagnosed, a rate of one in 3,300 Manitobans. Today, there is still no cure for TB. Antibiotic-resistant bacterial strains arise periodically and outbreaks recur, particularly in northern Indigenous communities.

The Ninette Sanatorium closed in 1972, by which time it was functioning mainly as a retirement home for its few elderly patients. Three ideas for alternative uses of the buildings were proposed: a retreat for artists, a personal care home for seniors, or a drug and alcohol addictions facility. From 1973 to 2000, it operated as the 70-bed Pelican Lake Training Centre, providing living accommodations and training to intellectually-disabled people,

Balconies, seen here in September 2012, were where tuberculosis patients at the Sanatorium were exposed to fresh air and sunshine in hopes of a cure. GOLDSBOROUGH

1982, along with the former Medical Superintendent's residence. The Gordon Cottage, renovated into a chapel in 1960, was cut into two pieces and moved to Dunrea, where it was reassembled into a community centre. The grounds facing Pelican Lake were developed as a seasonal trailer park and the Sanatorium's formal gardens were reclaimed by trees that concealed the four remaining buildings. In early 2000, shortly after the Lung Association withdrew its support, the Centre closed. Purchased two years later by a local couple, whose plans to board foreign workers from a Brandon meat-processing plant fell through, the buildings were then sold for $1 to a non-denominational religious group from Portage la Prairie and used as a conference centre and camp called "The Ridge." Some $700,000 was spent on renovations. The money ran out in mid-2006 and, after the group was unable to find someone to take over, and with looming bills to keep the buildings heated in winter, it was abandoned in September 2007. The place has been vacant and unheated

former residents of the over-crowded Manitoba Development Centre at Portage la Prairie. Only some of the buildings were used during this period and many of the others fell into disrepair. The East and West Infirmaries were demolished in

ever since. Purchased several years ago by a Saskatchewan resident, the seven-acre campus was put back on the market in late 2015.

In 2013, I had an opportunity to tour the main building of the old Sanatorium. It felt absolutely post-apocalyptic: perfectly usable items were strewn about as though its occupants left in a hurry. On a shelf in the main office, I found boxes of file cards containing Sanatorium employee records from the 1950s and '60s. A small museum contained scary-looking devices from a more primitive age of medicine. The uppermost level had been sealed off, after ankle-deep insulation had been spread all over its floors to improve the energy efficiency of the remaining levels. Washrooms and bedrooms had been renovated and they seemed ready for people to arrive at any moment. But much was unchanged. The dining room looked as it did in photographs from the 1920s, as did balconies where long rows of TB sufferers on recliners would take the "sunshine cure." For now, the building remains on life support. There is still hope that, like tuberculosis, some new miracle cure (or use) can be found as the old building suffers a slow, debilitating decline before an eventual death.

SOURCES

Annual Reports of the Manitoba Sanatorium at Ninette, 1923-1930. Elizabeth Dafoe Library, University of Manitoba.

Annual Reports of the Sanatorium Board of Manitoba, 1930-1971. Manitoba Legislative Library.

The Social Histories of Smallpox and Tuberculosis in Canada (Culture, Evolution and Disease) by Ethel L.M. Thorpe, MA Thesis in Anthropology, University of Manitoba, 1989.

Holy Ground: The Story of the Manitoba Sanatorium at Ninette by David B. Stewart, Killarney: J.A.V. David Museum, c1999.

"Ninette complex a reminder of TB scourge" by Bill Redekop, *Winnipeg Free Press*, 12 June 2005, page A1.

Memoir of a Living Disease: The Story of Earl Hershfield and Tuberculosis in Manitoba and Beyond by Maurice Mierau, Winnipeg: Great Plains Publications, 2005.

"Youth For Christ – Portage Inc. closes The Ridge camp and conference centre," *Baldur Gazette*, 27 November 2007, page 8.

ACKNOWLEDGEMENTS

I applaud Ronnie Aschenbrenner, without whom the old Manitoba Sanatorium might have fallen to ruin by now. She sees an opportunity to one day turn this storied place back into something productive. I greatly appreciated her willingness to drive several hours from her home to give me a tour. And, belatedly, I thank the late Dr. David Stewart who I met while living in Brandon. I knew nothing of his history at the time, or that of his like-named father, but I benefitted greatly from our friendly chats during my early career, and later from his insider's history of the beloved "Ninette San."

Paulson Bombing & Gunnery School

You would be hard-pressed to see them as you drove past this site on the south side of Highway 20, seven miles east of Dauphin, but they are clearly visible from the air: clumps of trees that are curiously straight-edged and form a large, open triangle. This triangular forest, sitting in the midst of 640 acres of prime farmland, now invades the runways of a Royal Canadian Air Force (RCAF) base what was once the largest of its kind in Canada for training pilots, observers, and gunners. It is the former Paulson Bombing & Gunnery School.

From the earliest days of the Second World War, it was clear that control of the skies would be essential for military victory on the ground. The federal government of William Lyon Mackenzie King saw an opportunity to support the war effort while keeping a large number of Canadians at home, by hosting training facilities of the British Commonwealth Air Training Plan (CATP). At its height in 1943, the Plan operated 107 schools and 184 ancillary facilities at 231 sites in nine provinces. Manitoba's contribution included two Air Observers Schools (Winnipeg and Southport), the Central Navigation School at Rivers, a Wireless School (Winnipeg), Elementary Flying Training Schools (Neepawa, Portage, and Virden), and Service Flying Training Schools (Brandon, Carberry, Dauphin, Gimli, Souris). Specialized training in bombing and gunnery was provided near Macdonald, northwest of Portage la Prairie, and at Paulson.

The Paulson School was known officially as Bombing and Gunnery School No. 7 but its informal name came from the nearby Paulson siding on the Canadian National Railway (CNR). Located about eight miles east of Service Flying Training School No. 10 south of Dauphin (now the Dauphin municipal airport), the site was chosen for its proximity to Lake Dauphin, just a mile away to the

The former Officer's Mess is the sole remaining building at the former Paulson Gunnery School, June 2015. GOLDSBOROUGH

northeast. The idea was that novice aircrews could take off from Paulson and practice attacks on floating rafts in the lake while instructors on the shore would keep close watch on them.

Construction of the Paulson facility began in late 1940 and most buildings were completed by January 1941. Six large aircraft hangars and a drill hall were constructed by the Claydon Construction Company of Winnipeg. Other buildings at the site—most with green walls and brick-red roofs—included barracks and mess halls for officers and enlisted men and women (each group with separate space), a 10-bed hospital, dental clinic, garages and workshops, recreation and dance hall, fire station, and stores surrounding a large parade ground. Two large concrete tanks held water for drinking, cleaning, and fire-fighting. A small sewage treatment plant on the north edge of the base sat beside a 25-yard range where machine

OPPOSITE Vegetation grows through the cracks of the floors for the vast aircraft hangars at the Paulson Gunnery School, June 2015. GOLDSBOROUGH

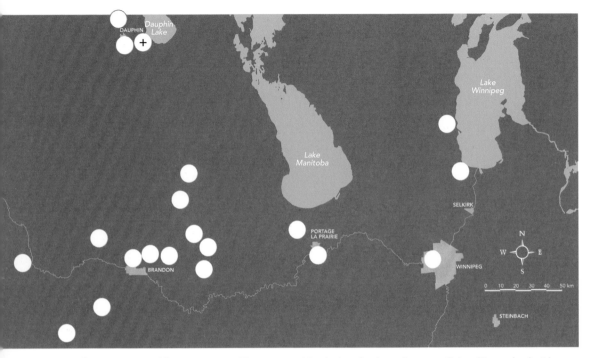

Map of Commonwealth Air Training Plan sites in Manitoba. Paulson Gunnery School is marked with +.
DRAWN BY GORDON GOLDSBOROUGH

guns aimed at a concrete wall, known as a "stop butt." A railway spur line transported cargo and personnel to and from the site. The total cost of construction was about $1.25 million. The RCAF took command from civilian contractors in early June 1941 and the base reached full operational status later that month. Initially powered by diesel generators, electrical power lines from the Manitoba Power Commission arrived in early November. The base operated 24 hours a day with an operating staff of 150 to 200 people. The first classes began in late June 1941.

The CATP brought thousands of men and women from all over the British Commonwealth—Canada as well as Great Britain, Australia, New Zealand, and South Africa, plus a large number of Americans—to Manitoba. (Canadian women were not fully integrated into military units and instead served in a Women's Division of the RCAF.) A man who enlisted in the RCAF spent three weeks learning basic drill procedures at one of three Manning Depots, including one at Brandon. Then, he spent four weeks at an Initial Training School where he learned military discipline, air force law, and the theory of flight and mechanics. Based on his aptitude, he was routed into one of three branches of service, as a pilot, observer, or gunner and wireless (radio) operator. A prospective pilot went to one of the 27 Elementary Flying Training Schools across the country, many of them operated by civilian companies affiliated with flying clubs, where he spent seven weeks learning the basics of flying before heading to one of ten Service Flying Training Schools to receive a further twelve weeks of advanced flight instruction. Meanwhile, an observer went to one of ten Air Observer Schools where he spent twelve weeks learning the nuances of air navigation, photography, and reconnaissance, while wireless operators (who doubled as onboard gunners) received 18 weeks of training in the operation and care of communications equipment. Observers also spent four weeks of advanced training at Air Navigation School. The three branches reunited at one of ten Bombing and Gunnery Schools across the country: pilots for two weeks, air observers for six weeks, and air gunners for four weeks. After six months of training, they were ready for deployment.

The Paulson School operated into early 1945. As it became clear the war was drawing to a conclusion, numbers of staff at the base diminished. The final aircrews received their wings on 2 February 1945 and the school closed a couple of weeks later. By April 1945, civilian employees were let go and the remaining military personnel were transferred elsewhere. The skies that had droned with the roar of aircraft for nearly four years fell silent.

Eventually, all but one of the buildings at the Paulson Bombing and Gunnery School were sold and moved away, or were demolished. It is rumoured that a large quantity of small equipment, for there was no further need, was simply buried in a hastily dug pit. The land, with its network of paved roads and runways still intact, was sold to a local farmer. When I visited the site in June 2015, the only remaining building was an Officers' Mess, which had been moved from its original site to the farmer's yard for use as storage space. Roads around the grounds were

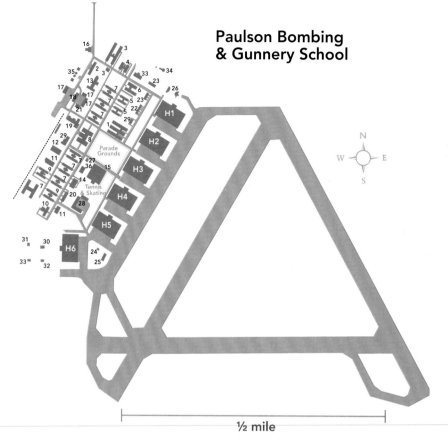

Paulson Bombing & Gunnery School

½ mile

H1	Hangar #1	8	Other Ranks' Mess	22	Turret
H2	Hangar #2	9	Women's Division Quarters	23	Spotlight Trainer
H3	Hangar #3	10	Civilian Mess	24	Gas Chamber
H4	Hangar #4	11	Canteen	25	Watch Office
H5	Hangar #5	12	Stores	26	Range & Stop Butt
H6	Hangar #6	13	Hospital	27	Dental Clinic
1	Ground Instructors School	14	Recreation Hall	28	W & B Maintenance
2	Headquarters	15	Drill Hall	29	Fire Station
3	Officers' Quarters	16	Guard House & Post Office	30	Bomb Stores
4	Officers' Mess	17	Garage	31	Detonator Stores
5	Non-Commissioned	18	Repair Shop	32	Fusing Hut
	Officers' Quarters	19	Supply Depot	33	Pyrotechnic Stores
6	Non-Commissioned	20	Workshop	34	Sewage Disposal
	Officers' Mess	21	Air Ministry Laboratory	35	Water Tanks & Pump House
7	Other Ranks' Quarters		Teacher	36	Chapel

Map of the Paulson Bombing and Gunnery School, July 1940.
REDRAWN FROM ORIGINAL IN POSSESSION OF RICHARD KUTCHER

Concrete everywhere: The gunnery range "Stop Butt" in the background and support columns from the aircraft hangars in the foreground are among the few remnants of the once vast Paulson Gunnery School, 2015.
GOLDSBOROUGH

cracked and mostly overgrown with vegetation, so much so that when the farmer gave me a tour, it seemed to me that he was driving his truck across bumpy prairie. (The occasional manhole cover, sewer drain, or fire hydrant did, however, give me pause.) The concrete floors of the six huge hangars and several of the smaller buildings were still readily visible, as was the sewage treatment plant and the gunnery range's stop butt. Plants had sprouted through cracks in the runways, growing into the triangular forest, and the land around the runways was mostly sown to agricultural crops. A site once devoted to swords has reverted to plowshares.

Today, some 70 years after the end of the Second World War, visible signs of the CATP training facilities are being slowly erased from Manitoba's landscape. Runways at Carberry, Chater, Eden, Hartney, Macdonald, Oberon, and Petrel have been removed or, like Paulson, are overgrown. Those at Dauphin, Gimli, Neepawa, Netley, Rivers, Souris, Southport, Virden, and Winnipeg have been converted to civilian uses. Once numbering in the hundreds, and designed for short-term use during what was hoped would be a short war, few CATP buildings survive. Well-preserved specimens form the basis of an excellent museum at Brandon. A remarkably intact hangar, now used to store farm equipment, stands at one of

Former RCAF hangar north of Chater, 2015, was one of two relief facilities for the Service Flying Training School No. 12 at Brandon. In addition to the hangar, the three runways are intact, and fire hydrants poking through crops of canola bear testament to the firefighting infrastructure that once existed here. GOLDSBOROUGH

The cracked concrete floors of the six large aircraft hangars are still visible at the former Paulson Gunnery School, along with other building foundations, and a network of roads. GOLDSBOROUGH

Brandon's relief fields, northeast of Chater, and a cluster of decaying barracks—used to film "For The Moment," a 1993 Hollywood movie (starring a young Russell Crowe) about airmen training in rural Manitoba—remain at the decommissioned CFB Rivers. But a maintenance building from the former Carberry base that I saw during a visit in mid-2015 was slated for demolition. So long as the inconspicuous remains of the Paulson Bombing and Gunnery School persist, the memory of Manitoba's role in Second World War aviation will not be lost.

SOURCES

"Biggest yet, Air School at Paulson opens," *Winnipeg Free Press*, 23 June 1941, page 3.

"Paulson Air School opens," *Winnipeg Tribune*, 24 June 1941, page 5.

"Power ready for Paulson Air School," *Winnipeg Free Press*, 31 October 1941, page 20.

"City briefs," *Winnipeg Free Press*, 17 March 1945, page 6.

Wings Over Dauphin: A History of a Forgotten Era by Elsie Lesyk, self-published, 1995.

Military abbreviations used in Service Files, Library and Archives Canada, http://www.bac-lac.gc.ca/eng/discover/military-heritage/pages/military-abbreviations.aspx [accessed 3 March 2016]

ACKNOWLEDGEMENTS

Were it not for Yvonne Lozinski, I would have never seen the Paulson Bombing and Gunnery School, despite having passed it on the highway many times. Her enthusiasm for this project is much appreciated, as is her hospitality during site-finding visits to the Dauphin area. Richard Kutcher, who owns the land formerly occupied by the School, was generous with his time and knowledge during a tour in 2015. He also provided a rare map of the base when it was fully operational. As always, I am grateful to Nathan Kramer for his careful and detailed research and I thank Barry Flett for his help in decoding arcane military acronyms.

Manitoba College of Pharmacy

If you have ever driven on Notre Dame Avenue in Winnipeg, between Carlton and Edmonton Streets, you have passed this building. But you might not have known it because, during the summer when the trees are fully in leaf, you can see virtually nothing beyond the sidewalk. The entire front yard is choked with copious foliage of long-unpruned trees. Only in winter does a one-storey brick building concealed by the trees become visible. This innocuous little building was the first place in the province dedicated to the training of pharmacists.

In 1878, eight years after Manitoba became a province, the Legislature passed The Manitoba Pharmacy Act. It created the Manitoba Pharmaceutical Association to regulate the profession of pharmacy in Manitoba, just as the Manitoba Medical Act of 1871 regulated the medical profession. The Act required prospective pharmacists to have a certain standard of education to work in Manitoba. But it made no provision to provide such education. Consequently, our first pharmacists were obliged to take their education outside Manitoba. Through the late 1880s and early 1890s, the Pharmaceutical Association fostered pharmacy-related courses, some in affiliation with the Manitoba Medical College that had been established in 1882. By 1894, the Association assumed full responsibility for training, and it hired lecturers who worked in space rented from the Medical College.

In 1899, the Association purchased a modest site on the south side of Notre Dame Avenue and had local architect Frank Peters design a 1,600-square-foot building with a full basement. Its main floor had a lecture room seating 35 students, a laboratory with space for 16 students at a time, and a small, combined storeroom and office used by the Association as well as the College. In the poorly-lighted, low-ceilinged basement was a waiting room, workshop, storeroom, furnace room, and lavatory. The facility opened with Henry Bletcher as principal and lecturer. Trained as a pharmacist in Ontario, Bletcher had

OPPOSITE The former Manitoba College of Pharmacy building, February 2016. GOLDSBOROUGH

The University of Manitoba's main science building in downtown Winnipeg, where the Faculty of Pharmacy moved when it abandoned the College building on Notre Dame Avenue. Constructed in 1900, the Broadway building was demolished in 1962 and its site is now occupied by Memorial Park. ROB MCINNES

come to Manitoba in 1891 and managed a drug company at Carman.

Pharmacy education at the college consisted of two sessions of four months each, from September to Christmas, and from January to April. Subjects included in these classes included botany, use of microscopes, chemistry, toxicology, posology (the medicine of dosage), materia medica (the study of remedial substances used in medicine), pharmacognosy (drugs obtained from plants and other natural sources), and pharmaceutical practice. After the formal training period ended, there was a mandatory period of apprenticeship under the supervision of a certified pharmacist. There were 13 men and one woman in the first graduating class of 1900. One of the men was Nellie McClung's brother-in-law, Herbert McClung. The sole woman—a rarity considering that women at this time had few opportunities for advanced education and professional careers—was Miss Margaret Woodhull. After graduation, she returned to her hometown of Hartney, in western Manitoba, and apprenticed with her brother Fred in his drugstore. Later, Woodhull managed drugstores in Saskatchewan. After Fred's death in 1920, she purchased the Hartney store and operated it until the mid-1930s when she sold out to her younger brother and retired.

In 1914, the College formally joined the University of Manitoba as its Department of Pharmacy, making Henry Bletcher the first University Professor of Pharmacy in the British Empire, and the College the first such

The former pharmacy building during its life as a brush and broom store, May 2011. GOLDSBOROUGH

facility to affiliate with a Canadian university. The building was leased to the University on a five-year term but the Association continued to pay for heat, light, and janitorial service. When that term expired in 1919, the Association gifted the building to the University on the assumption the University would continue using it to train pharmacists. In 1921, Bletcher was given a lecture room, office and library space in the University's building on Broadway, allowing all classes to be offered there. The original College building was retained for laboratory work. In his annual reports to university administrators, Henry Bletcher observed that students had to walk nearly a mile to get from classrooms on Broadway to the laboratories on Notre Dame. Finally, by January 1934, adequate space was provided at the Broadway site and the little building on Notre Dame was closed, having been a centre for pharmaceutical education in Manitoba for nearly 35 years.

After some mild renovations, from late 1934 the former

college building accommodated the Winnipeg branch of the Royal Canadian Legion. In January 1940, after the Legion had moved out, the University put the building up for sale, advising that it "might suit [a] small manufacturing plant." It sat empty for a couple of years then was bought in 1942 by Nicholas and Mary Syzek as a factory for their Winnipeg Brush Company (renamed the Winnipeg Modern Brush Company around 1948). The firm made "all types of brushes, machine & hand-made, for domestic and industrial purposes." By 1946, the Syzeks were living in a suite at the back of the building, employing a housekeeper to look after their two sons. Nicholas Syzek died in 1957 and Mary Sysek died in 2001 but the business, described in Mary's obituary as "Manitoba's oldest brush manufacturing company" went on. Their son Andrew continued to conduct business from the building—or, more correctly, the front yard where brooms, brushes, and maps festooned the fence along the public sidewalk—as recently as 2011. My request to see inside the building was rebuffed.

After the Second World War, the University of Manitoba consolidated its science teaching at its growing campus in south Winnipeg. In 1949, the former Department of Pharmacy, renamed the School of Pharmacy (the Faculty of Pharmacy as of 1970), moved into renovated former army huts at the Fort Garry campus then, in 1962, into a brand-new, two-storey building. There it remained until 2008 when pharmacists returned to downtown Winnipeg, to join the university's medical campus, just a few blocks away from the forlorn college building on Notre Dame. That's where I intersect with the story: the vacated two-storey building in Fort Garry became home to the Department of Biological Sciences where I have my office.

As I write this in early 2016, the City of Winnipeg considers the old college building on Notre Dame "vacant and boarded" and I learned it was sold to new owners earlier this year. One of the first things they did was to cut down the trees facing the street. So now more people can admire the building as they pass by.

SOURCES

"College of Pharmacy," *Manitoba Free Press*, 5 February 1900, page 6.

"Constant appearance of new buildings is proof of growth of university," *Winnipeg Tribune*, 31 October 1922, page 61.

"Building notes," *Winnipeg Tribune*, 15 September 1934, page 22.

"Meets before move," *Winnipeg Tribune*, 16 October 1934, page 3.

"For sale or rent [422 Notre Dame Avenue]," *Winnipeg Tribune*, 19 December 1939, page 21.

"Wanted, good housekeeper," *Winnipeg Tribune*, 13 March 1946, page 19.

"Wpg. Modern Brush Co.," *Winnipeg Tribune*, 28 January 1948, page 23.

The History of Pharmacy in Manitoba: 1878-1953, compiled by the Historical Committee of the Manitoba Pharmaceutical Association, Winnipeg, 1954.

"Brush firm founder dies at Selkirk," *Winnipeg Free Press*, 23 April 1957, page 32.

Obituary [Margaret Lucinda Woodhull], *Winnipeg Free Press*, 16 February 1963, page 32.

A Century of Living: Hartney, 1882-1982, Hartney and District Historical Committee, 1982, page 680.

History of the Faculty of Pharmacy: 1899-1999 by J.W. Steele, Faculty of Pharmacy, 1999.

Obituary [Mary Victoria Syzek], *Winnipeg Free Press*, 21 April 2001.

"Science comes to Manitoba," H.W. Duckworth and L.G. Goldsborough, *Manitoba History*, Number 47, Spring/Summer 2004.

"422 Notre Dame - Winnipeg Modern Brush Company" by Christian Cassidy, Winnipeg Downtown Places, http://winnipegdowntownplaces.blogspot.ca/2013/10/422-notre-dame-winnipeg-modern-brush.html (accessed 21 February 2016)

ACKNOWLEDGEMENTS

I thank Murray Peterson for information on the present status of the College of Pharmacy building, Lewis Stubbs for providing copies of University of Manitoba Annual Reports, and Rob McInnes for providing a scan of the former university science building on Broadway from his extensive collection of historical postcards.

Port Nelson

Aerial view of the artificial island at Port Nelson with the dredge in the foreground and the railway bridge in the background, June 2006. ANGELE WATRIN-PRODAEHL, STANTEC

Can you give an example of a government wasting vast sums of public money on some ill-conceived idea? Of course you can. But can you name one in which the physical evidence is still readily apparent one hundred years later? Consider the case of Port Nelson on the shore of Hudson Bay.

The Golden Boy atop Manitoba's Legislative Building is purposely facing north, illustrating the importance that its creators assumed the northern areas of the province would hold in our future. And to reach the limitless reserves of natural resources assumed to lie just beyond civilized parts of the province, boosters pushed for the construction of a railway line into the north, beyond The Pas. The interest in having a transportation corridor to Hudson Bay goes back to the 1870s but it was not until 1908 that the federal government began to consider seriously building one. It compared the cost of constructing a line to the mouth of each of the two major rivers that discharge into Hudson Bay from Manitoba, the Churchill and the Nelson. Although mariners preferred the Churchill harbour because it had deeper water, the government concluded that the Nelson option would be cheaper: $21 million versus $25 million to Churchill. Nelson was chosen in the fall of 1912.

Satellite photos of northern Manitoba reveal the story of what happened. You can see the railway heading northeast out of The Pas, heading toward the mouth of the Nelson River. Then, at a spot downstream of Gillam, it takes a hard-left turn and heads north to Churchill. Yet, if you look closely, a perceptible line continues northeast past the point where the railway turns northward. Following it, you end up at Hudson Bay, at what would have been the harbour at the mouth of the Nelson River, called Port Nelson.

Construction of the Hudson Bay Railway began on two fronts. One crew began building the rail line heading

Map of possible shipping routes on Hudson Bay, dubbed "Canada's Neglected Inland Sea," for cargo ships leaving Port Nelson to European and American ports, prepared by the On-To-The-Bay Association, no date.
R.W. PATERSON FONDS, ARCHIVES OF MANITOBA

out from The Pas while a second one began constructing at Hudson Bay. All of the construction materials for the port had to be shipped from eastern Canada. Delivery of equipment began in 1913. This included a 180-foot-long, two-thousand-ton suction dredge dubbed the *Port Nelson*, built at a Toronto shipyard and delivered to the mouth of the Nelson River at a cost of some one million dollars. The *Port Nelson* was believed to be the most powerful dredge in the world at that time. By early 1914, over 700 construction workers were on-site. Two and a half miles of narrow-gauge rail track and a dry dock were built. Numerous bunkhouses and dining halls accommodated

View of the 17 railway trestles from the mainland to the artificial island, 1924.
H.F. HAYWARD FONDS, ARCHIVES OF MANITOBA

and fed the enormous construction crew. There was also a machine shop, hospital, general store, water tower, and two-storey administration building. A telephone system was for local communications while a radio tower provided a link to the outside world. During off-work time, there was a billiard table and tennis courts for the workers. Construction continued through the winter of 1914-1915, with about 200 workmen, despite the onset of the First World War.

Engineers found deep water about a half-mile off shore so they used the *Port Nelson* to dredge material for an artificial island 7.5 acres in area, and they designed a half-mile-long, 17-span steel truss bridge (pre-fabricated by Dominion Bridge Company of Montreal) out to it. The plan was to build a terminal grain elevator on the island, to which railway cars would deliver grain. But the island consisted of not much more than a U-shaped wooden seawall by the time that work ceased in 1917, with about one-quarter of the project completed. The cost of building the port to that point was $6.3 million, while the railway had consumed an additional $13.8 million. Large numbers by any standard, they are roughly equivalent to $500 million in today's currency.

The stoppage of work at Port Nelson was the result of shortages that had become dire by late 1917, mostly the result of the Great War in Europe. It was simply no longer possible to divert precious resources like coal and steel that were needed badly for the war effort. Money was increasingly short and, perhaps most significantly, it was becoming difficult to find able-bodied construction workers. So Port Nelson was mothballed, even though the railway roadbed was finished all the way to Hudson Bay and merely awaited the laying of rails past the "end of steel" at Pikwitonei (Mile 214). A lone RCMP officer was stationed at Port Nelson (with his family) to provide security. A government supervisor and seven workmen were left behind to keep the machinery in running condition in anticipation of resuming work after the war ended. A Senate Commission concluded in 1920 that the whole matter of which site, Port Nelson or Churchill, was most desirable for a port should be re-evaluated. Parliament chose to ignore the Commission's report.

Because Port Nelson was so far away from the halls of power, none of the provincial and federal politicians really knew much about it, and could only form opinions from reports by civil servants who had visited the site. In what may be the first instance of that time-honoured tradition, the political junket, successive cohorts of politicians (usually accompanied by miscellaneous businessmen and boosters of northern development) embarked on "fact-finding missions" to Port Nelson. In August 1924, Premier John Bracken and federal Member of Parliament Robert A. Hoey climbed aboard a train in Winnipeg. They were accompanied on a three-week trip to Hudson Bay by businessman and First World War general Robert

Premier John Bracken (third from left) and MP Robert Hoey (second from right) at the "end of steel" of the Hudson Bay Railway, Mile 333, 30 August 1924. R.W. PATERSON FONDS, ARCHIVES OF MANITOBA

View of the "million-dollar" dredge at anchor alongside the artificial island, 1924. R.W. PATERSON FONDS, ARCHIVES OF MANITOBA

W. Paterson, president of the newly founded On-To-The-Bay Association that advocated for completion of the railway. After passing through The Pas, they disembarked at the "end of steel" at Mile 239, then continued down the Nelson River by canoe, arriving at Port Nelson and spending a few days touring the site. On return to Winnipeg, Bracken lamented that "it is very much to the discredit of Canadian public men that the Hudson Bay railway project should have been started, and so much money spent upon it, and then abandoned on the plea, that it is not a practicable route."

This photo shows one of the collapsed buildings at Port Nelson with the insulated water tower in the background, in 2006. NORTH-SOUTH CONSULTANTS

On 1 November 1924, just two months after Bracken's visit to Port Nelson, the site was hit by a severe windstorm that pushed up a wall of water 24 feet high. The *Port Nelson* dredge, which had been dry docked on land, floated free and, when the water receded, it was deposited astride the wooden seawall on the artificial island. There, it was left precariously balanced, hanging above the normal 20-foot tide mark. The railway bridge was largely undamaged except where the dredge had struck it while afloat.

The vast majority of the men on these junkets returned to Winnipeg full of enthusiasm and bold talk about the necessity and merit of completing the facility at Port Nelson. But the public at large, lacking first-hand experience, had little basis to share their enthusiasm. That could have changed when an expedition in late August 1925 included not only members of the media—who dutifully reported on what they were seeing in pages of the *Manitoba Free Press*—but also 17-year-old filmmaker Frank Holmes. His footage of the trip was made into the one-hour silent movie *The Seaport of the Prairies*. It showed Manitoba and Saskatchewan businessmen and politicians (including four sitting MLAs and Charles Gray, ex-mayor of Winnipeg and an electrical engineer) travelling to Port Nelson via train, then handcar, then canoe, and finally motorboat. Made for the North Country Tourist Association, a short-lived Winnipeg organization that advocated tourism to northern Manitoba, the film was not a commercial success and Holmes later had to go to court to extract payment for his work. However, Charles

This photo shows the lichen-encrusted railway trestle to the artificial island at Port Nelson, in 2006. The outhouse in the background, built by persons unknown, discharges its contents right into Hudson Bay. NORTH-SOUTH CONSULTANTS

Gray's comment upon his return home, on the potential of the Nelson River for hydroelectric power production, would prove prophetic: "There are millions of horsepower awaiting development at the Kettle, Long Spruce and Limestone rapids."

It took until 1926 before the federal government's attention returned to Port Nelson. In 1927, an eminent British engineer enlisted by the government to re-examine the whole affair concluded that Churchill was the only logical choice and the original decision to build at Port Nelson had been a bad one. The cost of building an entirely new port at Churchill was calculated to be about the same as finishing the one at Port Nelson. But a port at Churchill had the distinct advantage that it could be used over a wide range of tidal conditions whereas Port Nelson would only be reached by ships for about an hour at high tide. At Churchill, the deep water of Hudson Bay was only one and a half miles away, versus twenty miles through a dredged channel at Port Nelson. A decision was made. The railway was re-routed to Churchill and there a 2.5-million-bushel grain elevator—allegedly the second-largest in the world to that point—was built, establishing Canada's only deep-water port in the Arctic. The first token wheat shipment from Churchill occurred in September 1929 and two ships were loaded in September 1931, soon after

The "million dollar dredge" lies with its back broken over a seawall on the artificial island at Port Nelson, in 2006. NORTH-SOUTH CONSULTANTS

A wheelbarrow and other tools on the artificial island were abandoned by construction workers when they moved to the new port of Churchill. NORTH-SOUTH CONSULTANTS

the elevator complex was finished. During the massive construction project at Churchill, some equipment from Port Nelson, such as the tugboat *George W. Yates* that had lain on the beach for ten years, was put back into service. Eight hundred tons of timber was moved along the Hudson Bay coast to Churchill. But the 17-span bridge, artificial island, dredge *Port Nelson*, railway locomotive and cars, and various buildings were simply abandoned.

Today, the million-dollar dredge still sits at the mouth of the Nelson River, perched across the wooden seawall on which it was deposited in 1924. Over time, its back has broken and it now sags over the seawall as though melted in a giant furnace. An eagle has made a nest in its front boom. Inside, larger pieces of its giant steam engine remain in place. Scattered around the island are wheelbarrows, timbers, pipes, and other materials left when the construction halted in 1917. The trestles of the railway bridge are generally intact but years of impact from shifting ice during the spring melt, and lashing from periodic storm waves, has bent them to and fro. It would now be difficult to walk down the length of the bridge, much less take a train on it. Curiously, someone has built an outhouse atop one of its spans, probably to take advantage of the water below for easy waste disposal. On the south shore of the river, two lighters—small vessels used to offload supplies brought to Port Nelson by larger, ocean-going ships—remain upright on the gravel about a half-mile apart. Various wooden buildings scattered around the site are in advanced stages of decay. The two-storey wooden administration building and smaller nearby residences have collapsed but, surprisingly, the water tower, with its large wooden tank at the top, is still standing. The larger warehouses are gone. Trees and other vegetation are slowly hiding the narrow-gauge rails that once criss-crossed the site. Side-dump rail cars are still sitting on the tracks but, in the 1990s, their locomotive was moved to Gillam on a specially-designed sleigh pulled by a caterpillar tractor during late winter when the ground was frozen hard. It is now being restored for display at the Manitoba Agricultural Museum at Austin.

Now, only the adventurous can visit the governmental blunder that is Port Nelson. Getting there is not for the faint of heart. The old railway right-of-way is overgrown or washed out in so many places that it would be a tough 70-mile walk from Manitoba Hydro's Limestone generating station. (Parts of it are used by snowmobilers in the winter and ATVers in the summer.) It is a short helicopter ride, or for those on a more modest budget, a boat ride, down a tumultuous reach of the Nelson River. Either way, the lucky few who get to see Port Nelson come away impressed that, almost exactly 100 years after the railway bridge and artificial island were abandoned, they are surprisingly intact despite a complete lack of maintenance. They bear silent witness to the ingenuity and hard work of engineers and workmen who toiled for naught in the name of the grain trade and northern development. With the future of the large terminal at Churchill and its connecting railway in doubt as of late, the promise of a thriving port facility in northern Canada seems as elusive today as it was a century ago.

SOURCES

"Premier Bracken and party on Bay Railway," *Manitoba Free Press*, 15 September 1924, page 1.

"Severe storm does much damage at Port Nelson," *Manitoba Free Press*, 4 December 1924, page 1.

"Port Nelson is hit by storm," *Winnipeg Tribune*, 14 January 1925, page 9.

"Tourist trip north July 31," *Winnipeg Tribune*, 18 June 1925, page 6.

"Port Nelson today," *Manitoba Free Press*, 9 September 1925, page 13.

"Completion of H.B.R. necessary tourists state," *Winnipeg Tribune*, 9 September 1925, page 21.

Seaport of the Prairies (1925), Archives of Manitoba, http://www.youtube.com/watch?v=mkOiovvisBs

"The development of the Hudson Bay project" by D.W. McLachlan, *Engineering Journal* [Engineering Institute of Canada], volume 16(4), pages 155-166, 1933.

"Brig. Gen. Paterson dies; was organizer and first Fort Gary Horse leader," *Winnipeg Tribune*, 26 March 1936, page 3.

"Port Nelson and the Hudson Bay Railway" by David Malaher, *Manitoba History*, Number 8, Autumn 1984. [http://www.mhs.mb.ca/docs/mb_history/08/hudsonbayrailway.shtml]

"Manitoba's moving pictures," *Winnipeg Free Press*, 17 August 2013, page D8.

R.W. Paterson Fonds, C102, Archives of Manitoba.

Port Nelson Fonds, MG11 A29, Archives of Manitoba.

H.F. Hayward Fonds, C14, Archives of Manitoba.

Samuel H. Williamson, "Seven ways to compute the relative value of a U.S. dollar amount, 1774 to present," MeasuringWorth [https://www.measuringworth.com], 2016.

ACKNOWLEDGEMENTS

A large number of photos of modern-day Port Nelson were provided by Glen Cook at Manitoba Hydro; Don MacDonell, Mark Blanchard, Ron Bretecher, and Susan Hertam at North-South Consultants; and Angele Watrin-Prodaehl at Stantec. Jason Friesen shared his experience of tripping over rails concealed in vegetation during his visit to the site, and Ed Zelenesky told me about bringing the old Port Nelson locomotive to Gillam. David Ennis drew my attention to an informative engineering report.

Ramsay Grave

Cemeteries are great places to savour history. On the markers in most any cemetery around Manitoba, one witnesses the trials and tribulations of a community, its waxes and wanes. Cemeteries of long standing around Winnipeg, such as St. James Anglican, St. John's Anglican, Kildonan Presbyterian, Brookside, and Elmwood contain a vast archive of historical data.

Yet, sometimes, one has a more visceral and personal experience in a small, inconspicuous cemetery. This was how I felt as I stood on an isolated, wind-swept point known as Sandy Bar on the shore of Lake Winnipeg, in the Municipality of Bifrost-Riverton, about three miles southeast of Riverton. Beside me was the grave of an Indigenous woman named Betsey Ramsay. Surrounded by a white picket fence, about a mile from the nearest road, the spot is easily overlooked. But it has an important link to the early history of the Icelandic community in Manitoba, and it illustrates a touching story of grief and remembrance.

In 1875, Icelandic immigrants arrived in Manitoba and established a community named "New Iceland" on the west shore of Lake Winnipeg, centred around Gimli.

Inevitably, they faced difficult conditions to which they were inexperienced and unprepared. Among those who helped the Icelanders to adapt to the new land was John Ramsay, a prominent member of a Saulteaux band who resided in the region. Like Chief Peguis, who had helped the Selkirk Settlers to become established at the Red River Settlement (now Winnipeg) in the early 1800s, Ramsay and his family provided the settlers with meat and instructed them in survival skills: the building of warm log cabins, and local fishing and hunting techniques. In 1876, within a year of their arrival, the Icelanders faced a smallpox epidemic. Many died.

Members of the Indigenous community who had helped the Icelanders were also felled by the epidemic. In September 1876, John Ramsay lost his 35-year-old wife

Betsey and four of their five children. Betsey was buried at Sandy Bar where, for at least 25 years, the Ramsays had had a log cabin they used while ice fishing during the winter. In 1880, the grieving John Ramsay travelled to Lower Fort Garry, on the Red River 65 miles to the south, where he traded furs and purchased a white marble marker for Betsey's grave. He hauled the stone back to Sandy Bar on a small sled, set it on the grave and built a fence around it. The engraved marker was the first of its kind. Most burial markers used to that point were made of wood and were, like the fence that Ramsay built around Betsey's grave, unlikely to survive for long. In April 1894, John Ramsay died and was buried alongside Betsey.

Local lore holds that, in the summer of 1910, local carpenter and

farmer Trausti Vigfússon had an unusually vivid dream in which a tall stranger emerged from the bush near his home at Geysir, a few miles southwest of Sandy Bar. (In 2000, the Vigfússon house was moved to the Arborg and District Multicultural Heritage Village.) The stranger shook hands with Vigfússon and introduced himself as John Ramsay. He described the gravestone he had erected for Betsey and asked Vigfússon to replace the fence, which had deteriorated over time. After a delay of some seven years, Vigfússon, a skilled carpenter, carried out the work and the Ramsay grave with its wooden picket fence would stand for the next 81 years.

As I looked at the Ramsay grave during my visit to Sandy Bar in 2011, the gravestone seemed battered and bruised by its 130 years beside Lake Winnipeg. At one time, it had been broken into over five pieces. Yet, it still emanated a poignant love with which it had been placed here. The stone was eventually repaired and the grave was capped with concrete. In 1998, the wooden picket fence was rebuilt again, this time of recycled cedar by local residents Elizabeth and Joan Hibbert, and a plaque for John Ramsay was added by Ruth Christie, one of his great-granddaughters. The grave is evocative of many things, including the interactions that occurred between Indigenous people and early European settlers—without which the Europeans would not have survived. It also reminds us of the disastrous consequences of epidemic diseases in early Manitoba, and the power that dreams hold in some cultures. So, much as I enjoy absorbing history in a walk through a large, old cemetery, I find that a single, lonely grave can be just as powerful.

SOURCES

"The grave of Betsey Ramsay (A tale of Old Manitoba)" by Kristine Benson Kristofferson, *The Icelandic Canadian*, Volume 42, Number 3 (Spring 1984), pages 21-24.

Icelandic River Saga by Nelson S. Gerrard, Arborg: Saga Publications, 1985, pages 151, 459.

"Betsey Ramsay's grave," Manitoba Historic Resources Branch, http://www.gov.mb.ca/chc/hrb/mun/m028.html

ACKNOWLEDGEMENTS

I thank storyteller and historian Ruth Christie for providing details about her great-grandfather, John Ramsay, and Elizabeth Hibbert for sharing how she rebuilt the wooden fence around the Ramsay grave in 1998. Meghan Hansen at the Manitoba Legislative Library kindly provided a reference while I was far away from Manitoba as I wrote this chapter.

View of the Ramsay grave, May 2011. Note the misspelling of Ramsay as Rumsay on the old monument. GOLDSBOROUGH

Rapid City Consolidated School

It was near dusk as I pulled into the village of Cardale, 32 miles northwest of Brandon, in mid-October 2013. A small, two-storey brick building gleamed with a pinkish hue in the light of the setting sun. Beside it sat a large, mechanical beast with an extended metal hook, beckoning at the building. The following morning, the beast would begin to disassemble the structure. But today, I was here to take one last look, to say a final farewell to a place that had served its community faithfully for 98 years.

The front door of the former Rapid City Consolidated School, May 2012. GOLDSBOROUGH

As I stood at its front entrance, staring up at a sign that announced it as Cardale Consolidated School No. 1763, my memory conjured up a similar building not far away, that I had seen five months earlier. The Rapid City Consolidated School also stood empty but, unlike this building, there was still hope that it might survive. Together, the two buildings tell us an important story, about the changes in rural Manitoba that have been occurring for over a century, and which continue today: the story of consolidation and urbanization.

In 1870, when Manitoba joined the Canadian Confederation, 95 percent of the provincial population lived in rural areas. With a brief exception during the Great Depression, when some people moved from cities back to their rural roots, that percentage has been decreasing ever since. By 2001, fewer than thirty percent of Manitobans were rural. Large areas of rural Manitoba are depopulated. There are probably a lot of reasons for the trend. One is farm mechanization.

As horse-drawn farm equipment gave way to steam- and gasoline-powered machinery, the amount of work done by a single farmer increased so the number of workers needed on the farm decreased. A consequence of the declining rural population was that fewer one-room schools were needed in rural areas to educate farm kids, and more were needed in urban areas. Greater numbers of children in urban schools meant greater efficiency of school operation, and better education in a diverse range of subjects. As early as 1905, Manitoba educators touting the virtues of school consolidation—the aggregation of neighbouring rural school districts into one, centrally-located urban district—saw results in the construction of a consolidated school at Virden, the first in the province. In that first decade of the 20th century, there were nine school district consolidations, then 85 of them in the 1910s.

One of those joining the trend was Cardale Consolidated, established in late 1914 through the consolidation of three rural districts in

Exterior view of the former Cardale School, demolished in October 2013, the day after this photo was taken.
GOLDSBOROUGH

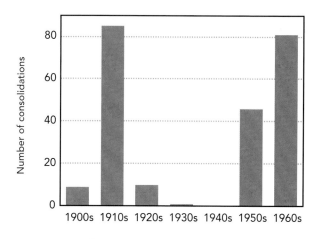

School district consolidations, 1900s to 1960s.

View of Rapid City School taken by School Inspector William Hartley, circa 1925. ARCHIVES OF MANITOBA

Canadian Association for Community Living) for use as a non-profit training facility called Rolling Dale Workshop. Clients drawn from a wide area were bused in daily and engaged in a number of activities, primarily producing craft items such as birdhouses that were sold from the premises and at community events. In the late 1970s, the workshop also became involved in paper recycling, serving as a recycling depot for that part of the province. Rolling Dale moved to the Town of Rivers in the early 1990s and, in 2002, the former school building was taken over by the Rural Municipality of Blanshard. It rented the building to a businessperson who ran a promotional merchandising business out of the two main-floor classrooms, while the upper floor was sealed off. After the business moved out in September 2013, and complaints were received from local residents on the perceived safety of the aging, poorly-maintained building, the municipality decided to demolish it.

I entered the story at this point. I had heard the building was no longer occupied and I hoped to have an opportunity to see its interior. I called the municipality's administrative office and explained what I wanted. The helpful person who took my call advised that I would have to act quickly because the demolition would begin the following morning. It was already afternoon. I immediately hopped in my car, and drove three hours to Cardale. I arrived as a local contractor was salvaging usable hardware and saleable items, such as trophies left when the school closed. Someone else had begun removing bricks from the

the vicinity of the village. The following year, a two-classroom, two-storey brick veneer building was constructed in Cardale to accommodate the burgeoning number of schoolchildren. Two additional classrooms were added in 1919, and the school operated until June 1969, by which time it had been absorbed into the Rolling River School Division. At that time, the school closed due to declining student enrollment and the building was used as a community centre. In 1973, it was leased for $1 to the Canadian Association for the Mentally Retarded (today's

exterior, probably so they could be reused. Hurrying against the looming darkness, I took more than 150 photos of the building's interior and exterior, then made careful measurements of each room and the entire building. As I drove home a few hours after arriving, I wondered if there could have been any means of saving the building. Was there any useful purpose to which it could have been put? In a small community like Cardale, I was inclined to think not.

That same thought had occurred to me five months earlier, as I pulled up to an amber-coloured, two-storey brick building in the Town of Rapid City, 15 miles from Cardale as the crow flies. I was there to meet two members of a committee trying to save the Rapid City Consolidated School building. They had offered to tour me through it. On the way into the building, I noticed out of the corner of my eye a six-sided commemorative plaque on the lawn near the entrance. I made a mental note to look at it after the tour.

My research in advance of that visit had revealed the building had been designed by noted Brandon architect William Elliott and constructed with $8,000 in debentures issued by the local School Board. The cornerstone dated its origin to 17 June 1902 and the official opening ceremony took place on 1 January 1903. The building had a full basement made of fieldstones, containing toilets and separate gymnasia for boys and girls, along with a room where a coal-fueled furnace produced central heat for the building. The upper two floors each had two classrooms, each being roughly 800 square feet in area, so the building as a whole was probably capable of accommodating over 100 children, assuming that classes in those early days could easily exceed 30 students. Each classroom had six windows to

Exterior of the Rapid City School, later a local museum. GOLDSBOROUGH

let in lots of light, a useful feature given that the building had no electrical lights when it was first constructed. Ceilings were high, probably around twelve feet, and were covered in elaborately-patterned, pressed-tin panels. A central staircase from the main floor led up to the second floor where, in addition to the classrooms, was a small room above the main entrance that had probably served as the Principal's office. There were hardwood floors throughout the two main floors, with lathe-and-plaster walls and wainscoting up to roughly waist height. The exterior brick walls were probably made with products of the local brick-maker, Robert Hales.

In 1960, after 57 years of continuous operation, Rapid City School joined the second wave of the consolidation movement to become Rapid City Consolidated School.

Eight years later, it was absorbed into the Rolling River School Division. After students were transferred to a newly constructed school in 1973, the old school was sold to the Town of Rapid City for $1. In June of that year, through the efforts of a local teacher and municipal councilor, the Rapid City Museum & Cultural Centre opened, staffed by community volunteers. The classrooms were turned into exhibit spaces to showcase local artifacts and documents. In its first year of seasonal operation, from June to September, the museum had 1,400 visitors. Within a year, the top-floor classrooms were renovated into space for the Rapid City Public Library. During renovations, two load-bearing walls that had delimited the cloakroom in each classroom were removed to provide more open space. The library eventually moved into another building and the museum expanded into the vacated space. Inevitably, as members of the museum board retired or passed away, and unpaid volunteers lost their resolve, the museum's momentum dissipated and it closed in 2004, although it reopened periodically on special occasions such as Canada Day.

By the time of my visit in May 2013, the building had been closed for nine years. There had been no significant renovations or additions to the original footprint other than the removal of walls on the top floor. Most of its windows had been bricked over, though, probably in hopes of improving energy efficiency. This made the interior rather dark. Each main floor classroom had one remaining window and the top floor classrooms had no windows. Metal mesh had been installed on the outside of these windows to deter vandalism. The furnace was no longer functional so the only heating was provided by small electric space heaters, used only when necessary. With no ventilation, the air was dank. A cluster of mushrooms had grown from a wall in the top floor lobby. The basement was especially humid with condensation and patches of black mold here and there. The lathe-and-plaster walls were cracked and broken in places, and paint was flaking

One of the large, fir rafters in the attic of the former school building is conspicuously cracked, possibly due to structural modifications made when it was renovated into a library. GOLDSBOROUGH

off the metal ceiling panels, probably because of temperature fluctuations in the unheated building. The removal of two load-bearing walls to make room for the library seems to have compromised the structural integrity of the roof. One of the large, fir rafters in the attic was conspicuously cracked and a cross-member under a vertical post in the attic was bowed visibly. There was missing mortar from bricks in the exterior walls. But despite all this, the interior walls and floors appeared level and plumb, and the basement walls had no cracks that would reveal foundation problems.

The committee members told me they want to maintain the building for future use. Their plan is to restore central heating to enable year-round use and reopen the bricked-over windows. They want to create two rental suites on the top floor, a renewed museum on the main floor, and a daycare facility and cultural/meeting space in the basement. The timeframe over which these renovations would take place is, as yet, unknown.

In 2012, they arranged to have the roof re-shingled. At the same time, eavestroughs were repaired and access holes that enabled pigeons to enter the attic were plugged. Fiberglass insulation installed in the attic was pulled out so large quantities of pigeon feces could be removed. But it appears the war against pigeons was being lost, as I saw active nests in the attic during my visit. Much more work remains to be done, for which funds must be raised beyond the small, annual grants received from the local municipality, which probably cover the power bills and not much more. (The municipality also mows the grass and provides insurance coverage.) The main thing, it seems to me, is that the group is enthusiastic and optimistic. They want to make the building relevant and useful to their community again, for which I commend them.

On my way out of the building, I was reminded of the six-sided plaque on the school grounds. Walking up to it, I saw that it commemorated Frederick Philip Grove, who I knew had served as Principal at Rapid City from 1922 to 1924, before retiring to devote himself to writing. Grove achieved only modest success as an author during his lifetime but there has since been renewed interest in his books, recognized for their gritty depictions of the pioneer experience in early Manitoba. But more recently, what has drawn public attention to Grove are revelations about his personal history. Much of what we knew about him has turned out to be fictional. Born Felix Paul Greve in the area of Europe once known as Prussia, in 1903 he was convicted of fraud and imprisoned for a year. He came to North America in 1909 and ended up in Manitoba, reinventing himself as Fred Grove. His fluency in German won him a teaching job in a small school near Winkler. He married a local woman in 1914 and had two children. He later taught at Winkler, Virden, Gladstone, a small rural school near Alonsa, and at Eden. The bushland country northeast of Gladstone appealed especially to Grove, and it became the setting for some of his finest work. His first Canadian novel, *Settlers of the Marsh*, was published in 1925. The partly autobiographical *A Search for America* came in 1927 followed by *Our Daily Bread* in 1928. Yet, his wife's salary as a school teacher continued to provide much of the family income. Awarded an honorary doctorate by the University of Manitoba in 1946, Grove died at his home at Simcoe, Ontario in August 1948. He was buried in the Rapid City Cemetery, alongside his daughter, who had died in 1927 at the age of 12.

On my drive home from Cardale a few months after my visit to Rapid City, I thought about what distinguished the two places, and their respective schools. At Cardale, I suspect the population base—fewer than 30 people—is simply too small to require a building of that size. Rapid City, on the other hand, had 417 people as of the 2011 census. Turning the former school into residential and day-care space makes it useful year-round and ensures the space is occupied rather than vacant. But the funds needed to bring the building into compliance with modern building codes will be considerable. And whether or not there will be municipal support for the plans may depend on events of the next few years. In October 2013, a week after my visit to Cardale, the office for the Town of Rapid City (including, ironically, the fire hall) burned to the ground. And Rapid City has been affected by the consolidation of services that continues as a result of rural depopulation. In essence, municipal amalgamation is doing for Manitoba's rural municipalities what school consolidation in the 1910s, and later the 1960s, did for education. In January 2015, Rapid City became part of the Rural Municipality of Oakview. The main municipal office moved to Oak River, 18 miles away. Some residents fear that municipal services will be compromised as a result of amalgamation but it is too early to draw conclusions. In the meantime, the old Rapid City Consolidated School building awaits a creative reuse, with hopes it does not follow the same path as at Cardale.

SOURCES

"Blanshard supports West-Man plan," *Rivers Gazette Reporter*, 30 August 1973, page 1.

Our Past for the Future: Rapid City and District by Rapid City Historical Book Society, 1978.

Foot Prints & Chalk Dust by Cardale Reunion Book Committee, circa 1981.

"Committee receiving letters," *Rivers Gazette Reporter*, 2 September 1981, page 6.

"Council clips," *Rivers Gazette Reporter*, 9 March 2002, page 2.

ACKNOWLEDGEMENTS

I thank Lenny De Schutter and Sue Armstrong for giving me a tour of the old Rapid City Consolidated School and for discussing their plans to resuscitate it. Diane Kuculym (Chief Administrative Officer for the RM of Oakview) provided information about the Cardale Consolidated School and alerted me to its impending demolition. Lynne Bereza (Association of Manitoba Municipalities) and Leona Devuyst informed me on the municipal amalgamations of 2015, and Rob McInnes gave me insight into the activities of the Rolling Dale Workshop.

Rose Hill Lime Kilns

Every time that I drove through the Interlake, along highway #6, I wondered about a mysterious concrete object beside the road, just north of Oak Point. It was a massive concrete block, about 30 feet to the top, supported on ten stout concrete legs. Surrounded by tall grass, it had not been used in a very long time.

OPPOSITE One of the derelict limestone kilns at the Rose Hill Quarry near The Narrows, August 2012. GOLDSBOROUGH

Nearby was a large, water-filled pit whose regular shape made clear it was not natural. Finally, my curiosity sufficiently piqued, I did some research and found that these are the remains of a plant used for the manufacture of lime—the mineral, not the citrus fruit. Developed in 1915 by the David Bowman Coal and Supply Company of Winnipeg, the facility operated for at least a decade, producing some 400 tons of lime per month. The pit is where the raw material, limestone rock, was quarried. There are other abandoned limestone plants around Manitoba,

Remains of the limestone quarry and processing plant at Oak Point, October 2011. GOLDSBOROUGH

most notably at Stonewall, that hosted an active industry from 1880 to 1967, where some six to ten tons of lime were manufactured each day. I was thinking of the Stonewall and Oak Point quarries as I drove to another site of lime manufacture, much less well known, associated with the basis for Manitoba's name.

Limestone is an abundant rock in southern Manitoba. Its chemical name is calcium carbonate, consisting of one calcium atom, one carbon atom, and three oxygen atoms in each molecule. Several buildings around the province, notably the Legislative Building in Winnipeg, are made from slabs of local limestone. When broken into smaller fragments, it is useful for gravelling roads. Crushed to a fine powder, it is a white colouring agent in toothpaste and paint. And limestone is the raw material for the manufacture of lime, an ingredient of plaster and mortar. A highly caustic powder, lime is also used to decompose organic matter. (One of its more notorious uses has been to destroy the evidence of mass murders.) Also known as calcium oxide—one atom each of calcium and oxygen—the conversion of limestone to lime, called calcination, requires exposure to high temperature, typically in the range of 1000 °C, over several days. Calcination is done in

Stonewall's limestone kilns, circa 1910. ARCHIVES OF MANITOBA

a kiln made of stones that can withstand the heat. Crushed limestone is put in the top of the kiln, and the heat is provided by burning wood or coal in the bottom.

The Narrows, the area where a narrow constriction links the north and south parts of Lake Manitoba, has an abundance of limestone and may be the place where the word Manitoba arose. One of several alternative explanations is that Manitoba derives from "Manito Wapow," a Cree phrase meaning "narrows of the Great Spirit." In

stormy weather, waves crashing on the limestone rocks at The Narrows resounds eerily, and early Indigenous people believed the sound came from a large drum beaten by Manitou.

Just east of the present-day bridge over The Narrows, about three miles off what is now Highway #68, brothers James and Bob Young (later joined by partner Charles Maloan) established the Rose Hill Quarry in 1897. They hoped to capitalize on a building boom during a period of economic prosperity in Manitoba, during which there was

an enormous demand for plaster. In commercial and domestic buildings alike, wooden straps were nailed horizontally across wall studs, then slathered with wet plaster. When dried, lathe-and-plaster made a fire-resistant, smooth wall. (Today, we achieve the same effect with drywall, a sandwich of gypsum between layers of paper.) In 1902, Maloan incorporated as the Manitoba Union Mining Company while the Youngs went chicken farming in California. The company operated as many as twelve kilns, turning out lime that was bagged and shipped by steamboat from The Narrows to a port on the Whitemud River, at the south end of Lake Manitoba. There, the lime was loaded onto trains for delivery to market. Unfortunately, the Rose Hill Quarry operated for a relatively short time, due to difficulty in mining the limestone deposits. The quarry's remote location, relative to more southerly ones at Stonewall and elsewhere, was probably a contributing factor, making transportation by ship during the short ice-free season prohibitively costly. When two of the company's barges sank in bad weather, the remaining fleet was sold to the Manitoba Gypsum Company, which operated a gypsum manufacturing plant farther north, at Gypsumville. Local homesteaders continued to use the Rose Hill kilns occasionally to produce lime for local consumption but they gradually fell into disuse. In 1952, ownership of the site was turned over to the local municipality.

Two kilns still stand at the former quarry site. Each is a square stack of limestone blocks, about twelve feet across and twelve feet high, with an opening barely three feet tall at the bottom. Crawling through the opening, you find that the stack is hollow and open at the top. The quarry itself is overgrown with vegetation. But someone has erected a small stone cairn beside one of the kilns with a plaque that provides some of their history. Standing inside the kiln during a visit in 2012, shielded from the sound of waves on the nearby lake, I pondered how the lime from this very kiln, in a secluded spot far from anywhere, played a significant role in the building of Manitoba. For that, I am inclined to toast the memory of those early limestone burners. Make that a cocktail, with a twist of lime.

SOURCES

"David Bowman Coal and Supply Co.," *Winnipeg Tribune*, 25 September 1915, page 80.

"Announcement" [Bowman-Mackenzie Coal Company], *Winnipeg Tribune*, 17 January 1925, page 2.

"How Manitoba got its name" by Frank Hall, *Manitoba Pageant*, Volume 15, Number 2, Winter 1970.

Taming a Wilderness, A History of Ashern and District by Ashern Historical Society, 1976.

"Site Review: The Quarry Park at Stonewall, Manitoba" by Robert Coutts, *Manitoba History*, Number 10, Autumn 1985.

ACKNOWLEDGEMENTS

I had heard about the Rose Hill kilns several years ago but did not know their location until local rancher Caron Clarke kindly provided directions. I obtained archival photos of the kilns at Stonewall from Ed Ledohowski.

Schepper's Agricultural College

Since the dawn of agriculture, farming methods have been passed down from generation to generation. That changed in the early 20th century when awareness of the latest scientific methods became an increasingly essential part of a farmer's education.

In 1905, the Manitoba Agricultural College was founded with the objective of educating students in modern farming practices. The first of its kind in western Canada and only the third in all of Canada, the College offered courses in horticulture, agricultural engineering, animal husbandry, farm management, and home economics. Until 1913, it occupied a site in southwest Winnipeg, now the home of the Asper Jewish Community Campus. With urban development engulfing it and needing more space for field work, the College moved to a more spacious location in south Winnipeg, which later became the Fort Garry Campus of the University of Manitoba. (The Administrative Building at the University still bears the College's name on its east side.)

In the view of at least some Manitoba farmers and clerics, however, the Manitoba Agricultural College had at least two shortcomings. Firstly, it was far away for those living in rural Manitoba and exposure to life in the big city—especially at a co-educational, nominally Protestant facility—might corrupt impressionable Catholic farm boys. Secondly, and perhaps more significantly, its language of instruction was exclusively in English. In the autumn of 1919, six years after the Manitoba Agricultural College moved to south Winnipeg, the Brothers of the Our Lady of Mercy arrived from Europe, having recently established colleges in their native Belgium, as well as England and Italy. Recruited by Archbishop Arthur

Beliveau, of the Archdiocese of St. Boniface, they purchased 320 acres of farm land northwest of Swan Lake in the Rural Municipality of Lorne, described by later reports as a "ten minutes walk" from town. There was a large francophone community in the region, as the first Belgian settlers had arrived here before 1890. The Brothers planned to establish a facility to provide boys with both general and agricultural training. (Francophone girls already had a school, run by nuns, at Bruxelles.) Farmers across the Archdiocese could send their sons to a small-town college to be educated, safe in the knowledge they would return home again. On 27 March 1920, the provincial legislature incorporated "Les Freres de Notre-Dame de la Misericorde" with the object of "performing various charitable works, of giving instruction to youth, of teaching catechism, of conducting orphanage schools, agricultural orphanage, industrial schools, and contemplate opening reformatory schools for young delinquents." Its officers were Joseph Serneels (known as Brother Mathieu), Joseph Grogna (Brother Cyprien), Auguste Moorkens (Brother Amedee), Jean Goes (Brother Narcisse), and Patrick Darmody (Brother Fintan).

In early 1920, St. James engineer Armand Boissonneau was commissioned to design an optimistically-large structure: a two-storey wood and brick veneer building on a foundation made from stones collected by the Brothers from the surrounding landscape. It measured 148 feet long and 82 feet wide, with high ceilings that made it difficult to keep the building warm in winter.

Construction by St. Boniface contractor Firmin Wyndels (also of Belgian ancestry) began later that year and was finished at a cost of some $80,000. The main building was surrounded by farm land and barns to provide food for the Brothers and a basis for instruction in farming methods. The new facility was consecrated by Archbishop Beliveau, who remarked that "Your students are all farmers' sons and will have to help their parents at the farm. Educate them thus theoretically and in practice. In so doing you will instill in them the love for the land and our countryside will remain Catholic." The college opened for classes in October 1920 with Brother Mathieu as Principal. Its formal name, carved into a

"SCHEPPERS"
COLLEGE

Swan Lake, Man.
Elementary and Secondary Section with Commercial :: Course ::
AGRICULTURAL SCHOOL
English and French Instruction
Fees Per Month—
    Boys under 12 years $15.00.
    Boys over 12 years $18.00.
    Pupils over 15 years $20.00.
    Ask for Prospectus:
    Bro. Director of the College.

Advertisement for the Agricultural College in the Northwest Review, the largest Catholic newspaper in western Canada, September 1923. LEGISLATIVE LIBRARY OF MANITOBA

stone over the entrance, was Collège du Sacré-Coeur (Sacred Heart College) but it was known widely and informally as Scheppers College, for the Order's European founder, Victor Cornelius Scheppers.

College tuition was $15 per month for children under 12, $18 for those 12 to 15, and $20 for students over 15. Optional services included laundry for $2 per month and bedding for $1.50 per month. Culturally-minded parents could have their sons take piano or violin lessons for $3 per month. Religious and language instruction in Flemish was also available. In the words of the College's promotional literature, "No efforts have been spared to ensure every comfort and convenience for the pupils."

Initial reception of the new College was promising. For several years, it had an enrollment of 60 to 75 boarders and 15 to 20 day students. In addition to its classes, the College hosted a hockey team that played other local teams. Unfortunately, optimism for the appeal of an agricultural education

would prove to be unfounded. In at least a few instances, some of the College's students, enamoured by monastic life over the prospect of returning to the farm, joined Our Lady of Mercy as its first Canadian recruits. Agricultural classes, as well as instruction in French, were phased out in 1926, much to the displeasure of Archbishop Beliveau, as the instructional focus shifted to commerce and sciences such as Physics and Chemistry, in English and Flemish. The livestock and farm machinery were sold to a local farmer on the condition that one-third of his produce would supply the College. Despite these changes, student enrollment dropped in the late 1920s, especially as farm commodity prices fell with the onset of the Great Depression in 1930. The Brothers had to borrow money to buy coal to heat the building and to pay for insurance and other necessities. The roof of the relatively new building leaked but there were no means to fix it.

The College closed permanently in October 1932. The Brothers were transferred to an orphanage at Huberdeau, Quebec, taking beds and mattresses with them, along with the contents of the chapel. The rest was sold at auction. The building sat vacant for several years, scavenged by the local priest for materials to build a church in town, and the surrounding farm land was sold. The building was finally demolished in 1939 but the altar from its chapel was salvaged and is supposedly still in use in the church at St. Alphonse.

The old College has been gone so long that few people recall its existence. I visited Swan Lake a couple of times, hoping to see what remains were visible, but was stymied by my ignorance of where to look. My obsession to know its exact location took me to the Manitoba Air Photo Library in Winnipeg. I hoped it would have an aerial photograph taken during the period when the College was operating or, at least, soon after its demolition. The nearest image I could find came from 1948 by which time the building had been gone for nine years. Luckily, although the scarred earth where the building had sat was healing with new vegetation, the extensive shelterbelt of trees that had protected it from the harsh prairie wind—now gone—was readily visible. So I was able to estimate the building's location. I am told that, by the 1950s, remnants of its concrete foundation were still visible. However, diligent work by the present owners have removed all traces of the vision of francophone farming that lived and died here.

SOURCES

"Brothers of Mercy at Swan Lake are building college," *Manitoba Free Press*, 16 March 1920, page 14.

Chapter 166, An Act to incorporate "Les Freres de Notre-Dame de la Misericorde," Statutes of Manitoba, 10 George v, 1920, assented 27 March 1920.

"Belgian college is near completion," *Winnipeg Tribune*, 28 August 1920, page 5.

1921 Canada census, Macdonald District, Subdistrict 18 (Townships 5-6, Range 10w), Ancestry.

"Swan Lake Midgets lose to college team," Winnipeg Tribune, 20 March 1924, page 15.

Pioneers, Oh! Pioneers! Historical Records and Accounts of the Early Pioneers of the District of Swan Lake, Manitoba, from its Early Settlement, 1873-1950 by Rev. George H. Hambley, 1952.

"Scheppers College," Rootsweb. [http://freepages.history. rootsweb.ancestry.com/~manbelghx/manbelghx/Manitoba/ Pages/scheppersCollege.htm, revised 15 April 2001]

"Archives of The Brothers of our Lady of Mercy in Canada" by Brother Rombaut Obbens, Rootsweb. [http://freepages.history. rootsweb.ancestry.com/~manbelghx/manbelghx/Manitoba/ Pages/scheppersCollege3.htm; revised 25 April 2001]

"Prospectus of the Sacred Heart College, Swan Lake, Man. under the direction of the Brothers of Our Lady of Mercy," Rootsweb. [http://freepages.history.rootsweb.ancestry. com/~manbelghx/manbelghx/Manitoba/Pages/ scheppersProspectus.htm, revised 7 March 2001]

"Belgian immigrants and language issues on the Canadian prairies" by Cornelius J. Jaenen, *Canadian Journal of Netherlandic Studies*, volume 33, number 1, 2012, pages 39-47.

ACKNOWLEDGEMENTS

I thank Monica Ball of the Manitoba Legislative Library for her dogged research on the Schepper's College, especially in French sources that were mostly unavailable to me. I also benefitted from the help of Karen Letourneau, Jim Wyndels, Theresa Early, and Chris Searens, along with the good folks at the Manitoba Air Photo Library, in determining the approximate site of the former college building.

The Churches of Sclater

The conversion of western Canada to agriculture began in 1812 with the arrival of the Selkirk Settlers at the junction of the Red and Assiniboine rivers. The pace quickened as settlers began to arrive aboard steamboats in the 1860s and 1870s, and trains from the late 1870s onwards. They came from far and wide, arriving with hopes of a new and better life.

Each of them had a promise from the Canadian government of 160 acres—one quarter of a square mile—of free farm land so long as they resided on it for several successive years, broke a certain acreage, and planted crops. Settlers did tend to congregate with others of their own kind. But this was not always so, because land was allocated on a first-come, first-served basis. It was possible that your neighbour spoke a different language, ate different food, and worshiped with different rites. The result was a prairie landscape that was an ethnic and cultural mosaic.

By the early 20th century, most of the easily farmable land in Manitoba was taken. Settlers arriving from central Europe—from the regions that today we call Poland and Ukraine—were obliged to take less desirable land such as in the Dauphin and Swan Valley regions of western Manitoba. Soils there were less well suited to immediate farming, being stonier and heavily wooded. After

OPPOSITE Our Lady of the Snows Roman Catholic Church, June 2015. GOLDSBOROUGH

these new Canadians had built shelter for themselves and their livestock, and cleared land for crops, their thoughts turned to other needs. The Canadian Northern Railway (precursor to today's Canadian National) arrived, providing transportation for agricultural produce to the outside world, and school districts were established to educate the growing numbers of children. General stores provided essential goods that could not be made or grown locally. Settlers met their spiritual needs by meeting in each other's homes and, in time, they built churches, often with associated community halls.

Inevitably, the enticements of larger urban centres led people away from these small, rural communities and scores of once-thriving villages are now distinguished only by a motley collection of abandoned buildings. In my travels throughout rural Manitoba, I have encountered so many abandoned churches, for example, that I have come to think of them as "low hanging fruit." So I did not think much of it when,

The Sclater area was predominantly forested in the 1930s when this photo was taken. ARCHIVES OF MANITOBA

in the summer of 2015, while driving on Highway 10 toward Swan River, I saw a disheveled little church standing forlornly along the road. Nevertheless, I decided to pull in for a quick look. That was my first introduction to the "ghost town" of Sclater and its three abandoned churches.

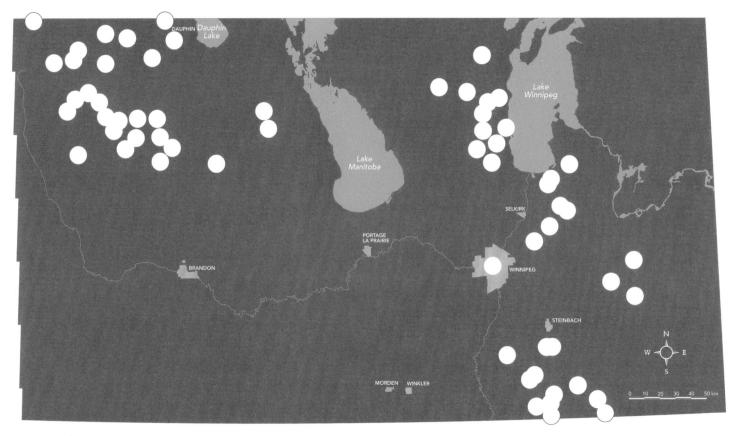

Sites of 110 Polish and Ukrainian churches (not all of which are abandoned) mapped by the Manitoba Historical Society since 2010. Their distribution pattern matches that of Polish and Ukrainian immigrant groups.

I had a hard time learning anything substantive about Sclater. It was always a very small place. Established in 1904 as a "flag station"—where the train only stopped when flagged down by someone at the station—and named for a railway contractor, the Sclater area never produced enough grain to warrant the construction of a grain elevator. In 1912, its population was 15 people, described as a mixture of "Canadians and Ukrainians." There was a single general store, run by postmaster William Hruszowy, and an agricultural implements dealership. The surrounding land was extensively wooded; by 1912 only about half of it was considered arable and, of that, only about two percent was under cultivation. Even by the 1920s, much of the land had not been taken up by settlers. The local economy was a mixture of farming—some 6,000 bushels of grain were shipped annually in the 1910s—and woodcutting; about 200 railway cars of timber were

shipped in 1912. Nothing much happened at Sclater other than the annual rituals of birth, marriage, and death. The progressive downgrading of Sclater in the *Gazetteer of Canada* is telling. In 1955, it was described as a "Hamlet." By 1968, it was a "Post Office." That post office closed in 1976. In 1981, Sclater was merely a "Locality."

The Catholic, Ukrainian Catholic, and Ukrainian Orthodox faiths have common attributes arising from their shared lineage but there are also differences, including their relative willingness to accept married priests. It is sometimes difficult, therefore, when visiting an abandoned church, to know its affiliation or name because identifying signs and banners were usually removed when it was deconsecrated. But subtle clues often remain. Walking up to the mysterious little church along Highway 10, my eye was drawn immediately to the cross on its steeple. It had a single crossbeam, meaning this former church was either Catholic or Ukrainian Catholic, not Ukrainian Orthodox, which would have two or three crossbeams, at least one of them not at right angles to the vertical beam. Stepping through a side door that was standing open, I saw that the structural integrity of the building was severely compromised. Floor boards were missing, along with some from the walls and ceiling. The cantor's (or choir) loft—a balcony at the rear of the church over the main entrance—was detached from the wall on one side. Outside light flooded through a gaping hole through the roof. Choosing my steps cautiously so I did not fall through a rotted section of the floor, I took several photos, then retreated back the

St. Michael's Ukrainian Orthodox Church, June 2015. GOLDSBOROUGH

way I had come. Another clue emerged just a few hundred feet down the highway. On the opposite side from the church stood a well-tended cemetery. A sign identified it as Holy Eucharist Ukrainian Cemetery. My working hypothesis was that the cemetery was associated with the church I had just visited, which I gave the tentative name of Holy Eucharist Ukrainian Catholic Church.

My curiosity was aroused. Were there any other churches in the vicinity? I turned off Highway 10 onto a gravel road heading to the former site of Sclater, two miles to the east. As I drove, I saw, on the left side of the road, another cemetery. A sign said it was the Sclater Pioneer Cemetery. Several stones bore the Orthodox cross and a few had Cyrillic inscriptions. Consulting my trusty cemetery directory that I carry routinely, compiled by the Manitoba Genealogical Society, and comparing its location against those of known cemeteries in the Rural Municipality of Mountain, I concluded this one was also known as the St. Michael's Ukrainian Orthodox Cemetery. Ah, I thought, then there is probably a St. Michael's Ukrainian Orthodox Church nearby.

Before heading off to search for it, I noticed on the right side of the road, several more graves, much less well tended than those in the St. Michael's Cemetery, being overgrown by small tree saplings. It must be a different denomination unconnected to the cemetery across the road. Otherwise, why would its caretakers let this part become so overgrown? I could see no Orthodox crosses or Cyrillic writing. Some of the names sounded Ukrainian but others did not. My cemetery directory provided no help in identifying it. Ahead a quarter mile stood what I suspected was the former St. Michael's Church. Inside, a tattered cloth hanging in front of the chancel (where the priest conducted the religious service) was emblazoned with the Orthodox cross. Like its counterpart on the highway, this building was open to the elements and was even more badly compromised; an entire section of its north wall was gone. Again, I took photos then pressed on to see if there was another church that might belong to the overgrown cemetery. I drove about a half mile but saw nothing but dense trees. Checking a satellite photo of the area on my smartphone, I could see the outline of what looked like a building, some distance back from the road. Stopping my car near where the building should be, I bushwhacked through the foliage and found a third church. This one was a different from the other two, simpler, with a tall roof line, and a Catholic-looking cross on its steeple. Its only door was closed but unlocked so I peered inside. Aside from junk strewn about the floor, it was mostly intact. The altar stood at the front. A structural beam running from side to side of the nave (where the parishioners sat) was painted with what appeared to be a motto: "Swieta Boza Rodzicielko Modl Sie Za Nami." Suspecting it was Polish, I photographed the beam and emailed it to my wife, who reads and speaks the language. Within minutes, she confirmed my suspicion and told me it said "Holy Mother of God, pray for us." I am fairly sure this was a Roman Catholic church, but I had no clue which one.

Holy Eucharist Ukrainian Catholic Church, June 2015. GOLDSBOROUGH

All three churches at Sclater were modest structures made of wood. In keeping with Ukrainian tradition, all have their main entrances facing west. None had a vestibule into which one entered from outside; instead, the entrance led directly into the nave. All had cantor's lofts over their entrances. The Roman Catholic church was architecturally simple—just a rectangular space for the nave and chancel. The Ukrainian Catholic building was more complex, being in the shape of a cross with a domed ceiling that gave it a distinct feeling of spaciousness, and a discrete chancel marked by a step up from the nave and a door leading into a small room where the priest would change into his robes. The Ukrainian Orthodox chancel was separated from the nave by a short partition wall with three low doorways. All three churches had been deconsecrated so their sacred items and images were gone. None had pews although I was told later by a friend that, a few years ago, the former Roman Catholic church had several hand-made wooden benches that have since been removed.

After my return home, I tried to find more information about the three small churches. My first avenue of inquiry was the Archdiocese of Winnipeg, which had once held jurisdiction over the Roman Catholic church at Sclater. A helpful archivist dug through numerous boxes of old files and found sacramental registry indexes listing baptisms for the Sclater area from 1915 to 1917. She also found land title records indicating the Archdiocese had owned the property in 1947, and perhaps as early as 1931. A 1950 report written by the priest at nearby Pine River stated that the Sclater church had been built in 1921. Most significantly, the Archdiocese's archivist was able to identify it as Our Lady of the Snows, named for a noted Basilica in Rome. Our Lady had been a "mission church" that did not have its own priest but was instead served through the years by priests from Roblin, Sifton, Pine River, or Winnipegosis. A 1960 memoir by Polish immigrant Edward Hubicz, who served as the priest at Sclater in the 1940s, clarified that although the building was built in 1921, it was not blessed until July 1925 and its construction continued into the 1950s with the addition of a steeple.

The Archdiocese archives contained a letter from 1973 indicating that Our Lady of the Snows

had closed in that year and its four remaining families joined the congregation at Pine River. Five years later, the Archdiocese looked into selling the property but local Catholics wanted it kept, so the site remained under the care of the Sifton Parish through the 1980s. Sifton later became a mission of St. Viator's Parish in Dauphin and Archdiocese records indicate the Sclater property was considered for sale in 1993 but do not state if the sale actually took place. I found contradictory information from other sources. A friend who works as an antiques dealer told me that, a few years ago, he met a couple at Sclater who claimed to own the former Catholic church and its land. On the other hand, a friend at Ethelbert recently asked the Reeve for the RM of Mountain about the church's status and was told that the municipality owns all three church sites.

My efforts to find information on the other two churches at Sclater were somewhat less fruitful. The generous archivist at the Ukrainian Catholic Archeparchy of Winnipeg gave me

a copy of a book about Ukrainian Catholic churches in Manitoba. It had been compiled in 1991 based on a visit to the church, organized by the priest from Pine River, in 1988. The book stated that the Holy Eucharist Ukrainian Catholic Church was constructed in 1918 on land donated by founding parishioner Peter Hrechka. In addition to the cemetery that had provided my first clue on the church's identity, the church had a second cemetery some three miles to the southeast. By 1941, the parish had 15 members and 30 school-aged children as part of the Pine River pastoral charge but, by 1988, there were just a "handful" of elderly people who typically attended services at "neighboring parishes." So it seems likely that Holy Eucharist Ukrainian Catholic Church closed in the late 1980s or early 1990s. Least successful were my inquiries on behalf of St. Michael's Ukrainian Orthodox Church. Although the state of the building would indicate its origins date to roughly the same time period as the other two churches, I could find no actual date of construction, nor information on its operations through the years. However, a short article in the Swan Valley newspaper from December 1988 provided a clue on its final fate when it reported that sacred items from St. Michael's had been donated to four churches in Saskatchewan at Yorkton, Prince Albert, and Saskatoon to be used "for the glory of God and the furtherance of the Orthodox Church." Presumably, St. Michael's had been deconsecrated around this time.

Today, with church attendance of the mainstream denominations at all-time lows, the role of organized religion in our daily lives seems to be on the wane. So I find it interesting that, in a former time, a sparsely populated place like Sclater could support no fewer than three churches. Clearly, religion was important to those early settlers. In their homelands, they had lived in groups that were more homogenous—ethnically and spiritually—than what they found in Canada, where homesteaders settled in a way that promoted interspersion. Neighbours could be, and often were, of different faiths. So churches provided a means for settlers in diverse communities to preserve their cultural identity and traditions from their homelands. Faith even maintained a distinction between neighbours that persisted beyond death, as shown by three graveyards at Sclater.

SOURCES

Henderson's Western Canada Gazetteer & Directory, 1908. Legislative Library of Manitoba.

Polish Churches in Manitoba: A Collection of Historical Sketches by Edward M. Hubicz, London, Veritas Foundation Publication Centre, 1960.

"Towns along the CNR in Swan River Valley," *Swan Valley Star & Times*, 23 July 1981, page 18.

Ukrainian Churches of Manitoba: An Overview Study by M. Christopher Kotecki and Randy R. Rostecki, Historic Resources Branch, Department of Culture, Heritage, and Recreation, Volume II, 1984. Legislative Library of Manitoba.

Ukrainian Catholic Churches of Winnipeg Archeparchy by Anna Maria Kowcz-Baran, Saskatoon, 1991.

Pioneer Settlers: Ukrainians in the Dauphin Area, 1896-1926 by Michael Ewanchuk, 1988.

"Cards of thanks," *Swan Valley Star & Times*, 1 December 1988, page 28.

Geographic Names of Manitoba, Manitoba Conservation, 2000.

"Tale of two churches: Ukrainian Catholic and Orthodox congregations still embrace their differences" by Bill Redekop, *Winnipeg Free Press*, 14 November 2009.

Gazetteer of Canada: 1955, 1968, 1981, 1994, 1999, Legislative Library of Manitoba.

ACKNOWLEDGEMENTS

I thank Tyyne Petrowski (Archdiocese of Winnipeg Archives) for providing information about Our Lady of the Snows and Gloria Romaniuk (Ukrainian Catholic Archeparchy of Winnipeg Archives) for providing information about Holy Eucharist Ukrainian Catholic. Mike Lisowski educated me on the meaning of a "flag station" in railway parlance.

Star Mound

Those poor kids! That's what I thought as I drove up the side of Star Mound, a 100-foot-high, gently sloping mound of shale standing out in a vast ocean of prairie four miles from the American border, about three miles west of Snowflake, Manitoba. There, perched in the centre of the hill's eight-acre flat top, was the one-room Star Mound School.

Modern view of Star Mound (July 2016): distant view from the northwest. GOLDSBOROUGH

I thought about generations of school children struggling up the mound on foot, while I rode up in ease and comfort in my car. Later, I learned that the former schoolhouse had been moved atop the mound in 1967, after it had closed, to be used as a community museum. It was probably moved there for the same reason that people have been coming for millennia to Star Mound: for the spectacular, panoramic view.

When you are in a place as flat as Manitoba, insignificant bumps on the landscape tend to be given misleadingly grandiose names like Riding Mountain. But a place with as much history as Star Mound deserves its star status. Visible for miles in every direction, about a mile in total length and a half mile wide, Star Mound is a knob of shale from the Cretaceous Period, millions of years old, sculpted during the Ice Age over 10,000 years ago. Mounds large and small abound in this region of southern Manitoba, most notably a few miles northwest of Star Mound from which the town of Pilot Mound gets its name.

Speaking of names, Star Mound has several, including Nebogwawin Butte, Nebogwawin Hill, Merry Dance Hill, and Dry Dance Hill, all of which harken back to its long period of use by Indigenous peoples. In fact, Star Mound is a mound on top of a mound. On top of the natural glacial feature, Indigenous people piled mounds of soil to create burial places for their dead. Anthropologists use the name Star Mound specifically for a cluster of burial mounds on the hill, rather than the hill itself. But Star

The supposedly beaver-shaped burial mound atop Star Mound requires a substantial amount of imagination.
GOLDSBOROUGH

Mound seems to be the name by which locals refer to it, so that's the name I use here.

It is clear that Star Mound has attracted people for a very long time, at least in part because it provides a commanding view, enabling one to see people (and weather) coming from far away. As archaeologist W.B. Nickerson observed in the early 20th century: "The habitation of this exposed, windswept hill-top doubtless indicates that these people had enemies against whom it was necessary to be ever on the alert. Nothing else, it would seem, could induce anyone to make this shelterless spot a place of abode." It is believed that, at one time, there was an Indigenous campsite on the mound-top, perhaps occupied seasonally. The camp was abandoned at the time of a 1738 visit by Quebec explorer Pierre Gaultier De Varennes La Vérendrye. Two centuries later, in August 1857, Irish

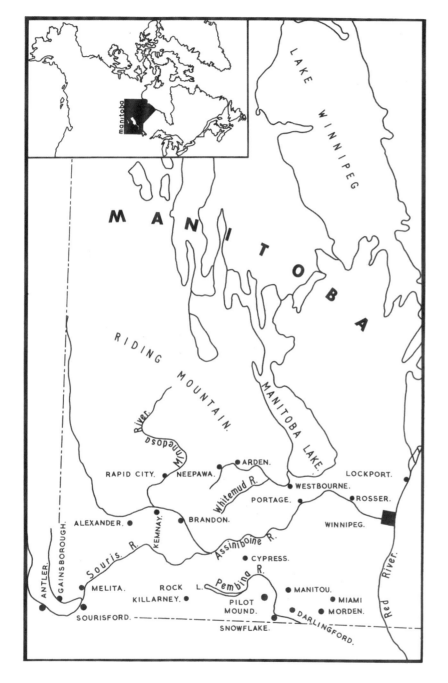

explorer John Palliser, during his scientific expedition across the prairies on behalf of the Royal Geographical Society, saw the hill on the horizon and referred to it as Paquewin Hill, or the "Hill of the Great Medicine Dance." The mound was mentioned by another visiting Irishman, Paul Kane, in his 1859 book *Wanderings of an Artist among the Indians of North America*.

There are burial mounds all over southern Manitoba so it was inevitable that, as Europeans flooded into the area through the 1800s, the mounds attracted attention. Henry Youle Hind, a Toronto college professor who visited the Red River Settlement in 1857, excavated a mound on the banks of the Souris River. In the 1870s and 1880s, members of the newly-founded Historical and Scientific Society of Manitoba, including such notables as John Schultz (protagonist of Louis Riel and later Manitoba Lieutenant Governor) and cleric and college professor George Bryce were enthusiastic excavators of mounds in the Red, Rainy, and Souris river regions. Modern anthropologists have dismissed their findings as "racist hodge-podge" because the men filtered what they saw through a Euro-centric lens, concluding the mounds could not possibly have been built by the "savage" peoples of Manitoba, but by some long-lost race of Europeans or Asians. Another Historical Society member, Charles Bell, who

Map of Manitoba burial mound sites visited between 1912 and 1915 by W.B. Nickerson. K.H. CAPES, NATIONAL MUSEUM OF CANADA

had come to Manitoba with the Wolseley Expedition of 1870, carried out his own excavations in the late 1880s. Rejecting the Mound Builder theories of his peers, Bell concluded that the mounds had indeed been built by local people. It was thought the mounds were built between 500 and 1730 AD by nomadic, bison-hunting people related to—or at least influenced by—a Sioux culture that thrived in the mid-reaches of the Mississippi River valley, in what is now the central United States.

In the early 20th century, the burial mounds at Star Mound drew the attention of *bona fide* anthropologists with formal training and expertise. In 1909, Henry Montgomery from the University of Toronto made a brief visit. Most of what we know about the human use of Star Mound comes from the work of American archaeologist William Baker Nickerson. Born in Connecticut in 1865, he trained at Harvard University in the 1880s but, there being no opportunities for employment as an archaeologist, he supported himself by

working as a railway surveyor, signal tower operator, and telegraph agent. During his four-decade working life, Nickerson excavated burial mounds wherever his work took him in the central interior of the United States, in Illinois, Iowa, Michigan, Minnesota, Ohio, and Wisconsin. His sole sojourn outside the country, at the behest of the National Museum of Canada in Ottawa, was to Manitoba. Between 1912 and 1915, he excavated sites near Lockport, Manitou, Morden, Darlingford, Pilot Mound, and Melita, focusing on the Pembina Valley and north of the Assiniboine River.

Nickerson visited Star Mound during his initial survey in 1912 and he returned two years later for more extensive work. He observed that the top of Star Mound, although private property, had never been broken for agriculture. Large boulders on its sides were polished smooth from years of rubbing by bison. A large burial mound near the centre, some 70 feet in diameter and up to five feet high, was formed in the shape of a

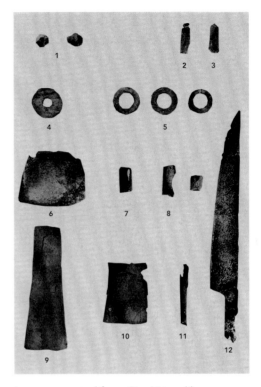

Items excavated from Star Mound by W.B. Nickerson included an axe made of "native copper," shown here in the lower-left corner of a page from a 1963 report about his pioneering archaeological work in Manitoba.
K.H. CAPES, NATIONAL MUSEUM OF CANADA

beaver, known as an "effigy mound," thought to be the only such example in Manitoba. The soil to construct the mound had been gathered in the surrounding area, though it was found to also contain "several bushels of food bones, mostly buffalo, and some fish

Interior of the former Star Mound School, now a community museum, May 2012. GOLDSBOROUGH

and bird." Digging into the mound with shovels, Nickerson uncovered several graves. Each contained a single human skeleton that he thought had been interred in a sitting position. Some were children and others were adults. One of the skeletons had the tip of an arrowhead embedded in it but bone growth around the wound indicated it was not the cause of death. Removed from the graves were such artifacts as arrowheads, assorted bone tools, stone blades, sharpened stones to scrape the flesh from bison skins, a large stone

spear point, and some pottery shards. Noteworthy among the finds was a decorative marine shell—indicating that items were traded from far away—and an axe head made from "native copper" that had been hammered into shape rather than forged with heat. Only one of the burial pits showed evidence of prior tampering, said to have occurred some twenty years earlier, by a man named Graves—an appropriate moniker for a grave-robber.

Nickerson excavated a large portion of the effigy mound and, after he was done, the soil was replaced and contoured using a horse-drawn scraper, so much of the original appearance was lost. Three smaller, circular mounds nearby, in a triangular layout, have likewise been destroyed over time. So there is not much visible to be seen other than an innocuous mound of earth. Studies of other Manitoba burial mounds were made in the 1940s by pioneering Manitoba archaeologist Chris Vickers, and more recently by Manitoba Museum curator Leigh Syms and Brandon University professor Bev Nicholson. A mound site near Melita has been designated as a national historic site but visits to it are discouraged in hopes of preventing vandalism and theft of buried artifacts. No such restrictions apply at Star Mound, which has been so thoroughly disturbed that the likelihood of finding artifacts is low. In 1999, a bison bone from a Star Mound burial pit was determined by radiocarbon dating to have been put there around 885 AD. This is now believed to be when the burial mounds were first constructed on Star Mound. But the identity of the people who built them is still in question.

Originally situated about a mile south of the hill, in 1962 Star Mound School was moved into nearby Snowflake to be used as a classroom for high school students. Four years later, the rural school consolidation movement was in high gear and senior students from Snowflake were bused to Crystal City. The schoolhouse was donated to a local group who formed the Star Mound Historical Society. In 1967, they moved it to the top of the mound and held a reunion of former students and teachers, culminating activities begun on New Year's Eve when Canada's 100th birthday was marked with a giant bonfire on Star Mound. Now a municipally-designated historic site equipped to look as it did when it was an active school, Star Mound School Museum is definitely worth a visit. There, you can savor the great view and ponder the geology and long history of human activity in southern Manitoba.

SOURCES

"Among the Mound Builders' remains" by George Bryce, *Transactions of the Historical and Scientific Society of Manitoba*, Series 1, No. 18, May 1885.

"Among the Mound Builders' remains" by George Bryce, *Transactions of the Historical and Scientific Society of Manitoba*, Series 1, No. 66, February 1904.

"Archaeology in the Rock and Pelican Lake Area of Southern Manitoba" by Chris Vickers, *Transactions of the Historical and Scientific Society of Manitoba*, Series 3, 1944-1945 Season.

"The W.B. Nickerson survey and excavations, 1912-15, of the southern Manitoba mounds region" by Katherine H. Capes, Anthropology Papers, National Museum of Canada, Department of Northern Affairs and National Resources, Number 4, November 1963, 178 pages.

"Prairies and passes: Retracing the route of Palliser's British North American Exploring Expedition 1857-60" by Mrs. Graham Spry, *Journal of the Royal Society of Arts*, volume 113, number 5110, September 1965, pages 807-828.

"The Devils Lake – Sourisford burial complex on the northeastern plains" by Leigh Syms, *Plains Anthropologist*, volume 24, number 86, November 1979, pages 283-308.

A Diary of Snowflake, Manitoba edited by Landon Booker, no date.

"Orientation of burials and patterning in the selection of sites for late prehistoric burial mounds in south-central Manitoba" by Bev A. Nicholson, *Plains Anthropologist*, volume 39, number 148, May 1994, pages 161-171.

"The Manitoba Mound Builders: The making of an archaeological myth, 1857-1900" by Gwen Rempel, *Manitoba History*, Number 28, Autumn 1994.

"A radiocarbon date from Star Mound (DgLq-1), Manitoba" by Ian Dyck, *Manitoba Archaeological Journal*, volume 9, number 1, 1999, pages 1-11.

"A mound of mystery?," *Morden Times*, 24 June 2002, page 2.

"The origin of the 'Chicago method' excavation techniques: Contributions of William Nickerson and Frederick Starr" by David Browman, *Bulletin of the History of Archaeology*, volume 23, number 2, pages 1-9, 17 September 2013 [http://www.archaeologybulletin.org/articles/10.5334/bha.2324/]

"Linear mounds one of Manitoba's best-kept archeological secrets" by Bartley Kives, *Winnipeg Free Press*, 21 September 2013.

ACKNOWLEDGEMENTS

I thank Judith Harrison for putting me in touch with her sister Beverly Stow who generously loaned me her treasured copy of the Capes report on the early excavations of Star Mound by W.B. Nickerson. Al Thorleifson provided a digitized copy of *A Diary of Snowflake*.

Union Stock Yards

I remember the smell. It was a pervasive, overwhelming, ungodly stench.

As a kid, I spent summers on the family farm near Winnipeg. Periodically, I would accompany my uncle to the city to get livestock feed and deliver his cattle to market. As we drove east along Marion Street approaching Lagimodiere Boulevard, my nose would be assailed by a warm, fleshy aroma; complex with vague undertones of unfamiliar food cooking.

Aerial view of the former Union Stock Yard site, June 2015. PAIGE KOWAL

It was always there, every time we visited that place. I wondered how anyone living in the area could ever get used to such a smell. Odour is one of the strongest cues for memory and that particular stink from decades ago is what I remembered as I turned off Marion into the former site of the Union Stock Yards, once the largest of its kind in the British Empire.

Where does your meat come from? Okay, I know, from a butcher. But where does the butcher get it? At the centre of the meat supply chain are packers who purchase live animals, slaughter and process the carcasses, and package the meat for wholesale and retail sale. Traditionally, the packers bought the animals at an auction held at a large, central stock yard where animals arriving from farms and ranches were kept prior to sale. When the Canadian Pacific Railway arrived at Winnipeg in the 1880s, the company built stock pens near its Weston yards on McPhillips Avenue. These pens were basic, consisting of not much more than fences to enclose the animals. There was no facility to protect them from the elements or feed and water them. Farmers complained of the lower prices they received from the sale of their animals due to shrinkage caused by the stress encountered in transport and holding. By 1910, a group of stockmen called on provincial premier Rodmond Roblin (grandfather of later premier Duff Roblin) and encouraged him to do something. He established a three-man commission of inquiry, headed by lawyer R.A.C. "Pat" Manning, to make recommendations for a better system. The commissioners studied conditions at public stock yards at Montreal and New York and vowed to create equal or better facilities here. They proposed building a large, public facility but, finding no suitable space in Winnipeg, turned to a site in the then-independent City of St. Boniface, much to the chagrin of Winnipeg boosters who decried the loss of tax revenue.

In early 1912, the government accepted the commission's

Caricature of beef merchant J.T. Gordon, founding president of the Winnipeg Livestock Exchange, circa 1908. MANITOBANS AS WE SEE 'EM, 1908-1909

recommendations and selected a 232-acre site for the new stock yards. A company named Public Markets Limited was incorporated to develop and operate the site. Its shareholders were the three major railways— Canadian Northern, Canadian Pacific, and Grand Trunk Pacific— which would construct lines to the site and later deliver livestock on

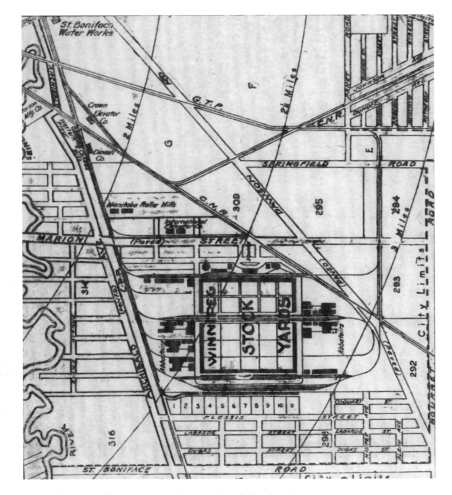

Map of the newly-constructed Union Stock Yards, 1913. WINNIPEG TRIBUNE

The new facility became a small city unto itself, with miles of railway tracks, paved roads, streetcar lines, sewer lines, and more. To handle the animals as they arrived, platforms, chutes, yards, pens, and sheds were constructed. A power house generated electricity for lights around the site. Water was acquired from a 250-foot-deep well, and collected in a 90-foot-tall tower, from which it ran through a network of pipes to buildings and fire hydrants. A two-storey building housed administrative staff and government inspectors and also contained a restaurant and bank. By the time it was fully developed, the stock yards had room for 450 railway cars of livestock. Roofed pens accommodated 1,800 cattle and 6,000 sheep while open pens held another 1,300 cattle and 7,000 sheep.

More than a thousand people attended an opening ceremony for the Union Stock Yards in August 1913, presided over by a proud Premier Roblin. Initially, the facility employed 1,500 people. This would rise to some 3,000 workers at its peak, becoming a major employer in St. Boniface. Within two years, 12,000 rail cars of cattle were handled. To oversee the efficient transaction in livestock, in October 1914 several commission agents, traders, and buyers met and formed the Winnipeg Live Stock Exchange. Its first president was James Thomas Gordon, whose firm Gordon, Ironside & Fares was the nation's largest cattle exporter, with its headquarters in Winnipeg and branches in nine other Canadian cities. Gordon had previously operated the biggest meat-packing plant in Winnipeg in the period leading up to the First World War. If that was not

those lines. (The collaboration of several railways led to the site being called the Union Stock Yards.) Initially reluctant to abandon its own stock yards, the CPR came on board although a cattle feedlot operated at its former site until the 1930s.

enough, by the time of his election to the Exchange, he had already served three terms as an MLA in the Legislature. In 1919, a group of several hundred livestock merchants, shippers, farmers, ranchers, packers, railwaymen, administrators, and others with interests in livestock founded the Hoof and Horn Club to foster social activities among its members. The club hosted a large annual picnic, during which the Stock Yards' auction rings closed, and it fielded football, softball, curling, and soccer teams.

To be fair, it was not really the Stock Yards that stank, at least no more than the average barnyard. The atrocious smell that sticks in people's minds did not begin until meat packers built abattoirs (slaughter houses) next to the Stock Yards, taking advantage of close proximity for greatest efficiency. By late 1916, two abattoirs were operating. To handle the increase in business, several more buildings were constructed in 1918 and a second bank branch opened in 1922. In 1925, Gordon, Ironsides & Fares built a new meat-packing plant on the northwest corner of the Stock Yard site, along Archibald Street, and renamed itself Harris Abattoir (Western Limited). Two years later, it merged with several meat-packers from eastern Canada to form Canada Packers. By 1929, six meat packers were handling over 260,000 cattle, 56,000 calves, 305,000 hogs, and over 52,000 sheep and lambs each year, with a cumulative value of nearly $20 million. In 1935, an American meat packer, Swift's, built a large plant next door to Canada Packers, at the southwest corner of the site. The value would increase to some $100 million by

1948, making it Canada's largest and busiest stock market. By that time, the yard's pens covered 56 acres and were capable of holding 14,000 cattle, 8,000 hogs, and 2,000 sheep. (Occasionally, the yards were called on to house other animals, including horses, bison, and zoo animals in transit through Winnipeg.)

The growth in business continued through the 1960s. In a show of civic pride for Canada's centenary in 1967,

View of cattle pens with water tower in background, 1942. ARCHIVES OF MANITOBA

Aerial view of Union Stock Yards, with the Canada Packers plant at lower left
and Swifts Meats at right, and surviving water tower (2015) at left middle, 1963.
MANITOBA DEPARTMENT OF INDUSTRY AND COMMERCE

members of the Hoof and Horn Club unveiled a six-foot-high statue of a Hereford at the entrance to the Stock Yards. (Later, cheeky accounts would claim the statue was originally a bull but that, over time, removal of its horns and "undercarriage" turned it into a steer.) In 1975, the yards handled 537,212 cattle, 317,159 calves, 10,265 hogs, 47,975 lambs, and 1,615 horses—a total of 914,226 head.

Mechanization reduced the need for manual labour so that, by this time, the yard was operated by only 100 workers. And the primary means by which livestock arrived at the site changed radically. Railway cars were replaced by large trucks as the main way for farmers to transport their animals to market. There was greater competition for animals too, from sources like the Manitoba Beef Commission that guaranteed a price to producers, so the number arriving at the Union Stock Yards was declining. In 1985, only 249,190 head of livestock were processed, a 73 percent reduction in just ten years, and fewer than 20 percent of the animals were delivered by rail. By August 1988, when the Stock Yards closed, only 20 staff remained. Its function was replaced with a $1.8-million auction facility, opened in September 1988, in the Rural Municipality of Rosser west of Winnipeg. One single meat-processing plant remains today along Lagimodiere Boulevard. Canada Packers struggled before being purchased by a British company and merged with Maple Leaf Mills to form Maple Leaf Foods, which today operates a meat processing plant at Brandon. A final symbolic indignity to the once-proud engine of St. Boniface

commerce occurred in the wee hours of 2 September 1989. Vandals attacked and destroyed the Hereford statue.

The City of Winnipeg was left to clean up the mess. In a dramatic demolition covered by local television stations, in May 1994 the old Swift's plant fell within seconds, becoming the first building in the city to be demolished by explosives. The Canada Packers building

Cattle moving between pens at the Union Stock Yards, 1964. UNIVERSITY OF MANITOBA ARCHIVES & SPECIAL COLLECTIONS

Sign at the entrance to the Union Stock Yards, 1964. UNIVERSITY OF MANITOBA ARCHIVES & SPECIAL COLLECTIONS

was bought by a local entrepreneur but was later seized by the city government for back taxes. After a thorough environmental cleanup involving removal of contaminated soil, hazardous waste, asbestos, and piles and piles of pigeon poop, the building was torn down in early 2001. Area residents cheered as the derelict building, so long a source of local employment, came down. Considered an "eyesore" with graffiti-strewn interiors walls and large gaping holes through its floors, the building was a threat to anyone who ventured inside.

The former Union Stock Yard site is now largely vacant except for a vehicle storage depot at its southwest corner. Early plans to develop a $130-million residential, commercial, and recreational space there fell apart when proponents could not agree on terms with the city, and an idea to build a sports stadium on the site never gained traction. Virtually all of the yard infrastructure is gone, except for the odd relict sign here and there, a water tower still emblazoned

"Union Stock Yards," and large expanses of abandoned pavement that are mostly hidden by vegetation growing through its cracks. Oh, and the smell? It too is long gone.

SOURCES

"Public abattoir commission," *Winnipeg Tribune*, 19 March 1910, page 2.

"Personnel of commission," *Winnipeg Tribune*, 23 March 1910, page 2.

"Abattoir commission has a lengthy report – Recommends establishment of public abattoir and market in St. Boniface under control of the Lieutenant-Governor-in-Council," *Winnipeg Tribune*, 24 June 1910, page 1.

"Commission on abattoirs here," *Winnipeg Tribune*, 2 September 1910, page 1.

"Union stockyards in St. Boniface officially opened by the premier," *Winnipeg Tribune*, 14 August 1913, page 1.

"Livestock exchange," *Manitoba Free Press*, 27 October 1914, page 12.

"Winnipeg's first public abattoir," *Manitoba Free Press*, 2 December 1916, page 18.

"Do you know Winnipeg?" *Winnipeg Tribune*, 14 January 1929, page 13.

"Cattle buyers have birthday," *Winnipeg Tribune*, 15 October 1949, page 15.

"Union Stock Yards growing old gracefully," *Winnipeg Free Press*, 3 August 1985, page 56.

"Vandals destroy steer statue," *Winnipeg Free Press*, 7 September 1989, page 11.

Public Markets Limited Fonds, University of Manitoba Archives & Special Collections.

"Canada Packers plant demolition to get nod," *Winnipeg Free Press*, 14 November 2000, page 12.

"St. B. to be Bombers' home?" *Winnipeg Free Press*, 31 March 2007, page 3.

Canadian Pacific Railway Stock Yards, *Henderson's Directory of Winnipeg*, 1910.

Photo of fibreglass bull monument, 1967. WESTERN CANADA PICTORIAL INDEX, ARCHIVES OF MANITOBA

Winnipeg Swift Meat Plant Demolition, Television News Excerpts, YouTube (https://www.youtube.com/watch?v=v-JQolA2940).

ACKNOWLEDGEMENTS

I thank Nathan Kramer for assistance with research, and Paige Kowal for skillful drone piloting.

Valleyview Building

Mental illness is no laughing matter but I intend no offence when I say that most family trees have a few nuts. My own family is no exception, with cases on both paternal and maternal lines. (Close friends will probably say that that explains a lot about me.)

My maternal great-grandparents immigrated to Manitoba from northern England in 1928 and, within three years of their arrival, my great-grandmother was committed to the mental hospital at Brandon. She died there. I thought of this as I walked toward the Valleyview Building at the former Brandon Mental Health Centre (BMHC, the name it acquired in 1972), on the north hill overlooking Brandon. Opened in 1925, it was the place where newly admitted patients—undoubtedly including my great-grandmother just a few years later—spent their first few days as medical staff decided their course of treatment. This building, vacant since 1994, represented a revolutionary transformation in the way that mental illness was treated in Manitoba, going from a "custodial" approach where patients were treated essentially like inmates to be clothed and fed but little else, to a "remedial" approach that viewed mental illness in some ways like a physical affliction, that could be cured with respectful treatment.

The BMHC originated in 1890 as the Brandon Reformatory for Boys, where juvenile delinquents would be housed. In fact, the facility only ever had one admission, a nine-year-old boy named William "Billy" Milligan who had been caught stealing a letter from a postbox, for which he received five years of imprisonment. It is unlikely that young Billy caused further trouble, as he was overseen by a staff of six people supervised by the father of Manitoba's Attorney General. The political

Valleyview Building under construction, 1922. BRANDON MENTAL HEALTH CENTRE COLLECTION, BMHC SLIDES, S.J. MCKEE ARCHIVES, BRANDON UNIVERSITY

embarrassment that ensued saw the Reformatory closed soon after its opening, and reopened the following year as the Brandon Asylum for the Insane. It was intended to house people from throughout Manitoba and the North West Territories (today's Saskatchewan and Alberta) who suffered from various types of mental illness. The first patient was a Mrs. Ackney, who was admitted on 13 July 1891 and remained there until her death in 1937 at the age of 86. Under physician Gordon Bell (who would later achieve fame as the provincial bacteriologist, and be commemorated by a Winnipeg high school), the main form of treatment, especially for physically aggressive patients, was physical restraint in strait jackets, restrictive arm muffs, or beds covered in cages. The new Parkland Building that

OPPOSITE Exterior of the unoccupied Valleyview Building, April 2016. GOLDSBOROUGH

opened at Brandon in 1912, replacing one destroyed by fire in November 1910, was described just six years later as "dark, dismal, and without anything to vary the monotony of the patients' lives." Little had changed by February 1919 when two psychiatrists from Toronto, Dr. Clarence Hincks and Dr. Charles Clarke, submitted a frank 57-page report on the state of affairs at the Manitoba's two asylums—at Brandon and Selkirk—that recommended sweeping reforms. During a tour of the Brandon facility, they had noted that 711 patients were under the care of a single physician with the aid of just two trained nurses, and the physician was so busy doing administrative work that there was no time for actual interaction

Charles A. Baragar (1885-1936), Medical Superintendent of the Brandon Hospital for Mental Diseases from 1920 to 1930, under whose authority the facility was transformed from an asylum to a hospital. BRANDON MENTAL HEALTH CENTRE COLLECTION, S.J. MCKEE ARCHIVES, BRANDON UNIVERSITY

with patients. The provincial government responded promptly. In March 1919, it passed "An Act respecting the Care and Treatment of Mentally Diseased Persons," among which was the directive to rename the Brandon Asylum as the Brandon Hospital for Mental Diseases. A new Medical Superintendent, Dr. Charles Baragar, was put in charge at Brandon and a new training program for psychiatric nurses and attendants was established, with the first seven graduates completing the two-year program in 1923. (They were all female nurses; the first male attendants graduated

Aerial view of the Brandon Mental Hospital, with the Nurses' Residence at left, Parkland Building in centre, and the Valleyview Building at right. At this time, the facility had 1,650 beds. GOLDSBOROUGH

in 1924.) The transformation of the facility from an asylum to a hospital continued with construction of the Valleyview, as well as the medical staff and facilities that it housed. Other reforms were instituted at the same time. To reduce the stigma associated with treatment for mental illness, which at the time required a person to be committed to a mental facility by a judge or magistrate, provision was now made for people to admit themselves voluntarily, or with the advice of a physician. This addressed a criticism levied at the Brandon facility by Drs. Hincks and Clarke in 1919:

> "[T]he method of admitting patients … is not to be commended, as it really classifies insanity as a crime rather than a disease, and humiliates both friends and patients."

Known originally as the Receiving Unit, Receiving Hospital, or Psychiatric Unit, the new building was renamed the Valleyview later. Designed by a pair of Winnipeg architects, Lewis Jordan and Percy Over, construction began in 1920. Government austerity during the early 1920s meant that it took four years to be completed, and opened in mid-January 1925. The three-storey brick and concrete structure consisted of three blocks connected by corridors. The northernmost block contained staff accommodations, laboratories, a dental clinic, dispensary, and morgue. The central block contained kitchens and dining rooms on the first floor and an operating room and therapy rooms on the second floor. An infirmary for sick staff members was on the top floor. The southernmost block housed 73 female patients on its east wing and 63 male patients on the west wing. The main floor housed the "most acutely disturbed cases" in seven single rooms and one three-bed dormitory to avoid overcrowding that could cause problems. Three dormitories on the second floor were for patients with more acceptable behaviour, while the dormitories on the third floor comprised the "parole

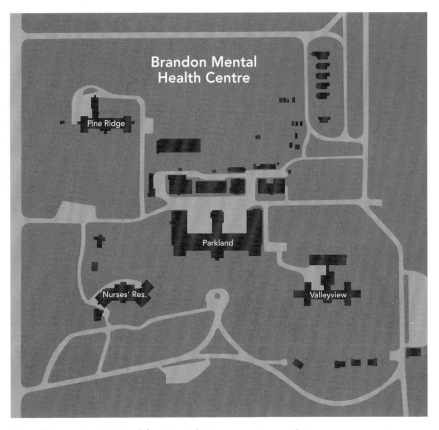

Map of Brandon Hospital for Mental Diseases site, no date. ADAPTED FROM BRANDON MENTAL HEALTH CENTRE COLLECTION, S.J. MCKEE ARCHIVES, BRANDON UNIVERSITY

ward" where doors were unlocked and patients could come and go as they pleased during daylight hours.

The primary purpose of the Valleyview was to enable new procedures for the admission and diagnosis of patients. It also provided more space for three of the facility's departments. The occupational department, established in 1921, gave patients practical activities to engage them, usually the making of crafts and other items that could be sold to generate revenue for the hospital. A farm that raised dairy cattle, hogs, horses, and grain provided food for the facility and meaningful employment for the patients, while others were put to work hauling coal to the power house that generated heat and electricity for the entire facility. The hydrotherapy and electrotherapy departments, which had previously occupied small spaces in the Parkland Building, became more active in the larger spaces made available in the Valleyview. Hydrotherapy in the 1920s consisted of immersing the patient in circulating baths of 100 °F water for several hours, then applying hot and cold wet packs for days to weeks. This was thought to help control restlessness, agitation, and hyperactivity. The medical staff was impressed to find that such treatments mostly eliminated the need for restraints for certain types of patients.

At the same time as the Valleyview opened, the staff commenced conferences one or two times each week to discuss admissions. New patients were given "immediate and greater amounts of personal, medical, and nursing attention" in hopes of a faster return to health so as to incur less social stigma from having been admitted to a mental hospital. The net result was to create an environment that was "more pleasant, less crowded, isolated from the chronic and deteriorated cases, and generally geared toward personal study and care." As a patient showed improved behaviour, they were rewarded by being moved to more pleasant surroundings, and "each progressive step

brought them into closer contact with normal living conditions." In 1920, the facility adopted the practice of releasing patients deemed to have been treated successfully on "parole" and, if they had not been readmitted within six months, they were formally discharged and removed from hospital books.

The Valleyview's medical laboratory, supervised by Miss Reta McCulloch, was considered the "scientific centre of the Hospital" that the hospital's medical superintendent described as being superior to any laboratory in the province, and "sufficient to provide facilities for a local branch of the Public Health Laboratory to supply the needs of the western part of the province." An operating room in the building, used for surgical and dental procedures into the 1960s, was as well-equipped as any found in a general hospital. In 1925, for example, it hosted two major operations, 130 minor operations, 130 lumbar punctures, 60 ear, nose, and throat exams, 4 fracture sets, 35 pelvic exams, and 654 dressings. For dental work, 660 patients were examined, resulting in 244 tooth extractions, 198 fillings, 277 polishings, 3 denture fittings, and 7 denture repairs.

In 1930, Dr. Ewen Cameron was appointed as "physician in charge of reception services," working in the Valleyview until his resignation in January 1936. Described as "aggressive and ambitious," Cameron embraced new techniques for the treatment of mental illness, such as allowing patients to have free movement within the facility. He was probably aware—and would undoubtedly have approved—treating those suffering from acute schizophrenia and manic depression with repeated injections of insulin to cause them to go into a brief coma. The practice was adopted at Brandon in October 1937 and was used until at least the mid-1950s. The drug metrazol given to manic-depressive patients caused them to have violent convulsions and amnesia. (Not surprisingly, a retired medical supervisor would later recall that "it was very difficult for staff to encourage patients to have a second treatment.") Dr. Cameron would go on to fame—or infamy, depending on one's views—for his brainwashing experiments in the 1950s and 1960s conducted under the secret sponsorship of the US Central Intelligence Agency. In 1942, Brandon introduced electro-convulsive therapy ("shock therapy") to induce seizures in depressed patients. Eighty-six patients received the treatment in 1950, increasing to 228 patients five years later. Lobotomies involving the surgical cutting of connections within the brain were first performed at Brandon in 1943, on 23 patients showing "destructiveness and untidy personal habits, violet temper, and confusion." By early 1956, 308 lobotomies had been done. Physical restraint with strait jackets remained commonplace until July 1952, when their use was finally abolished.

By 1966, the Valleyview Building hosted a Day Hospital ward, x-ray services, central supply, medical library, research office, dental clinic, electroencephalography lab, biochemical research lab, and a provincial public health lab. Its capacity was 115 patients. From the 1960s through the 1980s, patient numbers at Manitoba's two

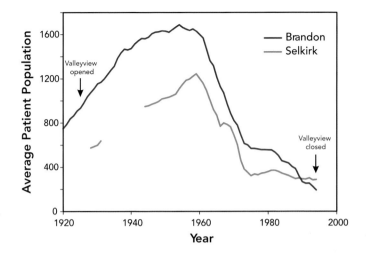

The average patient population at the Brandon Mental Health Centre (red line) and Selkirk Mental Health Centre (blue line) from 1920, when construction of the Valleyview Building was begun, to 1994, when the Valleyview closed. MANITOBA DEPARTMENT OF HEALTH AND PUBLIC WELFARE, ANNUAL REPORTS 1920-1994, MANITOBA LEGISLATIVE LIBRARY

large Mental Health Centres—Brandon and Selkirk—waned as mental health treatment shifted to regional, community-based programming. At Brandon, from a high of around 1650 patients in residence during the 1950s, there were half that number by 1970. By 1984, there were 458 residents and, by 1994 when the Valleyview closed, just 192. The BMHC patient population, as a percentage of the total provincial population, peaked in the mid-1940s at about one-fifth of one percent, and had decreased ten-fold by 1991. As the BMHC downsized, there was less need for space and administrators began to consider closing certain buildings. In 1984, the Manitoba Heritage Council recommended that the Valleyview's façade should be preserved

Interiors of the unoccupied Valleyview Building: laboratory (August 2014) and bathroom (July 2015). RÉMI TELLIER

as long as it continued to be used. Originally targeted for closure in 1989, a temporary reprieve occurred in mid-1989 when the building housed people fleeing forest fires in northern Manitoba. It continued to be used by small numbers of people until it was closed permanently in 1994.

Periodic proposals have been made to return the Valleyview to usefulness. A 1999 plan called for it to host a wellness centre, including spas, fitness centre, and medical clinic. It would also house condo-style housing for seniors.

The fact that the building was now over seventy years old meant that upgrades would be needed. Most pressing was a new roof and new windows. After the former BMHC campus was taken over by the Assiniboine Community College in 2006, an initial 10-year plan was for the Valleyview to be converted into student housing. As of 2009, it appeared the challenges of retrofitting an old building had convinced college administrators to construct new residential space instead. By 2010, a proposal was to outfit the Valleyview as a "theoretical research centre" but nothing has been done. I was told recently by a friend that asbestos insulation was removed from the building in 2015 but nothing else has happened. When I visited the campus in early 2016, the power was still connected but there was conspicuous damage to the roof that, at a minimum, would have to be addressed before it could be used for most anything. So, at present, this remarkable building—truly the first tangible step in

the transformation of mental health care in Manitoba—
stands empty.

We have moved away from the barbaric medical practices of the past, and the stigma that once attached to
those suffering from mental illness, as well as their family
and friends, has waned somewhat. It is now possible to
speak openly and compassionately about those suffering
from it, and to acknowledge the profound impacts that
it can have on human lives. My visit to the Valleyview
Building in early 2016, and my review of old documents
while preparing to write this chapter, left me with a
deeper appreciation of mental illness. I was struck by
the role, previously unknown, that the Valleyview had
played in my life. As I mentioned earlier, my great-grandmother died at the BMHC, possibly in the Valleyview, and
was buried in a cemetery near the farm that she and her
family had pioneered. Her son, my maternal grandfather,
was devastated. He had intended to return to his home
in England but, because he refused to leave her behind in
Canada, he stayed and met my grandmother. The rest, so
they say, is history.

SOURCES

"Report of the Canadian National Committee for Mental
Hygiene," Public Welfare Commission of Manitoba, Second
Interim Report, February 1919, pages 77-133. [Manitoba
Legislative Library SpR 1917 Public Welfare]

Brandon Hospital for Mental Diseases, 38th Annual Report,
1 May 1928. [Annual Report of the Department of Health and
Public Welfare, 30 April 1928, Manitoba Legislative Library]

A History of Mental Health Care in Manitoba by Cornelia B.
Johnson, MA thesis, University of Manitoba, 1980.

"Replace BMHC with community centres: report," Brandon Sun,
7 November 1983.

Buildings at the Brandon Mental Health Centre by David
Butterfield and Randy Rostecki, Manitoba Historic
Resources Branch Report, November 1988. [Manitoba
Legislative Library]

History of the Brandon Mental Health Centre, 1891-1991 by Kurtland
Refvik, BMHC Historical Museum, 1991.

"The Brandon Asylum Fire of 1910" by Kurtland Refvik, Manitoba
History, Number 21, Spring 1991.

"When Love and Skill Work Together:" Work, Skill and the
Occupational Culture of Mental Nurses at the Brandon
Hospital for Mental Diseases, 1919-1946 by Christopher P.A.
Dooley, MA thesis, University of Manitoba, 1998.

"BMHC deal close to reality," Brandon Sun, 26 July 2000, page 1.

"Future remains unknown," Brandon Sun, 1 May 2004, page 1.

"ACC plans unveiled," Brandon Sun, 8 March 2006, page 19.

"College covets funding," Brandon Sun, 7 February 2009, page 1.

"ACC unveils plans for North Hill," Brandon Sun, 5 June 2009,
page 21.

"ACC upgrades impress premier," Brandon Sun, 27 August 2010,
page 2.

ACKNOWLEDGEMENTS

I thank Rémi Tellier for drawing my attention to the Valleyview
Building, Beverley Hicks for sharing her experiences and recollections from her work at the BMHC, and Christy Henry (S. J. McKee
Archives) for providing access to the collection of BMHC reports
and memoirs held at Brandon University. As always, the help of
Monica Ball (Manitoba Legislative Library) in locating obscure
government records was very much appreciated.

Vulcan Iron Works

Several years ago, I was shown the results of soil analysis from a park in the Point Douglas area of Winnipeg. The soil contained astonishingly high levels of metals, so much so that gardening was not recommended because the vegetables grown from the soil might contain harmful levels.

View of the former Vulcan Iron Works, September 2015. GOLDSBOROUGH

A city map from 1906 provided an explanation: the park site had been occupied by a foundry, where metals were melted and formed into new products. The foundry building is now gone but across the street are two forlorn buildings of the Vulcan Iron Works, once one of the largest metal-fabricating plants in western Canada. Situated along Sutherland Avenue near the CPR tracks, the Iron Works had a key role in the building of our province, for which it seems to have left a worrisome legacy. It also contributed inadvertently to the development of labour relations in Manitoba.

The foundations of the Vulcan Iron Works trace back to 1874, just four years after Manitoba became a province, and a few months after Winnipeg was incorporated as a City. Two businessmen from Ontario, John McKechnie and William McMillan, established the Winnipeg Foundry and Machine Shop. Their original workshop is long gone but a surviving building in Point Douglas dates to 1881 or 1882, when the company was renamed for Vulcan, the Roman god of fire and metalworking. In January 1884, the Vulcan Iron Company of Manitoba was incorporated with shares held primarily by Montreal shipping magnate Andrew Allan and his Winnipeg son-in-law Frederick Brydges.

If you wanted most anything made of iron, steel, copper or wood, Vulcan Iron Works could do it for you. Its diverse product line included structural members for buildings and bridges, metal stairs and fire escapes, fire hydrants, tanks and steel plates, engine parts, grain elevator and mill machinery, railroad equipment, bolts and rivets, iron and brass castings, and ornamental iron and plaques. It was the first facility in Manitoba to manufacture high-pressure boilers used in steam-powered equipment such as railway locomotives and building furnaces. During the First and Second World Wars, it produced artillery shells for the Canadian military as well as anchors and other metal parts for naval and merchant vessels.

Advertisement for the Winnipeg Foundry and Machine Shop, June 1880.
WINNIPEG TIMES

In late 1902, the assets of the original company were taken over by the Vulcan Iron Works Limited, with John McKechnie and Edward Barrett as majority shareholders. Barrett had worked his way up the ranks, starting in 1882 as a 17-year-old office boy, eventually becoming the firm's president upon McKechnie's death in 1918. Vulcan's stated purpose was broad, involving "the business of iron-founders, mechanical engineers,

Vulcan Iron Works, 4 July 1920. ARCHIVES OF MANITOBA, FOOTE COLLECTION

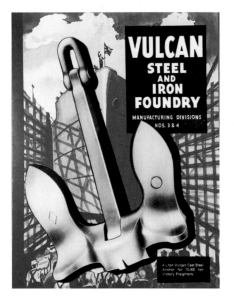

Cover of Vulcan Iron Works promotional literature ARCHIVES OF MANITOBA

and manufacturers of all kinds of machinery, tool makers, brass founders, metal workers, boiler makers, fitters, wire drawers, tube makers, galvanizers, mill-wrights, machinists, wood workers, platers, founders, metallurgists, electrical engineers, water supply engineers, gas makers, and to deal in machinery implements and hardware of all kinds and any goods, wares or merchandise in which iron, steel or wood is in any way used." With such a wide range of services, the company needed a large physical plant. By 1906, its buildings occupied two city blocks and included an office and warehouse, machine shop, woodworking shop, and foundry along Maple Avenue, a large boiler-making shop along Sutherland Avenue (constructed in 1904), and a warehouse and iron storage shed along Meade Avenue.

Vulcan's need for labour was correspondingly large. It was one of the largest employers of blue-collar workers in Winnipeg's North End, with a workforce of some 400 people by 1930 and peaking at over 600

during the Second World War, by which time its plant occupied three and a half city blocks, some nine acres in area, with 190,000 square feet of floor space. As one of the "Big Three" employers of metal workers in the city, along with Dominion Bridge and Manitoba Bridge and Iron Works, Vulcan set the standard for other employers, so any conflicts between management and labour were watched carefully. In mid-May 1906, mere weeks after Winnipeg's streetcar workers went on strike, 16 iron moulders at Vulcan (along with 20 of their counterparts at the other two firms) set down their tools, demanding that their 30 cent per hour wage be raised by five cents. A few days later, Vulcan's machinists and blacksmiths—who had been negotiating for better working conditions—were locked out. In early June, the company was given a court injunction to prevent union members from picketing around its premises. But hard feelings had subsided by the end of the year. In late December, plant foremen were given $50 in gold while assistant foremen and office staff received $25. Rank and file workers received no bonuses but did not have their regular pay deducted for the Christmas holiday. After three cheers for management, the assembled workers enjoyed a "sumptuous Christmas eve dinner." Despite the apparent equanimity, in late 1908 the company took three labour unions representing machinists, iron moulders, and blacksmiths to court, seeking $50,000 in damages and a perpetual injunction against further union activity on its premises. The case was heard by Judge Thomas Mathers, who would later preside in cases against leaders of the 1919 Winnipeg General Strike. Mathers ruled in favour of the company, causing labour unrest to simmer through the next decade, and ultimately come to a boil in 1918. In July of that year, the Metal Trades Council, acting on periodic complaints about low wages and long hours, demanded that the "Big Three" recognize it as a union representing the interests of metal workers or a general strike would be called. Vulcan's John McKechnie had just died, and Edward Barrett was newly installed as his successor. Barrett was not in a mood to placate the striking workers. His brother, general manager Leonard Barrett, announced that "the metal contract shops of this city are prepared to carry on their work indefinitely without the men who are out on strike" by adhering strictly to an "open shop" principle under which workers were hired on the basis of merit and not union membership. The matter came to a head during the summer of 1919 when Vulcan workers joined those of the other two factories

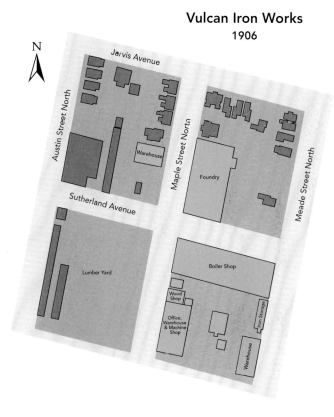

Vulcan Iron Works
1906

A fire insurance map from 1906 shows the spatial extent (in blue) of Vulcan Iron Works at that time. LIBRARY AND ARCHIVES CANADA

in a combined strike. Bolstered by members of the Metal Trades Council, it was a significant first step in the escalation that led ultimately to the Winnipeg General Strike.

In 1947, the company's assets were purchased by James Gairdner of Toronto and the firm was renamed the Vulcan Iron & Engineering Limited, with Gairdner as chairman of the board, but with long-time management staff remaining in place. A corporate reorganization

The interior of Vulcan Iron Works, circa 1952.
ARCHIVES OF MANITOBA

resulted in seven divisions: steel castings, iron castings, boilers, structural steel and ornamental blacksmithing and forging, machine shop, and warehousing. Seven years later, the company became the Western Division of Bridge & Tank Company of Canada Limited, formed from the merger of Vulcan with several companies from Hamilton, Ontario. Renamed Bridge & Tank Western Limited in 1958, the company moved its manufacturing plant to a

27-acre site in North Kildonan in October 1961, while the administrative office remained in Point Douglas. By the mid-1970s, however, the office was closed as operations were consolidated in North Kildonan. In July 1975, the old foundry building along Maple Avenue was demolished.

Its site became a public park named for Winnipeg lawyer and city councilor Joe Zuken, who might have appreciated the irony of commemorating an ardent Communist on the former site of a capitalist bastion. The large boiler shop and warehouses along Sutherland Avenue still stand, festooned with graffiti.

The "Big Three" metalworking firms are gone. But reminders of Vulcan Iron Works are all around us, including in the soil around its former foundry. Many of Winnipeg's fine old buildings from the early 20th century have steel skeletons made there. The water tower overlooking Winnipeg Beach was a product of its forges, and I am told that fire hydrants and manhole covers around the province bear its name. But what was once a major industry in western Canada is fast disappearing from memory. In today's globalized economy, low transportation costs combined with cheap overseas labour have revolutionized the metal fabrication industry. The other day, I met a fellow who works for a metalworking business in a small Manitoba town. He said that their main competitors operate plants on the other side of the planet, not in neighbouring towns. So the probability that we will ever again see the likes of Vulcan Iron Works in Manitoba is small indeed.

SOURCES

"Tenders," *Winnipeg Tribune*, 19 April 1904, page 4.

"Moulders still out," *Winnipeg Tribune*, 18 May 1906, page 10.

"Vulcan employees," *Winnipeg Tribune*, 27 December 1906, page 4.

"Important suit beings in court," *Winnipeg Tribune*, 16 November 1908, page 1.

"Vulcan Iron Works awarded damages," *Winnipeg Tribune*, 19 March 1909, page 1.

"To the public," *Winnipeg Tribune*, 9 August 1918, page 11.

"Metal employers ready to carry on," *Manitoba Free Press*, 10 August 1918, page 8.

"Vulcan Iron Works adheres to open shop principles," *Manitoba Free Press*, 25 April 1919, page 4.

"Established when Winnipeg was but a village," *Winnipeg Tribune*, 26 February 1930, page 86.

"E.G. Barrett, head of Vulcan foundry, dies," *Winnipeg Tribune*, 28 January 1935, page 13.

"Gairdner to retain Vulcan Iron control," *Winnipeg Free Press*, 30 October 1947, page 24.

"Gairdner Group will take over Vulcan on Nov. 1," *Winnipeg Tribune*, 29 October 1947, page 20.

"Steel … on a silver platter," *Winnipeg Free Press*, 8 March 1954, page 31.

Advertisement [Bridge & Tank Western Ltd.], *Winnipeg Free Press*, 19 June 1958, page 43.

"N. Slater Company, Limited," *Winnipeg Free Press*, 27 February 1961, page 25.

"Vulcan Iron Works being demolished," *Winnipeg Free Press*, 15 July 1975, page 5.

Letters Patent of Incorporation, Vulcan Iron Company of Manitoba Limited, 7 January 1884, Companies Office Corporation Documents, Archives of Manitoba, GR6427.

Letters Patent of Incorporation, Vulcan Iron Works Limited, 24 December 1902, Companies Office Corporation Documents, Archives of Manitoba, GR6427.

Vulcan Iron Works Fonds, 1944-1949, Archives of Manitoba MG11 C46.

ACKNOWLEDGEMENTS

I thank Victor Sawelo, Manager of Ross House Museum, for making me aware of the high metal concentrations in soil near the former foundry site.

Conclusion

The late American anthropologist William Rathje was famous for his research called the "Garbage Project." Over a period of many years, Rathje and his students looked at what people threw out, by analyzing the contents of their trash cans and by excavating in their landfills. There were numerous fascinating insights into human nature that arose from the project because, in effect, what we consider garbage is a statement of our priorities. We discard what we do not value. I think the same can be said for abandoned historic sites. I am not suggesting that sites like the ones described in this book are garbage. However, just as perfectly useful items can be thrown in the garbage, perfectly useful places can be abandoned. Or they may be used less intensively than they could be, or for a very different purpose than the one for which they were created. Like the garbage that one discards, looking at the places that are abandoned tells us something about the changing activities and priorities

of society at large. Each of the places profiled here, it seems to me, tells us something interesting and important about how Manitoba has changed and how the way we live our lives today came to be.

In considering abandoned places around Manitoba, we can explore how mechanization has affected the way our food is produced, by looking at the changing fortunes of the grain elevator at Helston, the Harrison Flour Mill at Holmfield, or the Union Stock Yards at Winnipeg. The evolution of our modern lifestyle that is highly dependent on energy and telecommunications is revealed by the hydroelectric power dam on the Little Saskatchewan River and the telephone repeater station near Morris. Our world is increasingly a global one, where the products we consume often come to us from far away and shipments of prairie grain are delivered to a hungry world via a northern Manitoba seaport. We can examine this change by considering innocuous things like the bricks that make

government records had told me was situated north of Treherne. I found the remains of the school across the road from the monument.

My third method is to be open to the advice of strangers. I have visited numerous places that I would never have found on my own. Talking to people while filling my car with gas, or stopping by a local museum, or posting an open-ended inquiry on the internet can all be effective at learning about some really important, and admittedly a few rather trivial places. (I try not to be judgmental about what constitutes "important" because I realize that we all assess this differently, and what seems trivial to me might have deep meaning to someone else.) This method has led me to some great places.

Finally, I cannot stress enough the value of research done in advance of field work. I never just drive randomly in search of something interesting. I always have a list of places that I want to check. For example, I have found many one-room schoolhouse sites using a Masters thesis written in 1978 by the late Mary Perfect. She combed diligently through Manitoba Department of Education files to compile a huge table of school locations. In the vast majority of cases, Mary's thesis was instrumental in leading me to the general vicinity, and my trusty GPS receiver got me the rest of the way. Local history books in my personal collection and at the Manitoba Legislative Library are excellent sources of tips on historic sites, as they refer to buildings, monuments, cemeteries, and other features. And in the past few years, Google Earth has been my single-best source to find obscure sites in out-of-the-way places. For some parts of Manitoba, the quality of the satellite photos that are freely available in Google Earth is easily good enough to see a wide range of structures. That is how, for instance, I have found numerous old bridges, by following rivers in Google Earth and seeing where something crosses them.

How do we document abandoned sites?

When I arrive at an abandoned site, I work on the assumption that I will never come back to it and that, someday soon, it will be gone. So I try, as much as possible, to collect as much information as I can about the place. My first priority is to measure its precise location—latitude and longitude—using my GPS receiver. In the old days, sites in rural parts of southern Manitoba were located using the system of sections, townships, and ranges established in the 1870s. This system is fine to get within a quarter mile or so of a spot, but I am not satisfied unless I can measure its location to within six to ten feet. So I use a high-quality GPS receiver with a good antenna that, by taking multiple measurements over a few minutes, can provide this level of accuracy. (Even the cheaper receivers can usually give good results if you are patient.)

The next step in my documentation of a site is to take *numerous* photos. In the age of digital photography, there is no reason not to take lots, as the cost is essentially nil. I want at least one general view that shows the entire site, along with whatever specific thing drew my attention to it. For buildings, I take a photo from each of its exterior corners, and close-ups of noteworthy details such as the type of foundation and wall material, unique features, and whatever damage may be visible. If it is possible to go inside a building, I take views from several angles and again focus on unique details. For the last year or so, I have had a new tool in my kit that, I think, provides a richer dimension to my photographic documentation: a drone for aerial photography. The cost of consumer-grade drones has dropped considerably over the past year and the quality of the still images and video they provide is excellent. They are remarkably easy to fly. Often, details that are invisible on the ground are readily visible from the air. For example, foundations of long-gone buildings may be obscured by tall grass but are often readily apparent in aerial photos.

Finally, I take notes about details that may not be apparent in photos, or for which I may need a reminder when looking at the photos years in the future. If some local person has provided useful information, I record their name and contact information, and a recap of the information, as I do not trust my memory to recall it months—or even days—later. Some monuments, for instance, contain caches of information about the circumstances of its creation, or details on the site that it commemorates. I photograph, for later transcription, everything that I find in such caches. (I warn those who create the caches to be mindful of the ravaging effects of weather over time, so a box or bag that appears durable and protective now will degrade over time, turning once-legible documents into unidentifiable sludge.)

How do we find information about an abandoned site?
Finding an abandoned place is only the first chapter of the story they tell. To get the whole story, one needs to dig deeper. By supplementing what can be found at the site itself, using information from other sources, a richer, more complex and engaging story will emerge.

For me, these other sources fall into four main groups. First, there is no substitute for local knowledge. In most any community, for example, there will be resources that provide a deeper understanding of an abandoned building that could ever be gained from just a visit to it. These resources include local history books, often written decades ago by people who have long since passed away, that contain details found nowhere else. Documents relating to the site may be held in the collections of a local museum (many of which are woefully underused), and personal anecdotes and experiences may exist only in the memories of people who have lived all their lives in the community. Second, large repositories of excellent information exist in regional, provincial, and national archives. The largest archives in Manitoba, by far, is the one operated by the provincial government, but excellent ones also exist at the University of Manitoba, University of Winnipeg, and Brandon University, and the archives maintained by religious denominations and companies may provide unique information. Most are open to the public. There can be challenges in using archival information to its full potential, ranging from arcane rules that restrict or prohibit access in the name of protecting personal privacy, to geographic restrictions for those who live far from the archives. Third, do not discount libraries—public and private—as useful sources. Again, I draw your attention to the universities and Winnipeg's Millennium Library. I would be remiss if I did not give ample credit to the Legislative Library of Manitoba which has extensive holdings especially well-suited to "historical detectives" such as us. I suspect it is used far less than it could be, because people do not know about it, or who think that it is not, like its federal counterpart in Ottawa, open to the public. Nothing could be further from the truth.

Fourth and finally, I am a big advocate for digital, online sources such as newspapers and local history books. These materials break the geographic barriers imposed by physical collections in archives and libraries, and often have the additional benefit of being much easier to search efficiently. On the other hand, do not think that all available historical information resides online. It is true that more information is becoming available every day but a vast trove is offline and probably always will be, because it is just too expensive to digitize, or the demand is too small for very specialized data. I suspect it will always be the case that the online materials are the veritable "tip of the iceberg" with the vast bulk of the berg on shelves and boxes in libraries, archives, and other collections. In a nutshell, what I am saying is that finishing the story of an historical site takes creativity, resourcefulness, and patience.

How do we share information about historic sites?
Many more interesting historic sites exist out there than can ever be presented in a book like this one. I believe firmly that information should be freely and widely shared. To that end, for the past six years I have been building an online database about historic sites in Manitoba—not just abandoned ones—for the Manitoba Historical Society. It is still very much a work in progress, but I encourage you to try it and let me know what you think. If you have suggestions on sites that you do not find in the database, please let me know about them. If you can contribute such information as a site's geographic location, some photographs, and more information about it, all the better. By working on this together, we can make this database an increasingly rich one for everyone. Good luck in your travels!

ACKNOWLEDGEMENTS

My wife, Maria Zbigniewicz, was my faithful sounding board on ideas for this book. Alan Mason has accompanied me on several of my adventures in rural Manitoba, in the process seeing large parts of the province that, as a Winnipegger, he had been wholly ignorant. The Manitoba Historical Society has given me the opportunity to travel in search of historic sites, not just abandoned ones featured here, but hosts of others, with financial support from the Manitoba Heritage Grants Program. If you are interested in seeing the full list, a prototype database can be found here: http://www.mb1870.org/mhs-map/search

Appendix: Site Coordinates

Additional information and photos for each of the sites are available on the website of the Manitoba Historical Society at the web links shown.

SITE	LATITUDE	LONGITUDE	URL
Alpha Shipwreck	49.69723	-99.03628	http://www.mhs.mb.ca/docs/sites/alpha.shtml
Atkinson House	50.15520	-100.56123	http://www.mhs.mb.ca/docs/sites/atkinsonhouse.shtml
Bender Hamlet	50.68398	-97.47344	http://www.mhs.mb.ca/docs/sites/benderhamlet.shtml
Birtle Residential School	50.43191	-101.04183	http://www.mhs.mb.ca/docs/sites/birtleresidentialschool.shtml
Bradley Grave	49.02266	-97.19633	http://www.mhs.mb.ca/docs/sites/bradleygrave.shtml
Copley Anglican Church	49.03012	-101.25183	http://www.mhs.mb.ca/docs/sites/copleyanglican.shtml
Cordite Plant	49.89394	-96.92578	http://www.mhs.mb.ca/docs/sites/corditeplant.shtml
Fort Daer	48.96544	-97.24051	http://www.mhs.mb.ca/docs/sites/fortdaer.shtml
Gervais Bowstring Bridge	49.94613	-98.05573	http://www.mhs.mb.ca/docs/sites/gervaisconcretebridge.shtml
Graysville Orange Hall	49.50907	-98.15858	http://www.mhs.mb.ca/docs/sites/orangelodgegraysville.shtml
Harrison Flour Mill	49.13753	-99.48421	http://www.mhs.mb.ca/docs/sites/harrisonmill.shtml
Hartney Town Hall	49.48196	-100.52340	http://www.mhs.mb.ca/docs/sites/hartneytownhall.shtml
Helston Grain Elevator	50.13216	-99.11679	http://www.mhs.mb.ca/docs/sites/helstonelevator.shtml
La Riviere Ski Slopes	49.24993	-98.67986	http://www.mhs.mb.ca/docs/sites/lariviereskislopes.shtml

SITE	LATITUDE	LONGITUDE	URL
Lakeside Fresh Air Camp	50.69555	-96.99472	http://www.mhs.mb.ca/docs/sites/lakesidefreshaircamp.shtml
Leacock House	50.42745	-101.05069	http://www.mhs.mb.ca/docs/sites/leacockhousebirtle.shtml
Leary Brickworks	49.47723	-98.42683	http://www.mhs.mb.ca/docs/sites/learybrickworks.shtml
Little Saskatchewan Hydro Dam	49.88658	-100.12368	http://www.mhs.mb.ca/docs/sites/littlesaskatchewanhydrodam.shtml
Mallard Lodge	50.18397	-98.38191	http://www.mhs.mb.ca/docs/sites/deltamarshfieldstation.shtml
Manitoba Glass Works	50.05303	-96.52311	http://www.mhs.mb.ca/docs/sites/manitobaglasscompany.shtml
Matchettville School	49.70976	-98.71037	http://www.mhs.mb.ca/docs/sites/matchettvilleschool.shtml
McArdle Salt Works	52.86797	-101.06025	http://www.mhs.mb.ca/docs/sites/mcardlesaltworks.shtml
Morris Repeater Station	49.44958	-97.36795	http://www.mhs.mb.ca/docs/sites/telecom4.shtml
Ninette Sanatorium	49.40317	-99.60705	http://www.mhs.mb.ca/docs/sites/ninettesanatorium.shtml
Paulson Bombing & Gunnery School	51.13406	-99.86553	http://www.mhs.mb.ca/docs/sites/paulsonairport.shtml
Pharmacy College	49.89800	-97.14866	http://www.mhs.mb.ca/docs/sites/pharmacycollege.shtml
Port Nelson	57.04880	-92.60033	http://www.mhs.mb.ca/docs/sites/portnelsonbridge.shtml
Ramsay Grave	50.96944	-96.93415	http://www.mhs.mb.ca/docs/sites/ramsaygrave.shtml
Rapid City School	50.11905	-100.03604	http://www.mhs.mb.ca/docs/sites/rapidcityschool.shtml
Rose Hill Kilns	51.11097	-98.74947	http://www.mhs.mb.ca/docs/sites/rosehillquarry.shtml
Schepper's College	49.41463	-98.80034	http://www.mhs.mb.ca/docs/sites/schepperscollege.shtml
Sclater Churches – Holy Eucharist	51.91191	-100.64368	http://www.mhs.mb.ca/docs/sites/holyeucharistsclater.shtml
Sclater Churches – Our Lady of the Snow	51.92909	-100.61206	http://www.mhs.mb.ca/docs/sites/sclaterromancatholic.shtml
Sclater Churches – St. Michael's	51.92906	-100.62176	http://www.mhs.mb.ca/docs/sites/stmichaelsukorthsclater.shtml
Star Mound	49.05975	-98.72491	http://www.mhs.mb.ca/docs/sites/starmound.shtml
Union Stock Yards	49.88038	-97.08946	http://www.mhs.mb.ca/docs/sites/unionstockyards.shtml
Valleyview Building	49.86865	-99.93345	http://www.mhs.mb.ca/docs/sites/brandonmentalhealthcentre.shtml
Vulcan Iron Works	49.90538	-97.13085	http://www.mhs.mb.ca/docs/sites/vulcanironworks.shtml

Index